BIG DATA FOR THE PUBLIC GOOD

Can researchers and innovators use UK public sector data to produce knowledge that improves policy making, scrutinises government work and promotes the public interest?

This open access book looks at interactions between UK public sector officials and researchers/innovators to shed light on barriers to data access and use. It asks: what are the frameworks that govern access to public sector big datasets for researchers and innovators? How are these frameworks applied in practice? What are the governance solutions for policy makers interested in harnessing the untapped potential of public sector big data to improve their policies and create public benefit?

Public sector data is a valuable resource that can help researchers and innovators create knowledge and solutions that benefit society. As public bodies collect increasingly more data about us, UK policy makers try to maximise the use of public sector big data for the benefit of the public. But accessing this data is not easy. There are many legal, technical and ethical barriers that prevent the use of public sector data for research and innovation.

This book is for researchers and innovators who want to understand and overcome the barriers to accessing UK public sector data. It is also for policy makers who are interested in how public sector data can be used to improve decision-making, scrutinise government work, and promote the public interest.

Hart Studies in Information Law and Regulation: Volume 4

Hart Studies in Information Law and Regulation

Series Editors

Tanya Aplin (General Editor)
Perry Keller (Advisory Editor)

This series concerns the transformative effects of the digital technology revolution on information law and regulation. Information law embraces multiple areas of law that affect the control and reuse of information, data and digital tools – intellectual property, data protection, privacy, freedom of information, state security, tort, contract and competition law. 'Regulation' is a similarly extensive concept in that it encompasses legal and non-legal modes of control, including technological design and codes of practice.

The series provides cross-cutting analysis and exploration of the complex and pressing issues that arise in a society where digital infrastructures are now pervasive and when massive volumes of digital information are shared globally. These issues include access to data; sharing, reuse, and governance of data; open source and public sector data; the legitimacy and transparency of training data; propertisation of data and digital tools; freedom of expression and information access rights; privacy rights and data protection regimes; and the role of the state and private entities in safeguarding the public interest in the uses of data.

In the spirit of representing the diverse nature of its topics, the series embraces various methodologies: doctrinal, comparative, empirical, theoretical, historical and socio-legal, and particularly welcomes monograph proposals.

The series is especially open to perspectives from jurisdictions or regions which have traditionally been underrepresented in the scholarly literature.

Recent titles in this series:

Constitutionalising Social Media
Edited by Edoardo Celeste, Amélie Heldt and Clara Iglesias Keller

Cybersecurity, Privacy and Data Protection in EU Law: A Law, Policy and Technology Analysis
Maria Grazia Porcedda

Critical Reflections on the EU's Data Protection Regime: GDPR in the Machine
Edited by Róisín Á Costello and Mark Leiser

Big Data for the Public Good: Regulating Access to Public Sector Big Data for Research and Innovation
Stergios Aidinlis

Big Data for the Public Good

Regulating Access to Public Sector Big Data for Research and Innovation

Stergios Aidinlis

•HART•
OXFORD • LONDON • NEW YORK • NEW DELHI • SYDNEY

HART PUBLISHING

Bloomsbury Publishing Plc

Kemp House, Chawley Park, Cumnor Hill, Oxford, OX2 9PH, UK

1385 Broadway, New York, NY 10018, USA

Bloomsbury Publishing Ireland Limited, 29 Earlsfort Terrace, Dublin 2, D02 AY28, Ireland

HART PUBLISHING, the Hart/Stag logo, BLOOMSBURY and the Diana logo are trademarks of Bloomsbury Publishing Plc

First published in Great Britain 2025

A catalogue record for this book is available from the British Library.

A catalogue record for this book is available from the Library of Congress.

Library of Congress Control Number: 2025932884

ISBN: HB: 978-1-50997-330-9
ePDF: 978-1-50997-332-3
ePub: 978-1-50997-331-6

Typeset by Compuscript Ltd, Shannon

ACKNOWLEDGEMENTS

The present book is inspired from my DPhil thesis at the Centre for Socio-Legal Studies at the Faculty of Law, University of Oxford. This project was supported generously by a UKRI grant at the University of Oxford and by scholarships from the Onassis and Leventis foundations in Greece. Open access was funded by UKRI. First and foremost, I want to thank my supervisors Jane Kaye and Bettina Lange for their intellectual guidance, support and rigorous feedback. I have also profited from having world-leading expert examiners providing robust checks on the direction of the project and its content: Graeme Laurie, Jessie Blackbourn, Joe Tomlinson, Edward Dove, Marina Kurkchiyan and Christopher Hodges. I also want to thank my friend Dimitrios Kyriazis for his unwavering support in times of intellectual challenge during our studies in Oxford.

Above all, this book is dedicated to my parents, Fotios Aidinlis and Elisavet Moysiadou, and my partner, Margarita Amaxopoulou, for their love, trust and support.

This work was supported by the Arts and Humanities Research Council [grant number ES/J500112/1].

CONTENTS

Acknowledgements v

PART 1
BACKGROUND

1. Introduction **3**
I. Public Sector Data: Definitional Boundaries 4
II. Public Sector Data Sharing for Research and Innovation in the UK: Policy Developments 6
III. Sharing Data for Research and Innovation Purposes? A Brief Anatomy 10
IV. Overview 12

2. Whose Data? Control Over Public Sector Data in the UK **16**
I. Personal or Non-personal Data? A Focal Distinction 17
II. The Meaning of Control 18
III. Control Over Public Sector Data in UK Law 19
IV. Viewing Data as a Public Good 21
V. Treating Data as Controlled by Public Sector Bodies 25
VI. Data as Controlled by Individual Citizens 28
VII. Conclusion 30

3. Researching Data Access Decisions for Research and Innovation in the UK Public Sector **32**
I. 'Regulating' Data Access for Research and Innovation 32
II. A Regulatory Space Analysis of Research Data Access Decisions 35
III. A Mixed-methods Historical Approach: Data Collection and Analysis 40
IV. Conclusion 42

PART 2
FRAMEWORKS

4. The Law of Public Sector Data Access for Research and Innovation **45**
I. Research and/or Innovation? 46
II. Elite versus Democratic Access? The Legal Addressees of Public Sector Data 47

III. Individual Rights to Access: The FOIA 2000 48
IV. Duties to Disclose: Private and Public Disclosure Mandates in the Law....................................51
V. Discretion to Disclose: The DEA 2017 and Other Legal Powers..........53
VI. Legal Limitations to Access Public Sector Information......................59
VII. Conclusion....................................64

5. Commercial Access to Public Sector Data for Research and Innovation 65
I. Commercial Access to Government Data for Research and Innovation: Organisational Challenges and Economic Incentives....................................66
II. Finding the 'Public Interest' in Research and Innovation Data Sharing....................................69
III. The Lawfulness of Commercial Access: 'Public' and 'Private' Interests in the GDPR....................................72
IV. Reconciling the Public with the Private? A Conceptualisation Based on 'Societal Welfare'....................................75
V. Conclusion....................................83

PART 3
APPLICATIONS

6. Research Data Sharing in the UK Public Sector: Main Phases of Historical Development....................................87
I. Informality: Ad Hoc Bargaining to Access Data for Research 89
II. The Origins of 'Independent Research': Demanding Independence, Settling for Informality....................................97
III. Widening Research Data Access: The View from the High Level....................................100
IV. Formalisation: Creating Formal Frameworks to Streamline Research Data Sharing in the UK....................................101
V. The ADRN (2013–2018) as an Agent of Systematic Formalisation....................................109
VI. Fragmentation: Unequal Access of Researchers to Administrative Data in the UK....................................112
VII. Conclusion....................................120

7. Rise of Different Data Sharing Cultures 121
I. Perceptions of Administrative Data 'Ownership': Sharing whose Data?....................................122
II. Data as 'Property': 'Our' Data and 'Their' Research............................130
III. Conclusion: The Salience of 'Research Data Sharing Cultures' for Regulating Decisions....................................143

8. Low-level Interactions and Communicative Possibilities 144
I. The Central Role of Data Analysts in Data Access Regulation for Research and Innovation 145
II. Informal Communications and Small-Scale Interactions 162
III. Conclusion: The Importance of Commonplace, Low-Level Interactions 174

PART 4
LOOKING AHEAD

9. Legal Reform to Widen Access to Data for Research and Innovation 179
I. Drawing Inspiration from the Freedom of Information Act (FOIA) 2000 180
II. A Legal Presumption for Data Availability for Research and Innovation 185
III. The Need for Organisational Change 188
IV. Conclusion 189

10. Research Data Access and Automating Public Services 190
I. Big Public-Sector Data and Automation: The Path to Adoption 192
II. Big Public-Sector Data and Automation: Applications........................ 194
III. Automation and Research (Data) Access: Rationale and Challenges 198
IV. Conclusion 201

Bibliography.. *202*
Index *219*

PART 1

Background

1

Introduction

The hunt for new data sources has become the gold rush of our era,[1] as innovative and powerful AI technologies like foundation models (e.g., GPT-4) have nearly exhausted the limits of currently available training data.[2] To prevent learning plateaus, however, models need to continually seek new, informative training data.[3] This urgency to unlock new data sources presents a valuable opportunity to harness cutting-edge technologies for public benefit. By tapping into hitherto unused public sector data,[4] governments can fuel innovations tailored to serve societal needs rather than solely commercial ends. For example, unlocking public healthcare data which is fragmented across institutions could enable advancements in treatments and therapies, resulting in reduced hospital re-admissions;[5] opening up public educational data stores could generate insights to improve literacy rates and learning outcomes for students.[6]

Some countries (e.g., the Nordic countries)[7] have made significant progress in widening access to public sector data for research and innovation.[8] However, according to the OECD, most countries are struggling due to legacy technologies,

[1] R Wigglesworth, 'Hedge Funds See a Gold Rush in Data Mining' *Financial Times* (28 August 2017) Available at: www.ft.com/content/d86ad460-8802-11e7-bf50-e1c239b45787 accessed 16 October 2024 [all links in this book were accessed on that date].

[2] UK Competition and Markets Authority, 'AI Foundation Models: Initial Review' 3.7.Available at: https://assets.publishing.service.gov.uk/media/650449e86771b90014fdab4c/Full_Non-Confidential_Report_PDFA.pdf; P Villalobos and others, 'Will We Run out of Data? An Analysis of the Limits of Scaling Datasets in Machine Learning'. Available at: https://arxiv.org/abs/2211.04325.

[3] R Bommasani and others, 'On the Opportunities and Risks of Foundation Models'. Available at: https://arxiv.org/abs/2108.07258.

[4] Public sector data is the data generated or collected throughout the operation of a national bureaucracy, eg, from the operation of administrative systems for such purposes as social security and tax collection.

[5] Welsh Government, 'Data Linking Demonstration Project: Examining Fuel Poverty Using Home Energy Efficiency Data (HEED) and Routinely Collected Health Data' (2013). Available at: www.gov.wales/sites/default/files/statistics-and-research/2019-01/data-linking-demonstration-project-examining-fuel-poverty-using-home-energy-efficiency-data-and-routinely-collected-health-data.pdf.

[6] D Figlio and others, 'Education Research and Administrative Data', in E Hanushek and others (eds), *Handbook of the Economics of Education, vol 5* (Elsevier 2016). Available at:https://linkinghub.elsevier.com/retrieve/pii/B9780444634597000026.

[7] ibid, where the two case studies come from Norway and Sweden.

[8] R Connelly and others, 'The Role of Administrative Data in the Big Data Revolution in Social Science Research' (2016) 59 *Social Science Research* 1.

skills shortfalls, and legal obstacles.[9] While the first two challenges can be addressed through committing to increased public investment or/and public-private partnerships, legal barriers remain a salient challenge in numerous countries. If governance structures enabled appropriate access, these hitherto unexploited public data could fuel innovation and provide tangible improvements to people worldwide.

In this book, I seek to set the groundwork for tackling such governance challenges from a legal perspective. Seeking to study the regulation of data access in the UK public sector, I enquire into the rules governing access to public sector data for research and innovation purposes, explaining how and by which actors these rules have been developed over time. After clarifying this book's focus on 'public sector' data and providing a brief overview of policy developments in this area, I provide a brief anatomy of a data access decision and the individuals involved in it, followed by an outline of the book's chapters.

I. Public Sector Data: Definitional Boundaries

The analysis in this book refers to public sector data typically generated throughout the operation of large-scale bureaucracies for such purposes as social security and tax collection.[10] It is not only confined to data collected and held by the UK central government such as the 25 ministerial departments, but includes a wide array of public bodies, e.g. executive agencies, local government bodies, non-departmental public bodies and non-ministerial departments.[11] However, the boundaries between 'public sector' data and data created or processed by private persons or entities may not always be clearly delineated, especially in the light of public services being contracted out to the private sector. Consider the following scenario of a public/private hybrid dataset that could be shared for research and innovation purposes:

> A regional government health agency contracts with a private healthcare analytics company to implement a new chronic disease screening program. The company handles logistics of testing kits and runs lab analyses on collected bio samples while also building a database platform to store and monitor patient test results over time. This database seamlessly integrates patient medical history data from public health records with new testing data generated by the

[9] OECD, 'A Data-Driven Public Sector: Enabling the Strategic Use of Data for Productive, Inclusive and Trustworthy Governance', vol 33 (2019) OECD Working Papers on Public Governance 33. Available at: www.oecd-ilibrary.org/governance/a-data-driven-public-sector_09ab162c-en.

[10] Connelly (n 8) 3.

[11] Cabinet Office, 'Departments, agencies and public bodies'. Available at: www.gov.uk/government/organisations.

private company's lab infrastructure. When external academics request access to this database to improve disease modelling techniques, it contains an inextricable combination of pre-existing public patient data as well as proprietary test data from the private contractor. This makes it difficult to parse which access protocols and restrictions should apply.

In practice, purely 'public' or 'private' data is becoming rare as digital services and administrative processes increasingly involve flows of data between state and non-state actors.[12] Public authorities rely on citizens and corporations to provide pertinent information on an ongoing basis, as well as to deliver essential public services that cannot be delivered based on in-house public sector capacities. This means data provenance chains are growing more complex with multiple overlapping origins.[13] As the provided scenario illustrates, even data created in the course of public services can incorporate inputs from private services. Definitions of purely 'public sector' data thus become increasingly difficult to articulate.

To demarcate its scope, this book focuses on data *directly produced by* or *collected by public authorities in the pursuance of their duties*. In the example, while a private company is generating some portion of new test data, that data collection and production process is happening explicitly under contract to fulfil public health agency duties and objectives around chronic disease screening and monitoring at a regional level. The entire hybrid database can reasonably be considered data that have been directly 'produced by' public authorities via delegated duties to private partners, even if certain lab testing components stem from private infrastructure.

Hence, the proposed demarcation does not focus on the hands that created the data (as in the hands of private sub-contractors) but on the political economy background of data creation: the mandate under which and the resources based on the data were created – both of which should be of public nature for the data to fall within the suggested demarcation. This is crucial for two reasons. First, from a legal perspective, data access considerations are influenced fundamentally by whether public tasks and resources were involved in the origination of data. Data created with and for the exercise of governmental administrative, regulatory and welfare state duties have a distinct standing compared to data which merely pass temporarily through public hands or incorporate some public and some private inputs. The fact that public sector bodies were originators and primary users shapes appropriate access frameworks regarding rights and oversight mechanisms. Second, compared to public sector data, private corporate data currently lacks developed governance frameworks enabling access for independent research and

[12] A Ballantyne and C Stewart, 'Big Data and Public-Private Partnerships in Healthcare and Research' (2019) 11 *Asian Bioethics Review* 315–326.

[13] I Susha and others, 'Achieving Voluntary Data Sharing in Cross Sector Partnerships: Three Partnership Models' (2023) 33(1) *Information and Organization* 100448.

innovation purposes. Rights and routes for researchers to negotiate data sharing with platforms, biopharma companies, private hospitals, banks, etc. remain limited and ad-hoc.[14] By contrast, public authorities are starting to develop data sharing mechanisms researchers can engage with, although, as will be shown, constraints persist. This book's spotlight on emerging governance regimes and norms around public sector data access will help to inform future discussions around private data sharing for research and innovation.

II. Public Sector Data Sharing for Research and Innovation in the UK: Policy Developments

In the UK, in the light of significant breakthroughs in big data analytics and AI over the last few decades, the government has sought to explore the potential of using 'big' government datasets to create economic and societal benefits.[15] A series of policy initiatives was developed, reflected in a series of high-profile reports and legislative instruments,[16] to make better use of UK public sector data. This policy has, particularly in the last few years, seen significant investment to facilitate public sector data sharing for research and innovation purposes.[17] Yet, there seems to be a gap between the policy drive and the legislative interventions to widen access to public sector data for external researchers/innovators and the actual 'on-the ground' experience of data sharing in the UK public sector. Empirical studies identify the existence of 'legal' and 'cultural' barriers to public sector data sharing for research and innovation purposes, raising questions about the forces that govern data access decisions.[18]

This book analyses the regulation of the activity of *sharing* data for research and innovation purposes in the UK public sector.[19] Decisions to share public

[14] See the example of Meta's Content Library. Available at: https://transparency.fb.com/researchtools/meta-content-library/.

[15] ibid 2.

[16] In terms of reports eg, R Thomas and M Walport, `Data Sharing Review Report' (2008). Available at: https://webarchive.nationalarchives.gov.uk/+/http:/www.justice.gov.uk/docs/data-sharing-review.pdf [5.24]; Law Commission, `Data Sharing Between Public Bodies: A Scoping Report' (2014). Available at: www.lawcom.gov.uk/app/uploads/2015/03/lc351_data-sharing.pdf [7.36]; legislative instruments include the Statistics and Registration Service Act (SRSA) 2007 and the Digital Economy Act (DEA) 2017.

[17] Some examples of public-sector investments are the multi-million ESRC Big Data Network. Available at: https://esrc.ukri.org/research/our-research/big-data-network/ and the Data Science Campus. Available at: www.ons.gov.uk/aboutus/whatwedo/datasciencecampus established by the Office for National Statistics in England.

[18] See the reports cited in n 16; more broadly on legal and cultural barriers to data sharing, see Centre for Excellence for Information Sharing, 'Overcoming Cultural Barriers to Information Sharing Within Regulatory Services' (2016). Available at: https://assets.publishing.service.gov.uk/government/uploads/system/uploads/attachment_data/file/535439/overcoming-cultural-barriers.pdf; G Laurie and L Stevens, 'Developing a Public Interest Mandate for the Governance and Use of Administrative Data in the United Kingdom' (2016) 43 *Journal of Law & Society* 360, 364 also provide a long list of references on the centrality of legal barriers to data sharing, predominantly in the public health sector.

[19] A decision to share data refers here to the 'provision of access to administrative datasets (…) by public bodies to other entities or individuals', see ICO, 'Data Sharing Code of Practice'. Available at:

sector data have arisen from the mundane, bureaucratic task of simply managing a database, which has gradually emerged as a distinct regulatory problem. Both the government and researchers, as well as civil society actors, have begun to understand the stakes involved in realising the untapped potential of public sector datasets. More specifically, in recent years, senior UK Government officials have announced the investment of significant resources to harness the untapped potential of massive public sector datasets. This potential was expected to contribute significantly to 'public service modernisation' and improve civil service delivery through insights produced by data-intensive research.[20] The promise of using such 'big' datasets to revolutionise our empirical understanding of complex social and economic problems has fuelled this ambition.[21]

Part of this digitalisation strategy was a £64 million investment by the British Economic and Social Research Council, via the Department for Business, Energy, and Industrial Strategy (BEIS), in the creation of a UK-wide infrastructure that would facilitate secure access to public sector administrative data for research purposes.[22] The infrastructure, called the Administrative Data Research Network (the ADRN), operated between 2013 and 2018. In this period, it demonstrated notable achievements, but also faced significant difficulties in facilitating access to public sector data for researchers. In fact, in its fourth year of operation, the Network had managed to get the data for approximately 19% of the ADRN-approved projects it had been facilitating.[23]

Academics and civil society organisations have also started to appreciate the significance of greater access to public sector data for research purposes. The increasing digitalisation of the civil service has made clear the significance of acquiring and maintaining more evidence on the basis of which we will be able to properly evaluate digital reforms, such as the HM Courts and Tribunals (HMCTS) £1.2bn digital modernisation investment.

Considering the heavy involvement of private companies in the digitalisation and, in some cases, the automation of civil services like benefit provision,[24] tensions

https://ico.org.uk/media/fororganisations/documents/1068/data_sharing_code_of_practice.pdf. It shall be stressed that 'data access' and 'data sharing' are two sides of the same coin, since data access requires that the public sector organisation share the data with an external actor.

[20] J Manzoni, 'Big Data in Government: The Challenges and Opportunities' (21 February 2017). Available at: www.gov.uk/government/speeches/big-data-in-government-the-challenges-and-opportunities. Also see E Dove, *Regulatory Stewardship of Health Research: Navigating Participant Protection and Research Promotion* (Edward Elgar 2020) 2 on how Research Ethics Committees (RECs) reviewing health research applications work 'under the umbrella of regulation that is becoming more streamlined and research-promoting' in England and Scotland.

[21] L Einav and J Levin, 'The Data Revolution and Economic Analysis' (2014) 14(1) *Innovation Policy and the Economy* 1, 7– 8.

[22] ADRN, 'History'. Available at: https://uksa.statisticsauthority.gov.uk/about-the-authority/committees/adrn/.

[23] UKSA, 'Thirteenth Meeting of the ADRN Board: Agenda and Papers' (2017). Available at: https://www.statisticsauthority.gov.uk/wp-content/uploads/2017/06/ADRN-05-06-2017.pdf 14.

[24] UN Special Rapporteur on Extreme Poverty and Human Rights, 'Digital technology, social protection and human rights: Report' (2019). Available at: https://www.ohchr.org/EN/Issues/Poverty/Pages/DigitalTechnology.aspx.

around data access for research purposes may arise. If we look at the handling of the coronavirus pandemic as an example, in April 2020 the UK Government declined to release information about the involvement of private companies like Google, Palantir and Faculty AI in the National Health Service (NHS) 'data store' which was built to help contain the outbreak. It took two months of negotiation and the threat of litigation by civil society organisations Foxglove and Open Democracy to have the contracts between the NHS and private companies disclosed.[25] Independent researchers, often affiliated with academic organisations, are both interested in and well-placed to critically scrutinise government policies that affect both individual rights and collective goods. To do so, however, they need access to data; this, it seems, is far from self-evident.

Private sector researchers and innovators have similarly demonstrated an appetite for access to public sector data. Private companies see the opportunity to use public data to develop new products and services, from traffic apps to healthcare analytics. For example, opening up transit data has allowed mobility start-ups to flourish.[26] In healthcare, researchers at pharmaceutical companies believe mining medical datasets could accelerate drug discovery.[27] AI firms want access to diverse public datasets to train machine-learning models for various applications. While potential economic benefits exist, private interests also raise additional concerns around privacy, the proprietary use of public assets, and conflicts of interest.[28] However, it can be argued that with proper controls, private sector data use can spur innovation and progress that ultimately serves the public good.[29]

These tensions and the significant attention that data sharing decisions have attracted in the last few years have led to such decisions becoming subject to legal regulation.[30] Access decisions are no longer a matter of internal discussions by public-sector organisations 'having physical and legal custody of data and deciding what is collected, aggregated and released'.[31] They are now a matter of extensive external debate. In the UK, data sharing was originally conceived of as an issue of public interest in the context of sharing confidential patient information for medical research purposes. Since the beginning of the twenty-first century, however,

[25] Open Democracy, 'Under pressure, UK government releases NHS COVID data deals with big tech'. Available at: www.opendemocracy.net/en/ournhs/under-pressure-uk-government-releases-nhs-covid-data-deals-big-tech/.

[26] G Tavmen, 'Data/Infrastructure in the Smart City: Understanding the Infrastructural Power of Citymapper App through Technicity of Data' (2020) 7 *Big Data & Society* 205395172096561.

[27] V Parvathaneni and others, 'Drug Repurposing: A Promising Tool to Accelerate the Drug Discovery Process' (2019) 24 *Drug Discovery Today* 2076.

[28] S Zuboff, *The Age of Surveillance Capitalism* (London: Profile 2019).

[29] S Aidinlis, 'Government-to-Business (G2B) Research Data Sharing and the GDPR: Reconciling the "Public" with the "Private"?' in E Kosta and R Leenes, *Research Handbook on EU Data Protection Law* (Edward Elgar 2022).

[30] Although not a central concern of the present monograph, the rise of a culture of recognising privacy rights to protect individual citizens' interests should also not be underestimated as a contributing force to making research data sharing decisions subject to legal regulation.

[31] M Burdon and others, 'Access Control in Federated Databases: How Legal Issues Shape Security' in M Wimmer and others (eds), *Electronic Government: 6th International Conference, EGOV 2007* (Springer 2007) 235.

the Department of Health has made the increased and more streamlined research use of NHS, primary care or social care data, a central aim of its research governance framework.[32] Legislative acts, such as the National Health Service Act (NHS Act) 2006 and the Health and Social Care Act (HSCA) 2012 delineate the powers of custodians to enable health data sharing for research purposes.[33] More recently, policy interest was extended to non-health data and its potential use by researchers and innovators. A series of White Papers, independent reviews and reports produced or commissioned by the UK Government suggested that the broader use of public sector data to facilitate research and policy development should be regarded as a priority.[34] Legal developments followed in the interest of providing a 'robust UK-wide evidence base to inform research, thereby guiding the development, implementation and evaluation of policy'.[35] Section 64 of the Digital Economy Act (DEA) 2017 established a generic legal power for public-sector custodians to disclose data they hold 'in the context of their functions' for research purposes, thus enhancing existing data sharing discretionary powers.

Based on these developments, does the law enable wider access to public sector data for research and innovation purposes? This question has been in the minds of policymakers in the UK for some time. In 2015, the Law Commission enquired into 'whether there are inappropriate *legal or other hurdles* to the transfer of information between public bodies and, potentially, between public bodies and private bodies engaged in public service delivery' (emphasis added).[36] The Commission identified legal and cultural hurdles by reference to a series of consultations and empirical studies,[37] as well as other academic and policy studies of risk aversion in UK public sector data sharing.[38] The Law Commission claimed that legal reform

[32] The Research Governance Framework operates like a code of conduct for the Department of Health, as it outlines principles of good governance related to research in health and social care, see Department of Health, 'Research Governance Framework for Health and Social Care' (2nd edn, 2005) 17; National Institute for Social Care and Health Research Wales, 'Maximising the Use of Routine Data for Research in Wales' (2013). Available at: www.healthandcareresearch.gov.wales/uploads/Policy%20%26%20Strategy/Use%20of%20routine%20data/Maximising%20the%20Use%20of%20Routine%20Data%20for%20Research%20in%20Wales.pdf 3.13: 'Maximising the use of routine data can play a key role in enhancing the evidence base and offering innovative approaches to policy development and evaluation'.

[33] Section 251 of the National Health Service Act 2006 and section 259 of the Health and Social Care Act 2012 are relevant here.

[34] Cabinet Office, 'Open Data: unleashing the potential' (28 June 2012); S Shakespeare, 'Shakespeare Review: An Independent Review of Public Sector Information' (May 2013); Administrative Data Taskforce, 'The UK Administrative Data Research Network: Improving Access for Research and Policy' (December 2012).

[35] Administrative Data Taskforce ibid 2.

[36] Law Commission (n 16) 1.2.

[37] House of Commons, 'The Bichard Inquiry Report' (2004). Available at: https://dera.ioe.ac.uk/6394/1/report.pdf; M Flynn, 'South Gloucestershire Safeguarding Adults Board, Winterbourne View Hospital, A Serious Case Review' (2012). Available at: https://hosted.southglos.gov.uk/wv/report.pdf; Birmingham Safeguarding Children Board, 'Serious Case Review in respect of the death of Keanu Williams' (2013). Available at: www.cscb-new.co.uk/downloads/Serious%20Case%20Reviews%20%20-%20exec.%20summaries/SCR_Archive/Birmingham%20SCR%20-%20KW%20(2013).pdf.

[38] Thomas and Walport (n 16) 5.24; Laurie and Stevens (n 18) 362.

can 'play a part in addressing problems of data sharing between public bodies'.[39] The Law Commission itself did not advocate for wider legal powers but for more clarity, also stressing that 'the problem is not one of lack of power to share so much as disinclination to use the powers'.[40] The Information Commissioner's Office, in its response to the Law Commission consultation, argued that 'a more prominent role for data protection law' would be critical to avoid confusion for practitioners.[41] Within the same report, various government departments and public bodies called for a codification of existing law to provide them with a 'map or single table of existing legislative data sharing powers'.[42]

While views echoing the centrality of legal hurdles to data sharing were not voiced for the first time,[43] the Law Commission report also recorded another view on the matter. This view highlights the centrality of an organisational *culture* that 'influences how personal information is viewed and handled'. In other words, there may be dominating ideas, norms and shared practices within organisations that pose barriers to data access. This culture creates barriers for research and innovation data sharing by aggravating 'perceptions by all parties of risk that will come from that activity'.[44] Authoritative policy reports written by senior UK Government officials,[45] which similarly highlight the significance of cultural barriers, concur that a culture shift within the UK public sector is more important than any legal amendment to alleviate data sharing barriers. Against this backdrop, this book will examine the existence of legal and cultural barriers to data access by drawing both on the legal and organisational frameworks for data sharing in the UK public sector, and their application in concrete organisational environments across the UK. In doing so, it will shed light on the factors influencing the regulation of data access decisions for research and innovation purposes.

III. Sharing Data for Research and Innovation Purposes? A Brief Anatomy

Who are the individuals involved in decisions to share data for research and innovation purposes in practice? How do they communicate with each other? What are their organisational affiliations and professional qualifications? The following scenario is illustrative of a potential data sharing request:

[39] Law Commission (n 16) 11.1.
[40] ibid 11.4.
[41] ibid 11.5.
[42] ibid 11.62.
[43] Administrative Data Taskforce (n 34) 16; Laurie and Stevens (n 18) 377 citing academic literature on data sharing in the public health sector.
[44] Laurie and Stevens ibid 362.
[45] Thomas and Walport (n 16) 5.24; also see Centre for Excellence in Information Sharing (n 18) 7.

Sarah is a researcher at a university who wants access to patient data from the national public health organisation to study trends in chronic diseases. She submits a request to the organisation describing her research goals and methodologies. The request goes to Emma, a data analyst at the organisation. Emma reviews the request and identifies which datasets within the organisation's databases would be most relevant for Sarah's research. Emma asks Sarah some clarifying questions about precisely which variables she needs. Once Emma understands Sarah's needs, she prepares the relevant datasets for disclosure. This involves selecting the required variables, removing any potentially identifying personal information, and reformatting the data into a user-friendly structure for Sarah.

Emma then passes the prepared datasets to Michael, an Information Governance official at the organisation. Michael thoroughly reviews the datasets to ensure no personally identifiable information remains that could pose a privacy risk if released. He also doublechecks that the disclosure would comply with all relevant data protection laws and the organisation's data sharing policies. Satisfied the disclosure meets legal and ethical requirements, Michael informs Sarah that her request has conditional approval pending final authorization from organisation leadership.

The request is sent to senior executives Li and Sanjay. They consider whether sharing the data would serve the public interest by advancing medical research. They confirm the public benefits outweigh any risks or costs to the organisation. Li and Sanjay grant final approval for Emma to securely grant access to the datasets to Sarah for her research. They inform Sarah she must sign a data sharing agreement restricting how she can use the data before she receives access.

'Data analysts' are the officials who are working most closely to the datasets. Although they may come from a variety of disciplinary backgrounds,[46] analysts share a common educational background which involves statistical knowledge and some familiarity with managing datasets.[47] Analysts are responsible for the core operational dimensions of data sharing. These dimensions include such tasks as identifying the desired variables within the datasets, matching particular variables with other variables of interest in other datasets and 'cleaning' the datasets (ie, fixing or removing incorrect, corrupted, incorrectly formatted, duplicate, or incomplete data) so that researchers or innovators can use them.[48]

[46] C Lindner, 'Where do Data Scientists Come From?'. Available at: https://medium.com/indeed-engineering/where-do-data-scientists-come-from-fc526023ace.

[47] P Besse and B Laurent, 'From Statistician to Data Scientist'. Available at: https://arxiv.org/abs/1509.07804.

[48] R Goerge and B Joo Lee, 'Matching and Cleaning Administrative Data' in M Ver Ploeg et al (eds), *Studies of Welfare Populations: Data Collection and Research Issues* (NAP 2002) 197.

The second group, which also works relatively closely to the datasets, is that of 'Information Governance' (IG) officials. They are responsible for ensuring that data sharing procedures are not only robust from an information security perspective, but also compliant with the law and, more broadly, with established standards of best practice.[49] Like data analysts, IG officials come from diverse backgrounds, which often include studies in law, systems architecture, and information management. Since public bodies are responsible for the lawfulness and technical propriety of data sharing, IG officials are mostly working for such bodies.[50]

Finally, yet importantly, policymakers are the ultimate decision-makers within the data sharing process, despite the fact that they are both physically distant and distant in terms of technical expertise and understanding from the datasets. They may have various job titles such as 'information asset owners' or 'data custodians'. While analysts advise about the feasibility of a proposed data disclosure and IG officials about the legal and technical safeguards that should be implemented before the disclosure takes place, policymakers concern themselves with the overall desirability and appropriateness of the request.[51] Crucially, policymakers assess whether the proposed disclosure is in the 'public interest', taking into account the potential benefits that the data use could yield and the costs that the public body would have to incur to share the data.

The analysis in Chapters 6–8 present how the above types of officials have interacted in stabilising or renegotiating the rules that govern data sharing for research and innovation purposes, while constructing and consolidating their own organisational identities. For example, policymakers consolidate a particular interpretation of the 'public benefit' requirement through their precedent decisions, while, at the same time, they draw on the conventions followed within their organisational environment, to decide on the desirability of granting or refusing a request. In other words, data sharing frameworks (either stemming from law, policy, or organisational guidance) structure and influence individual action. At the same time, these rules are not set in stone but are fluid and renegotiated through the multiplicity of interactions among individual an organisational actors in the data sharing space.

IV. Overview

This book is comprised of ten chapters. Following this introductory chapter, Chapters 2 and 3 lay the book's analytical foundations by presenting the issue of

[49] T Keyser and C Dainty, *The Information Governance Toolkit: Data Protection, Caldicott, Confidentiality* (CRC 2016) 20.

[50] Although other bodies such as academic research centres also specialise in information governance, see D Ford and others, 'The SAIL Databank: Building a National Architecture for e-health Research and Evaluation' (2009) 9 *British Medical Council Health Services Research* 157.

[51] N Waithira and others, 'Data Management and Sharing Policy: The First Step Towards Promoting Data Sharing' (2019) 17 *British Medical Council Medicine* 80.

public sector data ownership in the UK and provide the conceptual and methodological framework within which this enquiry has been undertaken respectively. Chapters 4 and 5 present the frameworks regulating access to public sector data for research and innovation purposes in the UK. Chapters 6, 7 and 8 present the empirical findings of my fieldwork by reference to concrete applications in real-world organisational environments across the UK public sector. Chapters 9 and 10 conclude the work by reflecting on proposed legal reforms and solutions for widening access to public sector data for research and innovation purposes in the advent of increasing public sector automation.

Chapter 2 unpacks the complex issue of control over public sector data by analysing three major perspectives. Each perspective makes different fundamental claims about whether public sector data should be seen as collectively, organizationally, or individually controlled. These claims have significant real-world implications for data sharing. The first view conceives public sector data as a public good benefiting all citizens and urges open data sharing, as seen in open data initiatives. The second view sees government bodies as owners of data to serve their interests, justifying restricted access policies. The third view draws on data protection laws to argue citizens own and control their personal data held by government, underpinning new rights like portability. As will be demonstrated in later chapters, these divergent assumptions about whether access should be open, restricted, or citizen controlled underlie and influence negotiations and attitudes regarding public sector data sharing. This foundational chapter elucidates the deeper data politics at play.

Chapter 3 concisely presents the analytical and methodological framework of the work. To conduct an analysis of public sector data regulation in the UK, the research adopts a theoretical lens that draws on the regulation theory concept of 'regulatory space'. Regulation of access decisions is examined in this thesis under three analytical dimensions of the 'data sharing space': the 'actors' which have populated the space and have been involved in shaping data sharing processes and frameworks over time; the 'institutions' or 'rules of the game' that filter access to public sector data for research and innovation purposes and the 'interactions' between the actors, through which the space has been shaped and recalibrated over time, e.g. at times 'opening up' to allow wider access and at other times 'closing down' to confine data access to specific uses. Regarding methodology, the monograph relies on a mixed-methods historical research design, which employed semi-structured interview (involving 42 participants) and documentary data about the regulation of data access decisions in the UK public sector.

Starting with frameworks, Chapter 4 analyses hard and soft legal frameworks, including organisational guidelines and policies and government guidance, applying to sharing public sector data in the UK for research and innovation purposes. This presentation is viewed from the perspective of the addressee of public sector data, ie, the interested researcher or innovator who wants to obtain access to such data. After providing an overview of different addressees, the chapter starts by analysing free-standing rights to access public sector data such as the ones enshrined in the Freedom of Information Act 2000. The analysis then turns to disclosure duties established in a vast number of legislative instruments such as the forthcoming online safety legislation. Then, the discussion turns to cases where public sector bodies have discretionary powers to disclose data, focusing on the legal powers established by the Digital Economy Act 2017. Finally, an analysis of legal barriers to access public sector data for research and innovation is offered, before assessing the impact of each of the different affordances analysed above to research and innovation.

Chapter 5 turns to a more specific and contentious legal issue. It elaborates upon the question of whether private entities are allowed access to public sector data for research and innovation purposes under applicable hard and soft law, and under which conditions. The chapter identifies that data protection law creates a divide between 'public interest' and 'private interests' as lawful grounds for processing. Public authorities are advised to rely on 'public interest' while private entities rely on 'legitimate interests'. This makes it difficult to justify providing access to public sector data for commercial entities pursuing privately funded research and innovation. The chapter proposes reconceptualising 'public interest' based on contribution to collective economic/societal welfare, not organisational identity. Adopting this interpretation requires clarifying the contribution of data sharing to public good, respecting data rights, implementing robust safeguards like pseudonymisation, and building public trust.

Moving towards the application of regulatory frameworks in the UK public sector, Chapter 6 considers the way in which the actors populating the data sharing space in the UK have shaped its historical development over the last four decades. Three main historical phases are identified: informality (when ad-hoc bargaining to access data for research and innovation was the dominant mode of access), formalisation (when the creation of formal frameworks sought to streamline data sharing) and fragmentation (when access to public sector data remains unequal). Under the lens of regulatory space, the chapter sketches the way in which particular organisational actors have defined the scope of central issues to the development of the space. Two central narratives invoked by actors stand out and determine who is 'in' and who is 'out' of the data sharing space: 'efficiency', referring to data-intensive research and innovation as a way to improve policymaking, and 'accountability', referring to research as a method of critically scrutinising the government's policies in the name of transparency and openness.

Chapter 7 identifies the emergence of different organisational data sharing cultures in the UK public sector, which often diverge from hard and soft rules, examining their potential to streamline or block data sharing on the ground. The two core constituents of these cultures are unpacked: unwritten, uncodified, and conventional normative assumptions about the ownership of public sector data and the relevance of research and innovation to policy-making priorities. Particular views as to the ownership of public sector data, or as to the desired alignment between research and a custodian's policy aims, are associated, as the chapters shows, with the creation and implementation of particular types of data sharing frameworks. For example, managers who see data as a public good tend to have transparent, accountable procedures for data access. Those who see it as their property resist accountability and keep processes opaque. Overall, the chapter shows how influential, yet uncodified cultural factors shape the implementation of data access frameworks, highlighting the divergence between legal rules and practical regulation.

Chapter 8 unpacks a common theme present in all applications chapters: the significance of daily interactions between researchers, innovators, and low-level technical stuff in the public sector for the development and application of data sharing frameworks, shifting the attention to the bottom-up and commonplace understanding of data sharing frameworks rather than merely analysing high-level legal and policy decisions. Disagreements, concerns, and crises are negotiated and perceptions about the desirability of data sharing are shifted through informal, small-scale iterations, not formal decision-making structures. Either with regard to 'opening up' the boundaries of the space to widen access to data for researchers and innovators, or in 'closing down' the same boundaries to confine data access to certain uses of data, such small-scale interactions matter. The chapter proceeds from unpacking the role of data analysts as the prominent network behind these interactions, before discussing the nature of the interactions themselves as informal and incremental, ie, likely to result in bigger changes through small steps.

Moving towards solutions, Chapter 9 proposes changes in legal frameworks and organisational-level policies to stimulate wider use of public sector data in the public interest through research and innovation. The chapter argues that freedom of information (FOI) legislation like the UK's FOIA has limitations in the digital state, as it enables enable static access to information, whereas researchers and innovators need ongoing access to massive, updated datasets to effectively pursue their goals. The chapter proposes legislative reform to create a legal presumption that government data shall be made available to researchers and innovators under reasonable conditions. This would be similar to the presumption in FOI law that government information should be disclosed unless an exemption applies. In this way, the onus would shift from researchers and innovators having to argue why they should get access, to public bodies having to argue why access should be justifiably withheld in a given case. The presumption would affirm access as a default starting point, rather than place this issue fully at the discretion of data controllers as it is currently the case.

Chapter 10 concludes the book by considering the challenges that are raised for public sector data sharing for research and innovation by the automation of an increasing number of public services. As powerful private technology companies are often contracted to develop automated systems for public sector use, their proprietary algorithms and corporate interests introduce obstacles to transparent external research. Furthermore, automated systems require massive, varied datasets to train and refine – far beyond what is needed for a human decision maker. Providing comprehensive data access is becoming more demanding. With automation blurring lines of accountability between algorithmic systems and human decision makers in the public sector, understanding information flows is a major challenge. Reflections are offered on these challenges as well as potential steps towards addressing them.

2

Whose Data? Control Over Public Sector Data in the UK

The question of who controls public sector data is vitally important, yet far from straightforward. As datasets proliferate within government, determining rights over and benefits from public sector information becomes ever more salient. In this chapter, I unpack the complex issue of control over public sector data through analysing three major perspectives: data as a public good benefiting all citizens, data as controlled by public sector bodies to serve their interests and data as controlled by individual citizens who can be identified by them. Each view makes fundamental claims about whether public sector data should be seen as collectively, organisationally, or individually controlled. These claims have significant real-world implications for whether and how such data are shared for research and innovation. Therefore, understanding the conceptual underpinnings of control over public sector data is an essential first step.

After introducing key background caveats and discussing the treatment of control over public sector data under UK law, I systematically examine the three viewpoints. The first view conceives of public sector data as a public good benefiting all citizens, urging governance modes like data commons and open data initiatives. The second view sees public sector data as owned by government bodies to serve their interests, justifying restricted access and public sector data commercialisation policies. The third view draws on data protection laws to argue that citizens own and control their personal data held by government, underpinning new data rights such as portability. Each view is substantiated through academic literature and real-world developments. While divergent assumptions become apparent about whether data access should be open, restricted, or citizen controlled, I will show that the three views are not mutually exclusive, but rather operate across a spectrum in which arguments overlap in various ways.

This framing sets the stage for the analysis to follow regarding data sharing practices across the UK public sector. The analysis of the different perspectives helps to interpret why participants espouse certain attitudes in the context of real-world data sharing for research and innovation. Fundamental notions of control underlie access negotiations, as will be demonstrated in later chapters. In this foundational chapter, thus, I elucidate the deeper data politics at play.

I. Personal or Non-personal Data? A Focal Distinction

An important caveat must be introduced before analysing differing views on control over public sector data. A key distinction exists between personal and non-personal data, which has significant implications for rights and control. While a lot of ink has been spilled on the concept of identifiability in data protection law,[1] the present discussion confines itself to the relevance of this distinction for the analysis in this chapter.

Under UK and EU law, personal data refers to any information relating to an identified or identifiable natural person.[2] In contrast, non-personal or anonymous data does not relate to an identified or identifiable individual. The EU's General Data Protection Regulation (GDPR) establishes a framework of rights for individuals over their personal data. However, such rights do not necessarily apply to non-personal, aggregated, or anonymized public sector datasets. This distinction affects discussions of control over data. For personal public sector data, such as health records or social security information, notions of individual rights and consent are relevant given the connection to specific citizens. But for non-personal public sector data such as transportation statistics or census data, individual rights-based perspectives carry less weight.

However, in practice, clearly delineating between personal and non-personal public sector data poses challenges. Public sector databases often contain a mix of directly and indirectly identifiable information.[3] Anonymisation techniques are imperfect and re-identification of supposedly anonymous data occurs.[4] New technologies that connect datasets can re-personalise aggregated information,[5] whereas metadata attached to non-personal records can render them personal.[6]

[1] M Mourby and others, 'Are 'Pseudonymised' Data Always Personal Data? Implications of the GDPR for Administrative Data Research in the UK' (2018) 34(2) *Computer Law & Security Review* 222–33; M Finck and F Pallas, 'They Who Must Not Be Identified – Distinguishing Personal from Non-Personal Data under the GDPR' (2020) 10 *International Data Privacy Law* 11.; M Hintze, 'Viewing the GDPR through a De-Identification Lens: A Tool for Compliance, Clarification, and Consistency' (2018) 8 *International Data Privacy Law* 86.

[2] Article 4(1) Regulation (EU) 2016/679 of the European Parliament and of the Council of 27 April 2016 on the protection of natural persons with regard to the processing of personal data and on the free movement of such data, and repealing Directive 95/46/EC (General Data Protection Regulation): '"personal data" means any information relating to an identified or identifiable natural person ('data subject'); an identifiable natural person is one who can be identified, directly or indirectly, in particular by reference to an identifier such as a name, an identification number, location data, an online identifier or to one or more factors specific to the physical, physiological, genetic, mental, economic, cultural, or social identity of that natural person'.

[3] P Conradie and S Choenni, 'On the Barriers for Local Government Releasing Open Data' (2014) 31 *Government Information Quarterly* S10.

[4] T Krizan and others, 'In-Situ Anonymization of Big Data', *2015 38th International Convention on Information and Communication Technology, Electronics and Microelectronics (MIPRO)* (IEEE 2015) http://ieeexplore.ieee.org/document/7160282/.

[5] P Schwartz and D Solove, 'The PII Problem: Privacy and a New Concept of Personally Identifiable Information' (2011) 86 *NYU Law Review* 1814.

[6] Finck and Pallas (n 1) 16.

Due to these practical difficulties disaggregating personal from non-personal data within public sector information systems, this discussion will proceed under the assumption that public sector data implicates personal data. While recognising that non-personal public sector data exists, the realities of public sector data make it difficult to separate entirely. Data types like transportation statistics or census datasets may seem non-personal at first glance. However, examining the granular, individual-level records behind aggregate figures, or connecting to other datasets, can often re-identify people. For example, transportation data may contain detailed logs with licence plate numbers or travel patterns for specific vehicles. Census datasets track individuals and households over time across geographic blocks. Connecting temporary anonymised IDs or machine IDs in these datasets with other information sources may enable re-identification.[7] Hence, the approach taken here aims to account for the intertwined nature of personal and non-personal data in the public sector context.

II. The Meaning of Control

Another important clarification relates to the understanding of control over data in this chapter and, more broadly, in this book. The notion refers to *decisional authority*. In other words, recognising that an entity controls certain data means that they get to decide how the data will be managed, whether access to such data will be provided to other parties, and how the data will be used or analysed to achieve certain outcomes. Control over data is interwoven into the core political dilemmas and questions of our time, particularly topical through the lens of 'surveillance capitalism',[8] where large private-sector companies 'claim human experience as raw material free for the taking' and seek to possess a 'right to own the behavioural data derived from human experience'.[9] The question becomes: Who controls the data collected and harvested by the public and private sectors? *Who should benefit* from the numerous advantages that their analysis might yield?

This notion is to be distinguished from the often-invoked notion of data ownership, which has been used as a powerful analytical and rhetorical vehicle that gives rise to 'protective rights that exclude others from an individual's personal informational sphere'.[10] As it will be shown, the terminology of ownership is not apt for describing control over public sector data in UK law, even if there are accounts of ownership which associate it with decisional authority akin to the notion of control adopted in this book.[11]

[7] Y De Montjoye and others, 'Unique in the Crowd: The Privacy Bounds of Human Mobility' (2013) 3 *Scientific Reports* 1376.

[8] S Zuboff, *The Age of Surveillance Capitalism* (London: Profile 2019).

[9] ibid Chapter 6.

[10] P Hummel and others, 'Own Data? Ethical Reflections on Data Ownership' (2020) 34(3) *Philosophy and Technology* 545–72.

[11] J Waldron, *The Right to Private Property* (Clarendon Press 1988) 41.

III. Control Over Public Sector Data in UK Law

European human rights law frameworks present data-related rights as part of fundamental rights, suggesting that they are 'inalienable and unsuitable for propertisation, commodification, commercialization'.[12] Perhaps due to this intricate connection with personhood, data ownership is not recognised in UK law which does not recognise property interests in 'mere facts or information'.[13]

In fact, and when one gets closer to public sector information, looking at legal or regulatory definitions, there is less emphasis on 'ownership' and more emphasis on 'possession' or 'collection' to refer to control over data. Statutory instruments prefer the terminology of information *held* (section 64 of the Digital Economy Act 2017) or *obtained* (section 38 of the Statistics and Registration Services Act 2007) by a public authority 'in relation to its functions'. Courts have also consistently denied the extension of property and other private law rights in similar cases. In *Fairstar*, the Court of Appeal sidestepped a proprietary claim to the content of business-related emails as a distraction from the real issue of rights within an agency relationship to inspect and copy emails related to one's business affairs.[14] The same Court drew a clear distinction between 'tangible' and 'intangible' property in *Your Response Ltd*; in rejecting a common-law lien over an electronic database, it clarified that rights in respect of data are contract-based and do not confer to the right-holder property in the data.[15] Similar were the findings in subsequent case law.[16]

Who, then, controls public sector data? In other words, who decides how public sector information should be managed and used under the law? While there is an abundance of data protection and privacy case law, the courts have seemingly intervened less in how public authorities use their discretionary powers to manage public sector datasets when a human-rights claim is not made. Does this mean that the matter lies entirely in the hands of administrators? In some cases, the courts themselves defer some decisions to administrators by saying that specific questions are *non-justiciable, and thus* they lack competence for judicial review. A prime example of such questions emerges from the allocation of public goods. If public sector information is seen as a public good, one might argue that the law

[12] N Purtova, 'Property in Personal Data. A European Perspective on the Instrumentalist Theory of Propertisation' (2010) 2 *European Journal of Legal Studies* 193; E Harbinja, 'Posthumous Medical Data Donation: The Case for a Legal Framework' in J Krutzinna and L Floridi (eds), *The Ethics of Medical Data Donation* (Springer Open 2019) 103–4.

[13] J Contreras and others, 'Patient Data Ownership' (2018) 319 *Journal of the American Medical Association* 935.

[14] *Fairstar Heavy Transport NV v Adkins* [2013] EWCA Civ 886 (Mummery LJ) at [46–50].

[15] *Your Response Ltd v Datateam Business Media Ltd* [2014] EWCA Civ 281 (Moore-Bick LJ) at [29–34].

[16] *Environment Agency v Churngold Recycling Ltd* [2014] EWCA Civ 909: copies of electronic data cannot be the subject matter of the tort of conversion; *Capita Plc v Darch* [2017] EWHC 1248 (Ch): recognising property over private emails would breach the Convention right to private life of the other correspondent.

affords almost unfettered discretion to public sector officials when it comes to the management of public sector data.

In the English administrative law context, the so-called non-justiciability doctrine was established by the Court of Appeal in *Cambridge Health Authority*.[17] The findings of the court in this case (to deny a challenge to health authority's resource allocation decisions) were endorsed in subsequent House of Lords case law where the courts were found to lack the competence to review the discretionary allocation of resources.[18] King argues that a proper reading of the case law makes it clear that the crucial non-justiciability factor is that '*cost* was a relevant and explicit concern of the authority's decision' (emphasis added).[19] He contrasts the above line of cases with the judgment of the Court of Appeal in *Anne Marie Rogers*.[20] The Court held in this case that when the availability of resources is irrelevant, a health authority's decision to refuse funding by reference to personal characteristics could not be regarded as 'rational'. Hence, the non-justiciability principle focusses on the notion of competing needs relating to distributing *limited resources* among many clients. Public sector data, however, can hardly be envisaged as a 'scarce resource'. It is not relinquished when another entity or individual is granted access; it can still be used for different purposes and satisfy the needs of different clients. This means that administrators' decisions about how to manage public sector information are, in principle, subject to judicial review and their decisional authority and control are not unlimited. To give an example, if, under section 39(7) of the Statistics and Registration Services Act 2007, the Office for National Statistics were to interpret the notion of a 'fit and proper researcher' by reference to the colour of the applicants' eyes, the courts would review this policy on the grounds of unreasonableness.

Nevertheless, the rigour of judicial review is a different question from justiciability and can be significantly weakened when the courts demonstrate excessive deference to the administrative decision maker. The two main reasons for judicial deference raised by Lord Sumption in *Lord Carlile*[21] are 'institutional capacity' and 'constitutional legitimacy' ie, institutional and constitutional limitations on a court's ability to substitute an executive decision. Such considerations as the expertise and sources of information of the decision maker or their advisors, whether the assessment is predictive and political, and technical expertise are crucial considerations here. In the advent of constantly evolving technologies, public sector data management is quite a complex, multi-layered procedure. The officials managing the data are able to make sense of it, understand how many variables need to be

[17] *R v Cambridge Health Authority, ex parte B* [1995] 1 WLR 898.

[18] *Ex p Tandy* [1998] 2 WLR 884 (Lord Browne-Wilkinson) at [749]; *R v Chief Constable of Sussex ex p International Trader's Ferry Ltd* [1999] 2 AC 418; [1998] 3 WLR 1260 (Lord Slynn of Hadley) at [430].

[19] J King, 'The Justiciability of Resource Allocation' (2007) 70(2) *The Modern Law Review* 197, 200.

[20] *R (on the application of Anne Marie Rogers) v Swindon NHS Primary Care Trust, Secretary of State for Health* [2006] EWCA Civ 392.

[21] *R (on the application of Lord Carlile of Berriew QC and others (Appellants) v Secretary of State for the Home Department (Respondent)* [2014] UKSC 60.

used for a specific purpose or what kind of procedural safeguards are necessary to ensure confidentiality. Lord Bingham clarified in *Smith* that '… the more remote the subject matter of a decision from ordinary judicial experience, the more hesitant the court must necessarily be in holding a decision to be irrational'.[22] This is illustrated by such examples as the administrative case law on planning; in reviewing discretionary decisions to grant or reject permission for new building projects, the courts show massive deference to the view of a local planning inspector or the Environment Secretary in respect of what is in the public interest.[23] Hence, one should not expect a very robust judicial review of discretion in managing public sector information; the courts are more likely than not to accept the defensibility of an administrative policy if the latter is not clearly problematic.

As this brief treatment of control over public sector data in UK law has shown, public officials managing public sector information are viewed by the law as authoritative controllers of the datasets, even if, strictly speaking, there is no legal ownership over data. The three different views on control over public sector data that are now analysed are inspired by legal and philosophical understandings of control over data, fusing these understandings with concrete normative aims and political agendas about the management of this significant resource.

IV. Viewing Data as a Public Good

The first view rejects the commodification of data and proceeds from a conception of public sector data as a public good, belonging to society as a whole. It claims that data is more than a commodity, as it embodies relations which make it a common resource that can benefit the public interest.[24] The proponents of this view advocate for a shift from the current individualist data governance paradigm towards more collective modes of governance, proposing such solutions as the so-called data commons.

Several scholars and public sector representatives have been treating data as public infrastructure to be used to improve knowledge of our society.[25] Writing about the use of public sector data for independent research, for example, Laurie and Stevens propose that public bodies endorse the 'public nature of administrative

[22] *R v Ministry of Defence Ex p Smith* [1996] QB 517 (Lord Bingham) at [556].

[23] *Tesco Stores v Environment Secretary* [1995] 1 WLR 759; *First Secretary of State v Hammersmatch Properties Ltd* [2005] EWCA Civ 1360; *R (Springhall) v London Borough of Richmond upon Thames* [2006] EWCA Civ 19.

[24] A Tarkowski and F Vogelezang, 'Public Data Commons: A Public Interest Framework for Business-to-Government Data Sharing in the Data Act.' (Open Future Policy Brief). Available at: https://openfuture.eu/wp-content/uploads/2022/05/Public-data-commons-A-public-interest-framework-for-B2G-data-sharing-in-the-Data-Act.1.pdf.

[25] P Arzberger and others, 'Promoting Access to Public Research Data for Scientific, Economic, and Social Development' (2004) 3 *Data Science Journal* 135. House of Commons Science and Technology Committee, 'The Big Data Dilemma: Fourth Report of Session 2015–16' 20.

data as a public resource … seeing data reuse as a core feature of the operations as a public authority'.[26] While she does not confine her argument to public sector information, Mazzucato elaborates on a vision of data as public good by reference to the economic resources which funded the production of data in the first place.[27] As she explains, the very technologies that underpin data production were created collectively using taxpayers' money, thus supporting the case that the public's data should be owned by a 'public repository' instead of belonging to different private and public data controllers.[28] In a similar vein, Rahman stresses the need to ensure social control over 'vital private industries' that provided foundational goods and services on which the rest of the society depends,[29] as is the case with data-driven services.

Other scholars highlight the potential of data to serve public interest objectives to justify its definition as a public good. Taylor puts forward the argument that data should be formally characterised as a public good due to its potential to alleviate poverty and combat disease, as well as inform emergency responses.[30] This view has been especially influential during the COVID-19 pandemic, amplifying voices that conceive health data as a 'global public good'.[31] Collington concurs that this potential social and economic value is not realised by the 'current modes of describing and conceptualising the data held by government bodies within policymaking'.[32] She calls for a conceptualisation of such data as a 'public asset' to enable 'collective forms of wealth and social endeavours'.[33]

Recently, the perspective of data as a public good found its way into proposed EU legislation and, more specifically, the proposed EU Data Act, albeit in a limited form. The Act establishes an exception to the norm of businesses controlling the flow of data in the market, empowering public authorities to mandate access and control of such data for the purposes of serving specific public interest aims.[34] Arguably, the scope of the proposed legislation is much narrower than the aspired contributions for public data to realise 'collective wealth and social endeavours': public authorities may exercise control over business data in case of 'exceptional need', ie to respond to a public emergency, to prevent it or to assist in its recovery,

[26] G Laurie and L Stevens, 'Developing a Public Interest Mandate for the Governance and Use of Administrative Data in the United Kingdom' (2016) 43 *Journal of Law and Society* 360, 383.

[27] M Mazzucato, 'Let's Make Private Data into a Public Good' [2018] *MIT Technology Review* 74–75.

[28] ibid.

[29] K Sabeel Rahman, 'The New Utilities: Private Power, Social Infrastructure, and the Revival of the Public Utility Concept' (2017) 39 *Cardozo Law Review* 1621.

[30] L Taylor, 'The Ethics of Big Data as a Public Good: Which Public? Whose Good?' (2016) 374 *Philosophical Transactions of the Royal Society A: Mathematical, Physical and Engineering Sciences* 20160126.

[31] World Health Organization, 'Health Data as a Global Public Good – A Call for Health Data Governance' (29 July 2021).

[32] R Collington, 'Digital Public Assets' (Commonwealth) (October 2019).

[33] ibid 4.

[34] A Petel, 'Chapter 5 of the Data Act – What Is the European Concept of "B2G Data Sharing" in the Data Act Proposal?' (*KU Leuven CITIP Blog*, 21 June 2022).

as well as to fulfil a public interest task that has been explicitly provided by law.[35] Still, this is a pocket of departure from the established individualist data protection and sharing paradigm in Europe. It is also indicative of a broader tendency in Europe, as countries such as France and Finland have established legislation to facilitate the public control of privately held data that are linked to the activities of public entities.[36]

Advocates of the view of data as a public good criticise the so-called 'responsibilisation of data protection',[37] whereby the burden of protecting personal data falls mostly on the shoulders of the data subject.[38] They argue that individualised approaches will never be able to combat systemic problems like excessive surveillance, unfair data-driven decision making and environmental externalities.[39] Instead, they call for 'alternative systems of value creation' from personal data through 'collective or communal' data ownership.[40] On the one hand, this is seen as addressing concerns about the individual commercialisation of data: loss of privacy,[41] unrealistic expectations about the worth of personal data,[42] and undermining one's personhood.[43] On the other hand, Taylor and others note that the boundaries for 'group ownership' of personal data may not be any easier to define than for individuals.[44]

Nonetheless, scholars and stakeholders have explored the idea of a data commons exercising collective control over data as a public/common good.[45] Zygmuntowski, Zoboli and Nemitz put forward the idea of public data commons relying on public actors to 'aggregate and steward citizen and commercial data'.[46]

[35] Article 15 of the Proposal for a REGULATION OF THE EUROPEAN PARLIAMENT AND OF THE COUNCIL on harmonised rules on fair access to and use of data (Data Act) COM/2022/68 final.

[36] The French law for a Digital Republic (Loi pour une République numérique) which allows public sector bodies to access data that is held privately but linked to a public entity and its activities, and the Finnish Forest Act, a sectoral regulation that establishes a public body tasked with gathering data about forestry.

[37] R Mahieu and others, 'Collectively Exercising the Right of Access: Individual Effort, Societal Effect' (2018) 7 *Internet Policy Review* https://policyreview.info/node/927.

[38] J Wong and others, 'Data Protection for the Common Good: Developing a Framework for a Data Protection-Focused Data Commons' (2022) 4 *Data & Policy* e3.

[39] J Tennison, 'We Need a More Collective Approach to Data Governance. How Might It Look?' (14 March 2022).

[40] J Hicks, 'The Future of Data Ownership: An Uncommon Research Agenda' (2023) 71 *The Sociological Review* 544.

[41] J Montgomery, 'Data Sharing and the Idea of Ownership' (2017) 23 *The New Bioethics* 81.

[42] B Evans, 'Much Ado about Data Ownership' (2011) 25 *Harvard Journal of Law & Technology* 69.

[43] L Floridi, *The Fourth Revolution How the Infosphere Is Reshaping Human Reality* (Oxford University Press 2014).

[44] L Taylor and others (eds), *Group Privacy: New Challenges of Data Technologies* (Springer International Publishing 2017). Available at: http://link.springer.com/10.1007/978-3-319-46608-8.

[45] S Mills, 'Who Owns the Future? Data Trusts, Data Commons, and the Future of Data Ownership' [2019] SSRN Electronic Journal. Available at: https://www.ssrn.com/abstract=3437936. E Morozov and F Bria, 'Rethinking the Smart City' (Rosa Luxembourg Stiftung). Available at: https://onlineopen.org/media/article/583/open_essay_2018_morozov_rethinking.pdf.

[46] J Zygmuntowski and others, 'Embedding European Values in Data Governance: A Case for Public Data Commons' (2021) 10(3) *Internet Policy Review* 1. Available at: https://policyreview.info/articles/analysis/embedding-european-values-data-governance-case-public-data-commons.

This is in line with a view of public institutions as being in a unique position to drive the use of data to generate non-economic value and ensure democratic control and accountability.[47] They stress that departing from the current 'rights-based' approach to data is necessary to 'break from the fictitious commodity form of data' and serve the public interest.[48] Viewing data as a 'shared asset' or 'common good',[49] they argue, with Purtova,[50] that a data commons can be seen as a common-pool resources (CPR) framework. Ostrom defined CPR as resources which have a high level of 'subtractability' (ie, rival consumption may threaten them), and a low level of excludability (ie, difficulty in limiting consumption).[51] In the case of data, 'subtractability' not only refers to the total depletion of resources, but also to conditions where overconsumption endangers sustainability of the commons.[52] Zygmuntowski, Zoboli and Nemitz point out that overconsumption by dominant actors affects the distribution of data-related gains such as innovation surplus and business insight.[53] The solution, in their view, is a trusted data-sharing space established in the public interest, with an active stewardship role of public actors, enabling a wide range of downstream goods and services.[54] Prainsack advocates for a similar view, stressing that a data commons approach would be integral to mitigating power asymmetries between large data processors and data subjects.[55]

Of course, the commons approach does not come without its own challenges, and more specifically, social dilemmas of governance in cases where a group of people share a resource. In his seminal article, 'The Tragedy of the Commons', Hardin showed how the self-interest of different users of a shared resource could lead to overexploitation, resulting in the resource no longer being useful. This is why, in practice, some actors opt for so-called 'semi-commons' approach, where stakeholders protect the quality of their data resources in a data commons through formal or informal exclusivity regimes, while accepting some level of cooperation for public interest purposes.[56]

Although the governance of data commons may pose salient challenges, it urges us to depart from the current individualist and commodifying paradigm of data and see data as a public asset. This is even more salient in the public sector,

[47] Tarkowski and Vogelezang (n 22).

[48] Zygmuntowski and others (n 46).

[49] T Bass, 'It's Time to Think About Our Data as a Common Good'. British Council (2020). Available at: www.britishcouncil.org/anyone-anywhere/explore/communities-connections/rethinking-data.

[50] N Purtova, 'Important Questions to Answer Before Talking of Data Commons' (2021). Available at: https://itforchange.net/sites/default/files/2021-06/Nadezhda-Purtova-Socializing-Data-Value-Provocation.pdf.

[51] *E Ostrom, Governing the Commons: The Evolution of Institutions for Collective Action*; [Nobel Prize Winner 2009] (Cambridge University Press 2011).

[52] Zygmuntowski, Zoboli and Nemitz (n 44).

[53] ibid.

[54] Tarkowski and Vogelezang (n 22).

[55] B Prainsack, 'Logged Out: Ownership, Exclusion and Public Value in the Digital Data and Information Commons' (2019) 6 *Big Data & Society* 205395171982977.

[56] A Ottolia and C Sappa, 'A Topography of Data Commons: From Regulation to Private Dynamism' (2022) 71 *GRUR International – Journal of European and International IP Law* 335.

where data should be seen as 'owned by everyone since it has been gathered about and from everyone'.[57] The next view sits at the other end of the spectrum, treating public sector data as a commodity that should be used to maximise the utility of its owner.

V. Treating Data as Controlled by Public Sector Bodies

An amalgam of different arguments views public sector data as being controlled by public sector bodies by emphasising the potential of such data to further the interests of these very bodies, either that refers to strictly speaking financial contributions to their budget or broader potential to improve the policy or administrative work of the bodies.[58] Some common threads connecting this heterogenous scholarship will be analysed in this section: public sector data is seen as a strategic resource to be preserved and exploited, often as a tradable commodity reflecting some commercial value, exclusively controlled by public bodies and by default closed to access for other parties. Three strands of scholarship will be drawn upon here to present this view: IP and commercialisation of public sector data, challenges to open government data and data sovereignty.

Intellectual property rights have been a major analytical framework to conceive of public sector data as falling under the exclusive control of public sector bodies. Facts and ideas are not protected under copyright law, as this would be detrimental to innovation, but compilations of facts, like administrative databases in the public sector, may satisfy the criterion of originality and thus attract copyright law protection.[59] This is reflected in Article 10(2) of the TRIPS agreement[60] where it is written that 'compilations of data … which by reason of the selection or arrangement of their contents constitute intellectual creations shall be protected as such'.[61] It should be noted, however, that this protection might be thin, as it does only cover the 'original selection or arrangement of the compilation' and does not protect from extraction of facts that could be then used differently in an independent selection,[62] eg, the extraction of certain variables from a public sector dataset that could then be analysed in a research project. In addition to copyright law, the UK has implemented EU law establishing a *sui generis* intellectual property right for database creators.[63] Database law, enshrined in the Copyright and Rights

[57] R Heeks, 'Government Data: Understanding the Barriers to Citizen Access and Use' [2000] SSRN Electronic Journal. Available at: www.ssrn.com/abstract=3540061.

[58] R Munné, 'Big Data in the Public Sector' in Jose Cavanillas (ed), *New Horizons for a Data-Driven Economy: A Roadmap for Usage and Exploitation of Big Data in Europe* (Springer Berlin Heidelberg 2015).

[59] T Scassa, 'Data Ownership' [2018] SSRN Electronic Journal. Available at: www.ssrn.com/abstract=3251542.

[60] Agreement on Trade-Related Aspects of Intellectual Property Rights, 15 April 1994, Marrakesh Agreement Establishing the World Trade Organization, Annex 1C, 1869 UNTS 299, 33 ILM 1197.

[61] ibid 7.

[62] ibid 6.

[63] Intellectual Property Office and Government Digital Service, 'Sui generis Database Rights' (2020).

in Databases Regulations 1997 in the UK,[64] seeks to protect 'substantial investment' in the creation of databases by granting exclusive rights over the data and preventing others from copying and reusing it.[65] The idea is that through this legal protection the curation and maintenance of an intangible asset is being rewarded.[66]

Based on intellectual property rights, public sector bodies in the UK have explored commercialising their data. One example is the information trading function of the Driver and Vehicle Licensing Agency (DVLA), which offers partial postcodes enabling the distribution of model, make and body type to be determined to interested marketing agents.[67] Another example is the information trading function of the Tariff and Statistical Office, a department within HM Customs, which validates and prepares for commercial use data collected from trader's declarations for UK Customs purposes.[68] There is also significant controversy around whether NHS data is being sold to third parties.[69] In all cases, the idea behind enabling access to public sector data for a fee is that this information holds great commercial value and can be used to create 'added-value informational products' that can be sold in the market.[70] This value emerges from the characteristics of public sector data: it is comprehensive, it covers long time periods (often decades) and it is usually quite accurate because of the significant resources that have been invested in its collection, curation and maintenance.[71] By utilising this value based on intellectual property, public bodies are entitled to receiving monetary compensation in the same way a private individual could monetise their personal information.[72]

Another strand of scholarship stems from the discussion of challenges to the movement of open government data. Open government data (OGD) initiatives have been proliferating in Europe and elsewhere since the early 2000s with a view to stimulating analytical engagement with public sector datasets and enhancing the transparency and accountability of governments.[73] Studies, including empirical studies, considering limitations and challenges to opening government data reflect the existence of perspectives viewing public sector data as exclusively controlled by public sector bodies. In some cases, public sector organisations see data as leverage

[64] The Copyright and Rights in Databases Regulations 1997 (SI 1997/3032).

[65] M Marcowitz-Bitton, 'Commercializing Public Sector Information' [2015] SSRN Electronic Journal. Available at: www.ssrn.com/abstract=2653555.

[66] J Tennison, 'Beyond Ownership: We Need Better Control and Rights over Data' (*ODI Knowledge and Opinion*). Available at: https://theodi.org/article/data-rights-we-need-to-build-a-coherent-framework/.

[67] Z Abd Hadi and N McBride, 'The Commercialisation of Public Sector Information within UK Government Departments' (2000) 13 *International Journal of Public Sector Management* 552.

[68] ibid.

[69] T Moberly, 'Should We Be Worried about the NHS Selling Patient Data?' (2020) *British Medical Journal* m113.

[70] Marcowitz-Bitton (n 65).

[71] Abd Hadi and McBride (n 67).

[72] R Farrelly and E Chew, 'Designing a Primary Personal Information Market as an Industry Platform: A Service Innovation Approach' (2017) *AIS Electronic Library* (AISeL).

[73] B Ubaldi, 'Open Government Data: Towards Empirical Analysis of Open Government Data Initiatives', vol 22 (2013) *OECD Working Papers on Public Governance* 22. Available at: www.oecd-ilibrary.org/governance/open-government-data_5k46bj4f03s7-en.

or bargaining tool with other organisations,[74] whereas other organisations are afraid of losing financial income that they currently draw from commercialising datasets.[75] Studying the 'politics' of open government data, Ruijer and others describe the strategic nature of public sector data as an organisational resource and sketch the resistance of public sector bodies to pressure for more transparency.[76] In their view, as information is a source of power and indispensability,[77] OGD initiatives are likely to succeed when supported by '(in)formal rules and organisational goals' of public sector bodies.[78] Institutional incentives such as 'economic gain' are required for public sector bodies to release OGD.[79]

The previously mentioned assumptions of the second view are present in the literature covering challenges to OGD initiatives. The 'perceived unprofitability' of OGD for public sector bodies sits at odds with the idea that data is a commodity from which commercial value can be extracted, as OGD means that the department 'cannot profit from the economic value created by the data'.[80] The public sector body is legitimised to seek the creation of economic value since it has 'invested money' in producing the data and the aim should be to earn 'valuable revenue' that will then be used for the organisational goals of the public body.[81] A game-based research study seeking to influence civil servants' behaviour concerning the opening of governmental data identified that public officials struggle to see a correlation between OGD initiatives and improvements in their job performance.[82] Considering themselves as exclusively in control of the data and failing to see the clear benefits from opening it to third parties, it is to be expected that cautiousness and fear of criticism dominate and result in barriers to OGD.[83] Even more so, in the context of broader access to public sector administrative data for research purposes, where the 'indirect' benefits of data access makes public servants to view the avoidance of risk as a 'personal objective'.[84]

[74] M Alamgir Hossain, and C Chan, 'Open Data Adoption in Australian Government Agencies: An Exploratory Study' (2015) *ACIS 2015 Proceedings* 60. Available at: https://aisel.aisnet.org/acis2015/60.

[75] C Martin, 'Barriers to the Open Government Data Agenda: Taking a Multi-Level Perspective: Barriers to the Open Government Data Agenda' (2014) 6 *Policy & Internet* 217.

[76] E Ruijer and others, 'The Politics of Open Government Data: Understanding Organizational Responses to Pressure for More Transparency' (2020) 50 *The American Review of Public Administration* 260.

[77] T Davenport and others, *Information Politics* (Taylor & Francis 1997).

[78] Ruijer and others (n 72).

[79] ibid.

[80] S Li and Y Chen, 'Explaining the Resistance of Data Providers to Open Government Data' (2021) 73 *Aslib Journal of Information Management* 560.

[81] Heeks (n 57).

[82] F Kleiman and others, 'Changing Civil Servants' Behaviour Concerning the Opening of Governmental Data: Evaluating the Effect of a Game by Comparing Civil Servants' Intentions before and after a Game Intervention' (2022) 88 *International Review of Administrative Sciences* 921.

[83] D Donald Shao and S Saxena, 'Barriers to Open Government Data (OGD) Initiative in Tanzania: Stakeholders' Perspectives' (2019) 50 *Growth and Change* 470.

[84] F Ritchie, 'Can a Change in Attitudes Improve Effective Access to Administrative Data for Research?' Available at: www2.uwe.ac.uk/faculties/BBS/BUS/Research/General/Economics%20papers%202016/1607.pdf.

Although not focusing so much on the 'tradable' aspect of data complication, the third strand, data sovereignty, also views data in an instrumental manner as a strategic resource that must be exclusively controlled by public bodies and be closely guarded to preserve government power and authority. Under international law, sovereignty encompasses both territorial integrity of a nation and the exercise of 'inherently governmental functions'.[85] With the outsourcing of public sector data storage to US-based cloud service providers, significant issues have emerged around the control of UK public sector data.[86] As sovereignty implies 'supreme authority to the exclusion of other sovereigns',[87] data sovereignty alludes to the exclusive control of public sector, more specifically government, data and the ability to decide who is allowed access to the data.[88] Scholars have gone as far as framing it as the 'right' of governments to collect and manage their own data.[89]

Arguably, the utility or interest served by public sector data in the sovereignty discourse is not individually confined to specific public bodies but refers to the government as a collective. In fact, data sovereignty has been framed as the government's quest for undiminished authority over government information assets. Essentially, this collective utility served by data sovereignty refers to some of the core functions of government, such as national security and law enforcement. Unless data are exclusively controlled by government bodies, these functions, as well as the integrity of the state, may be compromised.

Whether seen as a tradable commodity or a strategic resource crucial for governing, public sector data is conceived under the second view as exclusively controlled by public sector bodies (individually or collectively) to help them pursue their organisational goals. The next and final view presents a quite different perspective: public sector data as controlled by individual citizens.

VI. Data as Controlled by Individual Citizens

Even if public sector data are not, in practice, controlled by individual citizens, the public discourse around it abounds with voices urging governments to give citizens more control over 'their' data.[90] If the two previous views are expressed mostly in

[85] N Kushwaha, 'Up in the Air: Ensuring Government Data Sovereignty in the Cloud', *2020 12th International Conference on Cyber Conflict (CyCon)* (IEEE 2020). Available at: https://ieeexplore.ieee.org/document/9131718/.

[86] ibid.

[87] ibid 26.

[88] ibid.

[89] S Carroll Rainie and others, 'Data as a Strategic Resource: Self-Determination, Governance, and the Data Challenge for Indigenous Nations in the United States' (2017) 8(2) *International Indigenous Policy Journal* 1–29. Available at: https://ojs.lib.uwo.ca/index.php/iipj/article/view/7511.

[90] P Stephenson, 'The Future of Public Services Means Giving Citizens Control Over Their Own Data'. Available at: www.openaccessgovernment.org/giving-citizens-control-own-data/71660/; KPMG, 'Building trust in government's use of data'. Available at: https://kpmg.com/xx/en/home/insights/

the work of scholars and the activity of organisational stakeholders in public sector data management, the third view finds its expression in the approach adopted by the current data protection frameworks such as the UK Data Protection Act 2018 and the EU GDPR.[91]

Proponents of this view have advocated for viewing data protection rights under the GDPR as either *personal* or *proprietary* rights.[92] Both readings are underpinned by the liberal paradigm: they have an orientation towards 'economic efficiency, civil liberties, and avoidance of unjust interferences'.[93] Victor, expressing the proprietary view,[94] claims that the GDPR treats data very similar to property and data subjects enjoy default entitlements over personal data.[95] Under this view, data subject rights such as the right to access (Article 15), erasure (Article 17) and data portability (Article 20) can be seen as analogous to the owner's ability to demand their property if it is used and accessed by others.[96] On the other hand, proponents of the 'personal' view point out the broad concept of personal data in the GDPR,[97] pointing out that it sits at odds with the idea that data can be seen as a property that can be commodified and controlled.[98] Fezer, expressing such a view, develops a theory of *sui generis* ownership rights in data, viewing them as *behaviour-generated*, ie, as the result of citizen interactions and communications.[99] In his view, ownership over data is a facet of individual autonomy, providing a legally mediated space to enact freedom.[100]

In practice, individual ownership over data is translated as decisional authority and control. In his seminal essay on ownership, Honoré breaks down ownership into eleven different rights and duties:

> the right to possess, the right to use, the right to manage, the right to the income of the thing, the right to the capital, the right to security, the rights or incidents of transmissibility and absence of term, the prohibition of harmful use, liability to execution, and the incident of residuality.[101]

2018/06/building-trust-in-governments-use-of-data.html; M Jacobson, 'Who "owns" public data?' Available at: https://mrsc.org/stay-informed/mrsc-insight/october/who-owns-public-data.

[91] C Kuner, 'Protecting EU Data Outside EU Borders under the GDPR' (2023) 60 *Common Market Law Review* 77.

[92] H Pearce, 'Personality, Property and Other Provocations' (2018) 4 *European Data Protection Law Review* 190.

[93] Hummel, Braun and Dabrock (n 10).

[94] J Victor, 'The EU General Data Protection Regulation: Toward A Property Regime for Protecting Data Privacy' (2013) 123(2) *Yale Law Journal* 513–28.

[95] Purtova (n 12).

[96] See F Thouvenin and others, 'Data Ownership: Taking Stock and Mapping the Issues' in M Dehmer and F Emmert-Streib (eds), *Frontiers in Data Science* (CRC Press 2017) 111–45.

[97] Finck and Pallas (n 1).

[98] Hummel, Braun and Dabrock (n 10).

[99] K-H Fezer, 'Ein originäres Immaterialgüterrecht sui generis an verhaltensgenerierten Informationsdaten der Bürger' (2017) 3 *Zeitschrift für Datenschutz* 99–105.

[100] K-H Fezer, *Repräsentatives Dateneigentum. Ein zivilgesellschaftliches Bürgerrecht* (Konrad-Adenauer-Stiftung 2018).

[101] T Honoré, 'Ownership' in AG Guest (Ed.), *Oxford Essays in Jurisprudence* (Oxford University Press 1961) 107–47.

In this view, ownership can be seen as a *bundle* of rights and does not confer unconditional control over a resource. This is quite close to the protection of the right to data protection, which is an overarching fundamental right that is practically realised through data subject rights such as the ones to access and erasure.[102] For example, Honoré defined the right to capital and income from property. Similarly, the GDPR introduces new rights to data portability, allowing individuals to transfer data between service providers and profit from its value.[103] The GDPR also reflects Honoré's prohibition on harmful use and liability to execution. Its principles require lawful processing of data and hold controllers accountable for violations through fines and penalties.

Although having a solid foundation on existing legal frameworks, the liberal principles underlying individual data ownership are not fully realised in government data management practices. Citizens often lack meaningful control, access, or consent over government use of their personal data, contravening individualist control over data notions. Rights like rectification and erasure are rarely applicable; governments claim public interest exemptions to justify data use in ways that seem to exceed necessity and proportionality standards.

VII. Conclusion

In this chapter, I have shown that there is not one right answer to the question of who controls public sector data and who should benefit from them. This examination of the three major views on control over public sector data reveals inherent tensions in how we conceive of control over and rights to public sector datasets. Each view makes valid points, yet it also has limitations.

The first view conceives of public sector data as a public good that should benefit all. However, realising a true data commons faces the challenges of governance dilemmas and collective action problems. The second view reflects organisational interests of public bodies, but risks instrumentalising data in ways that limit transparency and access. The third view aligns with established data protection laws, yet in practice individual control is often lacking in public sector data use.

Ultimately, control over public sector data may likely require a hybrid approach. Elements of all three perspectives may be needed: stewardship for the public good, organisational data rights, and individual data rights can be balanced through novel governance frameworks. Rather than an all-or-nothing view, policymakers should seek pluralistic data ownership models that combine public, organisational, and individual interests through new institutional designs.

[102] M Tzanou, 'Data Protection as a Fundamental Right next to Privacy? "Reconstructing" a Not so New Right' (2013) 3 *International Data Privacy Law* 88.

[103] P De Hert and others, 'The Right to Data Portability in the GDPR: Towards User-Centric Interoperability of Digital Services' (2018) 34 *Computer Law & Security Review* 193.

In the following chapters, I will flesh out the application of these views in the UK public sector. As will be shown, the extent to which different participants in public sector data sharing espouse one of the above views may be integral to determining their attitude regarding the use and sharing of such data for research and innovation. Before that, I turn to the analytical and methodological frameworks of this book in Chapter 3.

3

Researching Data Access Decisions for Research and Innovation in the UK Public Sector

Regulation of data access for research and innovation involves complex interplay between formal rules and informal norms. On paper, laws like the Digital Economy Act 2017 grant considerable power to data custodians to decide whether and how to share data. However, the exercise of this discretion gets shaped through ongoing negotiations among custodians, researchers, innovators, and other parties. These negotiations continually redefine shared standards and expectations around data access.

To analyse these multifaceted negotiations, I introduce a theoretical framework drawing on the concept of 'regulatory space'. This concept views regulation not as top-down control, but rather as bargaining between interdependent public and private bodies with plural sources of authority. In this chapter, I also outline a mixed-methods approach combining legal analysis with data analysis from 42 qualitative semi-structured interviews and documents. This empirical work reveals how informal norms and formal strictures are mutually constructed through framings, knowledge exchange, and the institutionalisation of data sharing norms over time. For example, custodians face resource constraints and have internal risk calculations to guide data sharing decisions. However, framing data access as serving the 'public good' can press custodians to expand access beyond formal requirements. Over time, recurrent negotiations between custodians, researchers, and intermediaries shape shared repertoires and rationalities around data access.

I first explain the theoretical framework of regulatory space and why it is apt for illuminating data access negotiations. Then, I present the mixed-methods approach combining legal analysis with socio-legal empirical inquiry. Subsequent chapters show that informal norms and formal controls iteratively shape the emerging regulatory terrain around data sharing for research and innovation.

I. 'Regulating' Data Access for Research and Innovation

In the introduction to this book, I set out the literature finding that legal barriers have been central to hindering the development and application of consistent data sharing procedures for research and innovation, while other studies highlight the central role of cultural barriers.[1] This debate is to be understood from a regulatory perspective. Enquiring into the salience of law in governing a particular type of conduct that is subject to policy decisions raises questions about the centrality of law as an 'instrument of social control' within a regulatory regime that seeks to give these policies effect.[2]

Regulation is broadly defined here as establishing norms through setting rules or standards, as well as monitoring and enforcing compliance with them via both legal and non-legal processes.[3] Regulatory processes are designed to influence behaviour, including through facilitating and expressing certain 'clusters of ideas and assumptions about how things are to be done'.[4] Data sharing for research and innovation is an area where public policy objectives are explicitly pursued by the State, partly through a system of purposively designed legal norms, which may not, however, always be determinative of actual organisational data sharing frameworks and practices. Such frameworks and practices are defined in organisational studies as the 'rules, procedures, organisational standards, governance structures, conventions, and customs',[5] as well as the 'symbol systems, cognitive scripts and moral templates',[6] which operate within or interact with organisational environments and structure individual behaviour. These include 'both formal structures and informal rules and procedures that structure conduct'.[7]

What does it mean, however, to regulate 'data access decisions'? There are at least three potential dimensions of regulatory interest when exploring the different 'legal' and 'non-legal' influences on data access decisions in the UK public sector.

[1] This is not to say that this is necessarily a clear-cut dichotomy, yet proponents of these views are: Law Commission, 'Data Sharing Between Public Bodies: A Scoping Report' (2014). Available at: www.lawcom.gov.uk/app/uploads/2015/03/lc351_data-sharing.pdf 1.2; Administrative Data Taskforce, 'The UK Administrative Data Research Network: Improving Access for Research and Policy' (December 2012); see G Laurie and L Stevens, 'Developing a Public Interest Mandate for the Governance and Use of Administrative Data in the United Kingdom' (2016) 43 *Journal of Law & Society* 360, 362; R Thomas and M Walport, 'Data Sharing Review Report' (2008). Available at; https://webarchive.nationalarchives.gov.uk/+/http:/www.justice.gov.uk/docs/data-sharing-review.pdf 5.24.

[2] B Morgan and K Yeung, *An Introduction to Law and Regulation* (Cambridge University Press 2012) 1.

[3] B Lange and F Haines, 'Regulatory Transformations: An Introduction' in B Lange and others (eds), *Regulatory Transformations: Rethinking Economy–Society Interactions* (Hart 2015) 1, 7; similarly, and even more broadly, in E Dove, *Regulatory Stewardship of Health Research: Navigating Participant Protection and Research Promotion* (Edward Elgar 2020) 3 where regulation is defined as a 'set of rules, principles, mechanisms, strategies, or activities … that either affect behaviour as an incidental effect or are designed to steer behaviour in a … desirable way'.

[4] R Baldwin, M Cave and M Lodge, *Understanding Regulation: Theory, Strategy and Practice* (Oxford University Press 1999) 3.

[5] W Powell and P Dimaggio, 'The Iron Cage Revisited: Institutional Isomorphism and Collective Rationality in Organizational Fields' (1983) 48(2) *American Sociological Review* 147.

[6] P Hall and R Taylor, 'Political Science and the Three New Institutionalisms' (1996) *Political Studies* 936, 940.

[7] K Thelen and S Steinmo, 'Historical Institutionalism in Comparative Politics' in K Thelen and others (eds), *Structuring Politics: Historical Institutionalism in Comparative Analysis* (Cambridge University Press 1992) 2.

First, one could focus on individual decision-making outcomes, ie, 'access' vs 'non-access', by reference to the role of legal and other factors in steering them. Second, without focusing on individual outcomes, one could seek to explain the role of these factors in creating decision-making patterns, ie stable, and recurrent tendencies to respond to requests in a particular manner, granting or rejecting disclosure. This would also involve explaining what shapes decision outcomes, albeit only at a higher, more aggregate level. Third, shifting analytical attention away from the actual, individual, or aggregate, decision outcomes, one could seek to understand how the dominant, legal, or non-legal, *processes and frameworks* governing the activity of research data sharing are constituted. The latter analytical focus, ie the process through which data sharing frameworks are formed and become prevalent, is the one of the present work. Rather than asking what determines the outcome of particular access decisions, this type of enquiry is interested in what structures and justifies the process of deciding about access from the perspective of the actors in this space.

There are two reasons for choosing this focus. First, while the first two foci are arguably compelling, there is, presently, a lack of adequate information to pursue them. There is a dearth of information about actual research data access decision outcomes, with only a few public bodies in the UK publishing relevant information[8] and the majority being quite resistant to publicise concrete data. As a result, it is not possible to state, even by approximating the number of data custodian decision-makers,[9] or the number of requests particular bodies have received, granted, or rejected. Second, normative frameworks and organisational procedures matter regardless of their causal relationship to modifications in participant behaviour. As a representation of organisational efforts to 'enact order and coordinate action',[10] such frameworks and processes communicate both to internal and external actors an organisation's purposes, rationality and wider beliefs and values in respect of a particular activity.[11] At the very least, such communications provide fruitful insights into how organisations perceive themselves, their responsibilities and their roles in society, with scholars arguing that they have such significant functions as 'defining available modes of action', 'constraining' and 'empowering' behaviour.[12]

[8] The Department for Education (DfE) in England is a luminary in respect of publishing data on third-party requests and their data sharing decisions with regard to the 'National Pupil Database', Department for Education, 'DfE external data shares' (18 July 2019). Availabe at: https://gov.uk/government/publications/dfe-external-data-shares.

[9] See, eg, the website of the Dutch General Administrative Service which hosts an online database with the names and roles of high-ranking Dutch civil servants. Available at: www.algemenebestuursdienst.nl/.

[10] W Powell and J Colyvas, 'Microfoundations of Institutional Theory' in R Greenwood and others (eds), *The Sage Handbook of Organizational Institutionalism* (Sage 2008) 282.

[11] R Scott, *Institutions and Organizations* (Sage 1995) 134.

[12] ibid: 'Institutions construct actors and define their available modes of action; they constrain behaviour, but they also empower it.'

That being said, seeking to understand how the frameworks and processes governing the activity of data sharing for research and innovation are being formed and applied is associated with its own challenges. Data sharing has been developing in an incremental manner, with departments reactively responding to requests for sharing data rather than proactively developing their own procedures.[13] To take the example of research data sharing, even after the introduction of a generic legal power for public bodies to share data for research purposes in the UK Digital Economy Act (DEA) 2017,[14] there is not a public sector 'gold standard' on the appropriate decision-making actors and procedures or the relevant considerations that should govern data access decisions.[15] Instead, public bodies are expected to develop their own standards and procedures, ensuring that these conform to such broad principles, enshrined in the Code of Practice published by the UK statistics authority, as 'proportionality', 'transparency' and 'data minimisation'.[16] With a fair amount of uncertainty about the prevailing frameworks and processes being voiced,[17] it will be for this book to use existing secondary and primary original data collected by myself, to shed light on the frameworks that govern this form of decision-making in the UK public sector and their application in practice.[18]

II. A Regulatory Space Analysis of Research Data Access Decisions

'Regulatory space' is a very appropriate concept for understanding the process of making decisions about data sharing for research and innovation, where multiple organisations enter complex and long-standing relationships within which data sharing standards are (re)negotiated and conformity to them is demanded from more than one party. Originally developed by Hancher and Moran as a theoretical construct for understanding economic regulation by the State under advanced capitalism, 'regulatory space' analysis sees regulation as a 'process of intermediation and bargaining between large and powerful organisations'.[19] A 'regulatory

[13] MJ Taylor and others, 'Developing a Data Sharing Framework: A Case Study' (2014) 8 *Transforming Government: People, Process and Policy* 151.

[14] Section 64 of the Digital Economy Act 2017 established a generic legal power for public sector custodians to disclose data they hold 'in the context of their functions'.

[15] National Audit Office, 'Challenges in using data across government' (21 June 2019). Available at: https://nao.org.uk/wp-content/uploads/2019/06/Challenges-in-using-data-across-government.pdf 11.

[16] UK Statistics Authority, 'Research Code of Practice and Accreditation Criteria' (1 March 2018).

[17] MH Iveson and IJ Deary Iveson and Deary, 'Navigating the Landscape of Non-Health Administrative Data in Scotland: A Researcher's Narrative' (2019) *Wellcome Open Research* 97; F Ritchie, 'UK Official Microdata Release Practices'. Available at: www.academia.edu/1336375/UK_Official_Microdata_Release_Practices 3.

[18] O Williamson, 'Comparative Economic Organization: The Analysis of Discrete Structural Alternatives' (1991) 36 *Administrative Science Quarterly* 269 including 'customs, laws and politics' within the 'institutional rules of the game'.

[19] L Hancher and M Moran, 'Organizing Regulatory Space' in R Baldwin, C Scott and C Hood (eds), *A Reader on Regulation* (Oxford University Press 1998) 150.

space' is defined as an 'abstract conceptual space constructed by people, organisations and events acting in concert upon a set of specific regulatory issues subject to public decision'.[20]

Data access negotiations involve various stages of communication and negotiation, which are developed between data custodians, intermediary bodies, and researchers/innovators. Due to its nature as an activity, data sharing involves the co-ordination of technical processes and dynamic interactions between these stakeholders, who may have conflicting interests in accessing or withholding public sector data. These interactions may happen within either 'well drawn and institutionalised settings and through formalised processes' or 'more informal' processes, without necessarily resulting in the culmination of a formal or legally enforceable output.[21] Formal and informal means of regulation may 'exist in a symbiotic relationship',[22] with actors who lack the formal powers to shape the outcome of regulation often playing a critical role in so doing.

Three conceptual categories capture the application of data sharing frameworks for research and innovation in the UK, as also reflected in the empirical chapters of this book: *actors*, *institutions* and *interactions*. First, organisational *actors* are the 'primary drivers of regulatory actions' within a regulatory space approach.[23] A regulatory space approach observes regulatory processes from a 'closer perspective' and rejects a 'rigid hierarchical' analysis often assumed within regulatory studies.[24] This approach encourages empirical analysis of the roles and aims of a diverse number of actors within a specific regulatory regime.[25] The roles and aims of such actors as start-ups, research groups and consortia, public-sector data custodians and research funders as intermediaries will be analysed in this book.

In the case of research and innovation public sector data sharing in the UK, there are several actors who occupy the space. 'High-level standard-setters' encompass both the three core domestic branches of state authority and supranational bodies. Examples of high-level standard-setters may include ministerial departments such as the Department for Business, Energy, and Industrial Strategy (BEIS) in the UK or the Information Commissioner's Office. These actors set standards to be followed by data custodians but are also informed by the latter's organisational practices in doing so. Data custodians are central actors in the research and innovation data sharing space. As they are processing public sector datasets to

[20] J Young, 'Outlining Regulatory Space: Agenda Issues and the FASB' (1994) 19(1) *Accounting, Organizations and Society* 83, 84.

[21] N Chowdury and R Wessel, 'Conceptualizing Multilevel Regulation in the EU: A Legal Translation of Multilevel Governance?' (2012) 18(3) *European Law Journal* 335, 339.

[22] R MacKenzie and M Martinez Lucio, 'The Colonisation of Employment Regulation and Industrial Relations? Dynamics And Developments Over Five Decades of Change' (2014) 55(2) *Labour History* 189, 193.

[23] Chowdury and Wessel (n 21) 340.

[24] F Vibert, *The New Regulatory Space: Reframing Democratic Governance* (Edward Elgar 2014) 4.

[25] B Lange and C Cook, 'Mapping a Developing Governance Space: Managing Drought in the UK' (2015) 68 *Current Legal Problems* 229, 251–2.

perform functions in the public interest, they are entitled to decide whether to allow access for research and innovation purposes. There are numerous types of data custodians in the UK public sector, considering that the latter is comprised of 25 ministerial departments and more than 400 other public bodies, ie executive agencies, non-departmental public bodies, and non-ministerial departments.[26] If one adds local authorities and health and social care bodies to this list, it is clear that a comprehensive examination of custodians as actors becomes a very demanding task.

Researchers and innovators are another group of actors that is central in this space. Either via an intermediary body or directly, they interact with data custodians and seek to achieve a favourable data sharing decision. Regarding innovators, it shall be stressed that public-private data sharing partnerships are relatively scarce in so-far organisational practice in the UK.[27] Yet, the present monograph has sought to capture the trend of accessing public sector data for innovation purposes, both in terms of emerging frameworks and in terms of actual organisational practice. Finally, yet importantly, a wide range of other organisations mediate relationships between the previous actors in the interest of facilitating data sharing for research and innovation. This category of intermediary bodies is comprised of research funders, research networks or institutes, independent liaisons known as 'trusted third parties' and oversight bodies.

Second, such actors 'participate in public policymaking' not only creating, but also being themselves constituted by,[28] 'certain *institutions* in regulation' (emphasis added).[29] 'Institutions' are defined as the 'rules, procedures, organisational standards, governance structures, conventions and customs',[30] as well as the 'symbol systems, cognitive scripts and moral templates',[31] which operate within or interact with organisational environments and structure individual behaviour. Both formalised and informal institutions 'that structure conduct',[32] such as data sharing legal rules, collective assumptions about the value of data-driven research and perceptions of administrative data ownership, will be analysed.

There seems to be a variety of data sharing institutions at play, eg legal rules prescribing data sharing safeguards, organisational procedures structuring

[26] Cabinet Office, 'Departments, Agencies and Public Bodies'. Available at: www.gov.uk/government/organisations.

[27] See the collaboration between Swansea University (as 'data custodians' of the SAIL databank) and Quintiles, a major player in the healthcare industry, on managing patient engagement for research purposes across clinical studies; E Cascade and others, 'Combining Electronic Health Records and Patient-Reported Information in the UK: Preliminary Results from the WASPS (Wales SAIL + PRO Study' (2012) *Value in Health*.

[28] R Scott (n 11): 'Institutions construct actors and define their available modes of action; they constrain behaviour, but they also empower it.'

[29] C Scott, 'Analysing Regulatory Space: Fragmented Resources and Institutional Design' (2001) Public Law 283, 293.

[30] Powell and Dimaggio (n 5) 147.

[31] Hall and Taylor (n 6) 940

[32] Thelen and Steinmo (n 7) 2.

custodian decision-making, economic rationalities of prioritising resource allocation within custodian bodies or political ideas about the accountability of data custodians.[33] Institutions are reflected in and transported by multiple 'carriers' such as codified instruments (eg statutory acts like the DEA 2017), routines (eg routine assessment of the contribution of a request to the public interest within the civil service) and cultures (eg ideas and assumptions about public sector data ownership).[34] Some data sharing institutions may be settled, durable and articulated: legal rules, organisational procedures or formal networks between organisations with a view to facilitate research data sharing. Other institutions may be non-articulated, fluid, and dynamic: different subjective interpretations of legal requirements, customary assumptions about the value of research and innovation, conventions of approving particular types of requests or cognitive processes of knowledge exchange between data analysts working for different actors. Edelman draws a similar distinction between 'structures' and 'consciousness' in explaining the function of the 'legal environment of organizations'.[35] She associates 'rules, practices or procedures' with 'structures' and 'beliefs or ideas about technology, governance, management efficiency and … understandings about the meaning of law and ideas about how to make use of legal rules and rights' with 'culture'.[36] As Scott notes, such 'institutions … as culture and organisational form'[37] delimiting the regulatory issues in a space are to be understood empirically.[38] It is suggested here that the more dynamic institutions are not less important or influential than those that are articulated and durable. The former merit analytical focus as much as the latter.

Third, the *interactions* and interdependencies between multiple actors will be a focal aspect of studying regulatory processes in the research data sharing space.[39] This focus will allow an understanding of how certain groups or communities in the space, eg organised research groups or civil servants operating as data custodians, draw on 'plural systems of authority and of other resources'[40] in creating or implementing a regulatory regime.[41] Through their interactions, organisational actors create, modify and preserve institutions which structure and justify research data sharing in the UK public sector. The application of these three dimensions to the research data sharing space will now be elaborated upon.

[33] Hancher and Moran (n 19) 156; C Scott (n 29) 289.

[34] R Scott (n 11) 52: 'Institutions, whether regulative, normative, or cognitive perspectives are stressed, are embedded in various types of repositories or carriers.'

[35] L Edelman, *Working Law: Courts, Corporations and Symbolic Civil Rights* (Chicago University Press 2016) 155.

[36] ibid 163.

[37] C Scott (n 29) 288.

[38] ibid.

[39] J Kaye and S Gibbons, 'Mapping the Regulatory Space for Genetic Databases and Biobanks in England and Wales' (2008) 9(2) *Medical Law International* 111, 112.

[40] Scott (n 29) 287.

[41] J Black, 'Regulatory Conversations' (2002) 29 *Journal of Law and Society* 163; K Jonnergård and U Larsson-Olaison, 'Developing Codes of Conduct: Regulatory Conversations as Means for Detecting Institutional Change' (2007) 29(4) *Law & Policy* 460, 471.

Data access decisions are often made by individuals or small teams of individuals, often analysts working for government departments, with which requesting parties and intermediary bodies have to interact on an ad hoc basis and according to the requirements of each data custodian.[42] The idiosyncrasies of this multi-party relationship, structured around the minutiae of an everyday technical process performed by small groups of individuals, might not be adequately captured by a high-level view of the space and the interrelationships of some of its key decision-makers or high-level constituents.[43] Since data sharing institutions are created, interpreted, sustained and altered 'as they are enacted by individuals in concrete social situations',[44] emphasis will be shifted to the level of commonplace interactions between individuals negotiating data access, often involving representatives from two or more organisational actors. This can provide a rich understanding of how participants 'maintain or transform the institutional forces that guide daily practice'.[45]

Micro-level interactions in this space may involve various types of communication. For example, communication may foster facilitative relationships between trusted third parties and data custodians to ensure appropriate data security and confidentiality safeguards, as well as the broader social acceptability of public sector data research and innovation.[46] However, conflict and bargaining will often arise, eg, with regard to a request's aspiration to access data that data custodians would not like to see used to criticise their policy-making.[47] Similarly, tensions may emerge around the status of public sector data ownership; views expressed by high-level standard-setters or funders with regard to the status of such data as a 'public good' or 'public infrastructure'[48] are less likely to be shared by data custodians. In both cases, the space's constituents aim to leverage their organisational resources within their interactions with other data sharing participants in the interest of shaping norms, ideas, conventions, and procedures.[49]

[42] Eg for justice-related data, the HMCTS clarify on their website the precise steps a research request should follow. See HMCTS, 'Access to Courts and Tribunals for Academic Researchers'. Available at: www.gov.uk/guidance/access-to-courts-and-tribunals-for-academic-researchers.

[43] Regulatory space studies have been criticised for making more abstract and complex the task of understanding regulation, see J Black, 'Decentring Regulation: Understanding the Role of Regulation and Self-Regulation in a "Post-Regulatory" World' (2001) 54 *Current Legal Problems* 103, 109.

[44] Powell and Colyvas (n 10) 284.

[45] ibid.

[46] P Carter and others, 'The Social License for Research: Why Care.data Ran into Trouble' (2015) 41 *Journal of Medical Ethics* 404–9. Available at: https://jme.bmj.com/content/41/5/404; Administrative Data Taskforce (n 1).

[47] KH Jones and others, 'The Good, the Bad, the Clunky: Addressing Challenges in Using Administrative Data for Research' (2019) 4(1) *International Journal of Data Population Science* 587.

[48] House of Commons Science and Technology Committee, 'The Big Data Dilemma: Fourth Report of Session 2015–16'. Available at: https://publications.parliament.uk/pa/cm201516/cmselect/cmsctech/468/468.pdf 20; P Arzberger and others, 'Promoting Access to Public Research Data for Scientific, Economic and Social Development' (2004) 3 *Data Science Journal* 135, 136.

[49] Several institutional scholars have highlighted the significance of communication for creating, shaping, and disrupting institutions, emphasising that 'at its core, institutional theory is a theory of communication', see R Suddaby, 'How Communication Institutionalizes: A Response to Lammers' (2011) 25(1) *Management Communication Quarterly* 183, 188.

III. A Mixed-methods Historical Approach: Data Collection and Analysis

The present book is interdisciplinary, combining legal and qualitative empirical socio-legal research methodologies. For the empirical part of the book, the research adopted a mixed-methods historical approach based on the triangulation of data sources.[50] The approach relied on the combination of primary and secondary data sources. First, it involved 42 semi-structured interviews with individuals experienced in negotiating data access in the UK public sector. Second, it relied on the secondary literature about public sector data sharing in the UK, including grey literature, organisational reports and published accounts. Interviews and documents, as well as informal conversations with data sharing participants,[51] were used for collecting data about the regulation of data sharing decisions for research and innovation in the UK public-sector. Interviewing was employed to capture the thoughts and interpretations of data sharing participants in respect of how the prevalent criteria and the appropriate requirements in the context of data access decisions have been shaped over time.[52] Semi-structured interviews were employed to both focus discussion and allow respondents to elaborate on the issues they considered most important. With both interviewee and document selection, a strategy of *purposive sampling* was adopted. Emphasis was put on selecting data sources that had the potential to yield insight into the various factors that shape data sharing decisions, according to my constantly developing explanatory account.[53] A 'theoretically meaningful' sample was sought by involving 'certain characteristics or criteria which helped develop and test' my emerging theoretical account.[54]

The combination of primary interview data along with an analysis of secondary documents and accounts enabled me to reveal the incremental, small-scale interactions through which research data access rules have been established and revised over time. By interviewing 42 individuals with first-hand experience of negotiating data access, I was able to collect fine-grained qualitative insights into the negotiation processes, including the unwritten normative assumptions that shape decision-making but are not captured in formal policy documents. This approach is apt for answering the following questions: who are the individuals involved in research and innovation data sharing decisions in practice? How do

[50] U Kelle and others, 'How to Use Mixed-Methods and Triangulation Designs: An Introduction to History Education Research' (2019) *History Education Research Journal* 5–23.

[51] Mostly in the context of conferences which attract participation from both the research community and the civil sector. Note that these informal conversations were not strictly used as research data in this project but informed the overall understanding of my research data.

[52] J Aberbach and B Rockman, 'Conducting and Coding Elite Interviews' (2002) 35(4) *Political Science & Politics* 673.

[53] D Silverman, *Interpreting Qualitative Data* (Sage 2015) 62.

[54] J Mason, *Qualitative Researching* (Sage 1996) 93–4.

they communicate with each other? What are their organisational affiliations and professional qualifications?

Analysis of organisational reports and grey literature provided supporting evidence and allowed me to substantiate and contextualise key themes arising from the interviews. For example, the arguments around the 'concealment' of the political behind the technical were developed by identifying divergences between interviewee accounts of localised data access negotiations and the framing of data governance issues in public rhetoric and formal policy statements.

Triangulating the interview data with document analysis was crucial for comparing policy discourse with on-the-ground practice. Furthermore, the combination of data sources allowed me to trace changes over time in the governance of research data access. By drawing connections between current negotiation practices described by interviewees and historical rules and norms identified through document analysis, I could substantiate my claims around the incremental development of data access regulation based on evolving conventional assumptions.

This work initially involved an exploratory stage, identifying candidate factors which potentially explain the regulation of data access decisions for research and innovation purposes in the UK public sector. After identifying a set of factors, the research engaged in explanatory work, seeking to refine them, as well as developing a well-integrated set of propositions about the relationships between them and their relative salience in regulating data sharing decisions. Data analysis was *issue focused* rather than case focused.[55] In other words, analysis focused on the activity of data sharing for research and innovation as an overarching 'issue' triggering similar responses across the board, rather than on the particular responses of specific 'cases' of organisations in this space. The aim of this strategy was to strike a balance between the general and the contextual by seeking to portray 'what has been learned from all respondents about people in their situation'.[56]

In analysing the data, a 'thematic analysis' approach was followed, aiming to 'identify, analyse, and report patterns within data'.[57] This was an *inductive* and *grounded* approach to analysis, identifying patterns from the data from the bottom up, even if I did not follow all the procedures of a grounded theory approach. For example, I coded sentences or small paragraphs in lieu of performing exhaustive line-by-line coding. I did also not deliberately disregard the existing literature on the potential explanatory factors of the phenomenon.[58] Such literature provided me with broad directions in the early phases of coding. Analysis involved a succession of stages. Data were read and digested, taking note of items of potential interest to answer the research question by creating the relevant 'nodes' in the NVivo 12 software.

[55] R Weiss, *Learning from Strangers: The Art and Methods of Qualitative Interview Studies* (The Free Press 1994) 152.

[56] ibid 153.

[57] V Braun and V Clarke, 'Using Thematic Analysis in Psychology' (2006) 3 *Qualitative Research in Psychology* 77.

[58] Silverman (n 53) 119.

IV. Conclusion

In this chapter, I have laid out the theoretical and methodological framework for studying how frameworks and processes governing research data access decisions are formed and applied in the UK public sector.

Drawing on regulatory space theory, the analysis conceptualises data access decisions as occurring within a complex regulatory space involving multiple actors, institutions, and interactions. Key actors include data custodians, researchers/innovators, high-level standard setters, and intermediary bodies, who both shape and are shaped by formal and informal institutions governing data sharing. Their recurring interactions, from formal policymaking to informal knowledge exchange, construct shared understandings and justify particular data access frameworks and practices.

To study this regulatory space empirically, I adopt a mixed-methods historical approach combining legal analysis with qualitative empirical research based on interviews and documents. Thematic analysis of these data sources aims to provide an integrated account of the dominant factors steering data access decision making in context, how they interact and their relative influence.

PART 2

Frameworks

4

The Law of Public Sector Data Access for Research and Innovation

Chapter 3 conceptualised the public sector data access for research and innovation 'regulatory space' as a space where organisational actors shape the creation and implementation of certain institutions (rules, standards, governance structures) through their interactions. This chapter analyses the main aspects of one of the most important data sharing institutions: the legal framework.

The law provides a range of mechanisms enabling access to public sector data for research and innovation purposes. However, these mechanisms have important limitations and face uncertainties regarding the precise scope of access rights. A key finding is that while 'research' enjoys favourable treatment across data protection and human rights frameworks, 'innovation' lacks a clear legal basis. Innovators may have to frame their data access requests as research purposes to benefit from exemptions. Even then, commercial research faces more regulatory scrutiny compared to academic pursuits. In terms of modes of access, individual rights like the UK's Freedom of Information Act (FOIA) 2000 facilitate democratic access to data. However, one-off static disclosures under the FOIA have limitations in tracing the impacts of automated, dynamic government processes. Public disclosure duties may serve transparency but are often aggregate statistics of limited granularity.

For public sector bodies considering sharing data, the discretionary power to disclose under statutory gateways is the most appropriate legal basis. Relying solely on 'implied powers' is risky due to limited precedents. Common law powers apply exclusively to ministerial departments as data providers. Ultimately, all data sharing is conditional on respecting privacy rights and data protection principles. The research exemptions in data protection law offer helpful assurances for data sharing. But again, commercial reuse seems more restricted compared to non-profit research aiming for academic publications. Retention periods can be extended, but commercial sensitivity considerations may prevent open publication of analysis results.

After introducing a few background clarifications, I take a deeper dive into the law governing access to public sector data, highlighting tensions between furthering research and innovation in the public interest on the one hand and respecting privacy rights on the other. From individual rights to disclosure duties and discretionary legal powers to share data, the different legal affordances will be analysed and their applicability to research and innovation data processing will be evaluated. In this analysis, I suggest that there is significant scope for organisational actors to authoritatively interpret the law in a way that fits their interests, laying the foundations for subsequent empirical chapters where I focus on the interactions between such actors and their implications for data access for research and innovation in the UK.

I. Research and/or Innovation?

The first point that needs to be clarified is that, when it comes to the law of public sector data access, research and innovation are not born equal. While both are quite broad terms, 'research' has a solid foundation in data protection legislation, whereas 'innovation' does not benefit from such a legislative footing.

The General Data Protection Regulation (GDPR), transposed into UK law via the Data Protection Act (DPA) 2018, 'research' is treated favourably as a legitimate aim for personal data processing. Recital 159 of the Regulation defines research broadly, providing the (non-exhaustive) examples of 'technological development and demonstration, fundamental research, applied research and privately funded research and 'studies conducted … in the area of public health'.[1] Article 5(1)(b) of the Regulation prescribes a specific exemption from the purpose limitation principle, stressing that further processing for 'scientific or historical research purposes' shall not be deemed 'incompatible with the initial purposes' of processing.[2] Similar exemptions from the strict rules of the regulation are provided by Articles 14(5)(b), 17(3)(d) and 21(6) of the GDPR.[3]

By contrast, innovation, although a central notion in EU policy agendas,[4] does not feature in legislative language. In fact, scholars have pointed out the need to qualify the permissive language of the GDPR when it comes to privately funded research. Meszaros and Ho argue that commercial AI research should not qualify for the GDPR research exemptions unless it demonstrates a contribution to the public interest and adopts safeguards akin to those in academic research.[5] Wagner argues that accountability structures, such as ethics review committees, should apply to commercial research in the same way as they do to academic research, to ensure compliance with the GDPR.[6] Viewed in this light, one would follow the

[1] GDPR, Recital 159.

[2] ibid art 5(1)(b).

[3] ibid arts 14(5)(b), 17(3)(d) and 21(6).

[4] See, eg, European Commission, 'The New European Innovation Agenda' (2022). Available at: https://research-and-innovation.ec.europa.eu/strategy/support-policy-making/shaping-eu-research-and-innovation-policy/new-european-innovation-agenda_en.

[5] J Meszaros and C Ho, 'AI Research and Data Protection: Can the Same Rules Apply for Commercial and Academic Research under the GDPR?' (2021) 41 *Computer Law & Security Review* 105532.

[6] B Wagner, 'Accountability by Design in Technology Research' (2020) 37 *Computer Law & Security Review* 10.

approach taken in the new EU copyright directive in treating favourably research organisations that 'act either on a not-for-profit basis or in the context of a public-interest mission recognised by the State'.[7]

Although in Chapter 5 I argue against precluding the contribution of commercial, even for-profit, initiatives to the public interest,[8] it will be shown that legal powers and duties to share data are mostly structured around the notion of research, rather than the notion of innovation. With that in mind, innovators interested in accessing public sector data will have to frame their purposes as research purposes, invoking the broad ambit of 'research' in data protection legislation as explained above. Both the above considerations, and the following Chapter 5, show that research that is for profit and commercial may face more regulatory hurdles compared to non-profit or academic research.

II. Elite versus Democratic Access? The Legal Addressees of Public Sector Data

Another important background clarification relates to the mode of access from the perspective of the legal addressee of public sector data for research and innovation purposes. Based on the status of the addressee, access can be broadly distinguished into *elite*, where access is confined to a selected group of researchers and innovators who satisfy certain requirements, and *democratic*, in the context of which the broader public are allowed to access data and use it for research or innovation purposes.

There are arguments and reasons behind each type of access. Elite access promises expertise to conduct complex analyses, which can lead to high-quality, reliable insights, as well as ensures that resources are not wasted on duplicative efforts and that the data is used to its full potential. With respect to privacy risks, in principle, it is assumed that elite access is accompanied by institutional review boards or ethics committees, which may provide a layer of oversight regarding the lawful and ethical use of data. Democratic access, on the other hand, may allow a larger pool of individuals to bring a variety of perspectives, leading to a richer set of ideas and solutions. In terms of culture, it fosters an environment of transparency, allowing public scrutiny and accountability. Through diversity, the quality and applicability of research may be enhanced. Evidently, combining the two types of access is ideal to achieve both their advantages and mitigate their respective disadvantages (eg, a wider access pool can increase the risk of data breaches or the misuse of sensitive

[7] Directive (EU) 2019/790 of the European Parliament and of the Council of 17 April 2019 on copyright and related rights in the Digital Single Market and amending Directives 96/9/EC and 2001/29/EC, Recital 12.

[8] See Chapter 5.

or personal data). Indeed, UK law seems cognisant of this interplay and includes both elite and democratic access mechanisms, as the analysis below will show.

Apart from this distinction, one can also distinguish between the type of legal mechanism through which the addressee may access public sector information. There are three types of mechanisms: (a) individual rights of access ie, rights enshrined by law and creating claims of individuals to request information from public bodies; (b) duties to disclose public sector information, either to a specific individual or to the broader public and (c) discretionary legal powers to share information. As the analysis will show, the latter option is the most appropriate in the context of research and innovation data processing. The three mechanisms will be now discussed in turn.

III. Individual Rights to Access: The FOIA 2000

Starting with individual rights to access public sector information, the UK Freedom of Information Act (FOIA) 2000 was introduced in 1997 and passed in 2000 as an ambitious reform that was intended to make the UK a world leader in government transparency and information access.[9] It came into force in 2005, applying to over 110,000 bodies in the UK public sector.[10] The Act empowers 'any person', including legal persons, to receive a written response about the existence of specific information in the records of a public authority.[11] The requesting party does not have to be located in the UK. In case the public authority holds the requested records, the requester is entitled to receive them. If the information is exempt from the obligation of disclosure, or if the public authority does not hold it, the requester is entitled to a notice of denial.[12]

Exemptions lie at the heart of the Act's operation. In principle, there is a distinction between 'harm-based' and 'class-based' exemptions. In the case of 'harm-based' exemptions (eg, sections 26 and 27 of the Act concerning defence and international relations), authorities assess that the disclosure of information would cause harm or prejudice to such interests as national security, international relations, or national defence. In this case, there is a need to perform a balancing exercise to assess whether the harm caused by the release of the information would outweigh the public interest in disclosing the information.[13] 'Class-based' exemptions (eg, section 32 of the Act concerning court records) apply when public authorities have established that the requested information falls within the ambit

[9] D Vincent, *The Culture of Secrecy 1832–1997* (Oxford University Press 1998).

[10] B Worthy, 'More Open but Not More Trusted? The Effect of the Freedom of Information Act 2000 on the United Kingdom Central Government' (2010) 23 *Governance* 561–82.

[11] C Bessant (ed), *Information Sharing Handbook* (The Law Society 2009) 18.

[12] A Savage and R Hyde, 'Using Freedom of Information Requests to Facilitate Research'(2014) 17(3) *International Journal of Social Research Methodology* 303, 310.

[13] ibid.

of the class of information specified in the exemption, regardless of harms caused by the disclosure. Crucially, under section 40(2) of the Act, an absolute exemption applies if the disclosure of information would constitute a breach of the principles of the UK GDPR eg, in case there is no lawful basis for processing personal data and disclosing it.[14]

As Savage and Hyde point out, FOI legislation can be employed by virtually anyone who is interested in scrutinising government policies through research, not only established institutional actors such as universities or other research organisations and researchers working within their confines. It is, thus, no coincidence that scholars operating within disciplines traditionally concerned with power and accountability – including law,[15] sociology,[16] criminology,[17] criminal justice[18] and political science[19] – have pioneered the use of such legislation for research purposes. Scholars in different countries have used freedom of information legislation. In Canada, freedom of information requests have been used as a primary data source in a variety of research contexts, from policing and national security, to corporate security and post-secondary education.[20] In the United States, scholars employed freedom of information requests to look at the surveillance practices of the Federal Bureau of Investigation (FBI) against academics suspected to be radicals.[21] In the UK, scholars working in the area of policing from socio-legal and broader social-scientific perspectives have particularly utilised the FOIA. Savage used the FOIA to gain access to the whistleblowing policies of 39 UK police constabularies in 2015.[22] Kingston and others used the FOIA to interrogate how cost calculations block requests for information by the police in England and

[14] Information Commissioner's Office, 'The Guide to Freedom of Information' (updated July 2022). Available at: https://ico.org.uk/media/for-organisations/guide-to-freedom-of-information-4-9.pdf.

[15] K Walby and A Luscombe, 'Using Freedom of Information Requests in Socio-Legal Studies, Criminal Justice Studies, and Criminology' in M Deflem and D Silva (eds), *Methods of Criminology and Criminal Justice Research* (Emerald 2019) 33–46.

[16] P Greenberg, 'Strengthening Sociological Research Through Public Records Requests' (2016) 3(2) *Social Currents* 110–17.

[17] I Warren, 'Freedom of Information and Australian Criminology' in K Walby and A Luscombe (eds), *Freedom of Information and Social Science Research Design* (Routledge 2019) 75–85.

[18] L Cooke and P Sturges, 'Police and Media Relations in an Era of Freedom of Information' (2009) 19(4) *Policing & Society* 406–24.

[19] F Jiwani and T Krawchenko, 'Public Policy, Access to Government, and Qualitative Research Practices: Conducting Research Within A Culture Of Information Control' (2014) 40(1) *Canadian Public Policy* 57–66.

[20] K Walby and A Luscombe, 'Criteria for Quality in Qualitative Research and Use of Freedom of Information Requests in the Social Sciences' (2017) 17(5) *Qualitative Research* 537–53; J Piché, 'Accessing the State of Imprisonment in Canada: Information Barriers and Negotiation Strategies. Brokering Access: Politics, Power, and Freedom of Information in Canada' (2012) 234–60.

[21] S Diamond, *Compromised Campus: The Collaboration of Universities With The Intelligence Community* (Oxford University Press, 1992); J Keen and J Appleby, 'Freedom of Information. Quietly Does It' (1999) 109(5678) *The Health Service Journal* 24–26.

[22] A Savage, 'Whistle blowing in the Police Service: Developments and Challenges' (2016) 22(1) *European Journal of Current Legal Issues*. Online.

Wales in 2018.[23] Other scholars have used FOIA requests to assess the resources dedicated to combating economic crimes or the number of police station closures and reductions in opening hours.[24]

FOIA legislation is a prime example of democratic access for research purposes but, due to its rationale as an instrument that serves government transparency, it would have very limited use for broader innovation purposes. Even for research, however, the rise of the so-called 'digital state' in the UK, as in other countries, has imposed serious limitations on its empowering capacity. Simply put, the FOIA provides access to information in a more *static* manner: researchers can use the legislation to identify certain important pieces of information, or certain databases, and request access. In most cases, this request will refer to previously collected or created information, potentially reflecting public service delivery some years ago. The modernised State, however, is collecting and producing information in a much more *dynamic* fashion. Massive government datasets are updated daily and must be organised and curated to ensure that the contributions of thousands of civil servants and the data points of millions of citizens are registered during the routine operation of the government in a coherent and meaningful manner.[25] For example, if one were to scrutinise the fairness of immigration decisions by the UK border control authorities, one would have to enjoy ongoing access to massive datasets that are continuously updated through everyday border control activities, as well as in the process of bureaucratic decisions about eg, the settled status of EU citizens in the UK. Many of the relevant datasets will belong to different public bodies apart from the main decision maker (in this case the Home Office), such as HM Revenue and Customs and the Department for Work and Pensions.[26]

As continuous data sharing between public bodies is becoming the norm,[27] ongoing access to up-to-date government information will be required before a complete picture of the progress made by public policymaking and delivery can be ascertained. To make things even more complicated, the automation of certain civil service processes blurs the boundaries between human decision makers and algorithms, raising challenges for mapping information flows. For example, public bodies may use automated systems to triage user requests or augment

[23] S Kingston and others, '"Cost" Calculations as a Barrier to Gaining Information Under the Freedom of Information Act 2000 from the Police in England and Wales' (2019) 29(7) *Policing and Society* 834.

[24] R Smith and P Somerville, 'The Long Goodbye: A Note on the Closure of Rural Police Stations and the Decline of Rural Policing in Britain' (2013) 7(4) *Policing: A Journal of Policy and Practice* 348–58; M Button and others, '"The Not So Thin Blue Line After All?" Investigative Resources Dedicated to Fighting Fraud/Economic Crime in the United Kingdom' (2015) 9(2) *Policing: A Journal of Policy and Practice* 129–42.

[25] S Lowe, 'The Value of Safe Settings in Evidence-based Policy Making' (2018). Available at: http://eprints.ncrm.ac.uk/4255/.

[26] J Tomlinson, 'Quick and Uneasy Justice: An Administrative Justice Analysis of the EU Settlement Scheme' (2019) The Public Law Project. Available at: https://publiclawproject.org.uk/content/uploads/2019/07/Joe-Tomlinson-Quick-and-Uneasy-Justice-Full-Report-2019.pdf.

[27] Law Commission, 'Data Sharing Between Public Bodies: A Scoping Report' (2014). Available at: www.lawcom.gov.uk/app/uploads/2015/03/lc351_data-sharing.pdf.

(if not make) certain decisions affecting the rights and the obligations of citizens eg, regarding social welfare benefits.[28] With powerful private actors often being involved in the deployment of such systems,[29] it may be difficult for researchers to hold the exercise of public power accountable without on-going and regularly updated knowledge about existing data sharing practices. This type of access is not provided via FOI requests but needs a more sustained and long-term approach to data sharing.

Apart from FOI legislation, the Environmental Information Regulations 2004 (the EIRs) grant the public specific rights to access environmental information.[30] The scope of what constitutes environmental information under the EIRs is broad and encompasses data that may not initially appear to be related to the environment eg, 'cost–benefit and other economic analyses' related to measures and activities referred in the regulations. By contrast to the more general scope of the FOIA, the EIRs are exclusively applicable to environmental information.

IV. Duties to Disclose: Private and Public Disclosure Mandates in the Law

Public bodies may have an obligation to disclose data under the law, either to another specified entity or to the broader public. For example, sections 337–339ZG of the Proceeds of Crime Act 2002 mandate that public bodies disclose data as part of submitting a Suspicious Activity Report to the National Crime Agency, when there is knowledge or suspicion of an individual being involved in, or attempting, money laundering.[31] Similarly, section 17 of the Criminal Appeal Act 1995 requires a public body to supply information to the Criminal Cases Review Commission upon request, in relation to the commission's exercise of its duties.[32]

Beyond the individual rights mentioned in the previous section, legislation such as the FOIA 2000 and the EIRs establish public disclosure mandates in the name of open government and transparency. The Freedom of Information Act mandates that each public authority maintains a publication scheme approved by the Information Commissioner's Office (ICO). This scheme should outline their commitment to regularly provide access to specific categories of information, including policies and procedures, meeting minutes, annual reports, and financial

[28] R Booth, 'Benefits system automation could plunge claimants deeper into poverty' *The Guardian* 14 October 2019. Available at: www.theguardian.com/technology/2019/oct/14/fears-rise-in-benefits-system-automation-could-plunge-claimants-deeper-into-poverty.

[29] UN Special Rapporteur on Extreme Poverty and Human Rights, 'Digital technology, social protection and human rights: Report' (2019). Available at: www.ohchr.org/EN/Issues/Poverty/Pages/DigitalTechnology.aspx; HM Government, 'Guidelines for AI procurement' (8 June 2020). Available at: www.gov.uk/government/publications/guidelines-for-ai-procurement/guidelines-for-ai-procurement.

[30] The Environmental Information Regulations 2004 (SI 2004/3391).

[31] Proceeds of Crime Act 2002, Part 7.

[32] Criminal Appeal Act 1995, s 17.

data.[33] The majority of public authorities typically display their publication scheme on their website, often under sections labelled 'freedom of information', 'guide to information', or 'publication scheme'.[34] In a similar vein, section 4 of the EIRs stipulates that public authorities shall 'progressively' make available environmental information they hold to the public.[35]

Public authorities are also obligated under the Equality Act 2010 to fulfil certain disclosure responsibilities that assist them in adhering to the public sector equality duty. The public sector equality duty imposes an obligation on public authorities to reflect on how their policies or decisions impact individuals protected by the Equality Act. This duty does not apply to private organisations and individuals, who are not required to comply with it. The disclosure duties include annually publishing equality information to demonstrate their compliance with the equality duty,[36] as well as formulating and publishing equality objectives at least once every four years.[37] The Re-Use of Public Sector Information Regulations 2015 also require that public authorities release a list of the main information they hold within their public task, including information they publish proactively and unpublished information.[38] Under the same regulations, public sector bodies are obliged to allow re-use of documents unless restricted or excluded upon request.[39]

Obligations may also be jurisdiction specific to the devolved countries, such as the obligation of public bodies in Northern Ireland to comply with a request from the Chief Statistician to disclose information.[40] Another example derives from sections 31 and 32 of the Public Services Reform (Scotland) Act 2010 which mandate that the Scottish Government and specified public bodies are required to disclose information regarding their spending and other relevant issues as promptly as feasible following the conclusion of each financial year.[41]

It is worth considering whether duties to disclose information can be utilised for the purposes of research and innovation data processing. Arguably, public disclosure duties are more appropriate, as private disclosure mandates confine disclosure to specified entities for specified purposes, with the government having explicitly avoided to introduce such duties for research or innovation purposes.[42] Even in the

[33] Information Commissioner's Office, 'What Information Do We Need to Publish?'. Available at: https://ico.org.uk/for-organisations/foi-eir-and-access-to-information/guide-to-freedom-of-information/publication-scheme/.

[34] HM Government, 'HMRC Publication Scheme'. Available at: www.gov.uk/government/organisations/hm-revenue-customs/about/publication-scheme.

[35] Environmental Information Regulations 2004, reg 4(1).

[36] Equality Act 2010 (Specific Duties and Public Authorities) Regulations 2017 (SI 2010/353), reg 4.

[37] ibid.

[38] Re-Use of Public Sector Information 2015, s 16.

[39] ibid s 6.

[40] Law Commission (n 27) 30.

[41] Public Services Reform (Scotland) Act 2010, ss 31 and 32.

[42] 'Mandating the disclosure of data would not be appropriate', Department for Culture, Media & Sport, 'Digital Economy Bill – Factsheet – Digital Government: Research and Statistics (clauses 56–68)'. Available at: https://assets.publishing.service.gov.uk/government/uploads/system/uploads/attachment_data/file/535021/11._Research_and_Statistics.pdf.

case of public disclosure duties, however, there would be a need to identify a lawful basis to re-process the data for research and innovation purposes and this might prove challenging in practice, especially for commercial researchers and innovators, as I will explain in chapter 5.[43] Furthermore, the quality, format, and scope of the disclosed data are critical, as most cases of public disclosure mandates serve transparency and compliance purposes, thus they shall be expected to be more in the form of aggregate statistical information, rather than the sufficiently detailed data that are optimal for research and innovation purposes. With that in mind, the potential to utilise disclosure duties for research and innovation purposes is rather limited.

V. Discretion to Disclose: The DEA 2017 and Other Legal Powers

Discretionary legal powers to share public sector data stem from a variety of 'sources': statutory gateways, implied, common-law and prerogative powers.[44] The analysis presented here suggests that not all these sources are equally applicable in the research and innovation context; apart from statutory gateways, common-law powers might be a more appropriate source than implied powers, whereas prerogative powers are highly unlikely to be applicable.

A. Statutory Gateways

The most uncontroversial legal source of data sharing powers is (administrative) statutory law. In general, there are many different and context-specific legal powers to share administrative data deriving from statutory acts. To give a few examples, key 'gateways' are to be found in sections 251 of the National Health Service (NHS) Act 2006, 47 of the Children Act 1989, 175 of the Education Act 2002, 2 of the Local Government Act 2000 and 17 of the Crime and Disorder Act 1998, 39 of the Statistics and Registration Services Act (SRSA) 2007, 261 of the Health and Social Care (HSC) Act 2012, 3 of the Prescribed Persons Act 2009 and 64 of the Digital Economy Act (DEA) 2017.

Until the very recent enactment of the DEA, these gateways empowered only a few public bodies to share data for research purposes. For example, the 'approved researcher' gateway in the SRSA empowers the Office for National Statistics to share data for statistical research purposes. The NHS and HSC Acts are similarly limited in the scope of research allowed. Section 251(12) of the former confines its use to *medical* research; section 261 of the latter, after its amendment by section 122

[43] See Chapter 5.
[44] Law Commission (n 27) part 2.

of the Care Act 2014, requires that the purposes of data sharing are limited to the 'promotion of health', ie proposing improvements in the operation of the health and social care system.

The enactment of the DEA in April 2017 was a step-change to this piecemeal approach. Section 64(1) of the Act empowers all public authorities to disclose data they hold 'in the context of their functions' for research purposes. Crucially, the Act confines this authorisation quite narrowly from the perspective of encouraging research and innovation with public sector data. More specifically, research must be conducted in the public interest, with both the researcher and the research project being accredited by the UK Statistics Authority (UKSA) according to section 71(2) of the Act.[45] The Research Code of Practice and Accreditation Criteria, published by the UKSA,[46] elaborates on the accreditation conditions. To be accredited, a researcher must provide 'evidence of suitable research qualifications and/or experience' and agree to certain conditions such as to undertake compulsory training and be included on a public record.[47] The research project must serve the public interest, in one of the following ways:

- provide an evidence base for public policy decision making;
- provide an evidence base for public service delivery;
- provide an evidence base for decisions which are likely to significantly benefit the economy, society or quality of life of people in the UK, UK nationals or people born in the UK now living abroad;
- replicate, validate, challenge or review existing research and proposed research publications, including official statistics;
- significantly extend understanding of social or economic trends or events by improving knowledge or challenging widely accepted analyses; and/or
- improve the quality, coverage or presentation of existing research, including official or National Statistics.

It is evident that the Code envisages mostly non-profit or academic research as falling within the ambit of research that can be accredited, although commercial research can arguably satisfy some of these categories, on a case-by-case basis. A significant challenge for commercial researchers and innovators is the requirement that:

> When the project is complete, all results or outcomes of the research must be made openly and accessibly available in a way that could reasonably be expected to be permanent.

[45] DEA 2017, s 71(2).

[46] UK Statistics Authority, 'Research Code of Practice and Accreditation Criteria' (12 February 2020). Available at: www.gov.uk/government/publications/digital-economy-act-2017-part-5-codes-of-practice/research-code-of-practice-and-accreditation-criteria.

[47] ibid.

This requirement may clash with the protection of trade secrets and it would be really interesting to see how this balancing of interests would operate in a legal judgment. Public bodies may disclose data in accordance with the conditions outlined in sections 64(3)–(10), as well as with the Data Protection Act 2018 which implements the EU General Data Protection Regulation into domestic law. The most important requirements under article 64(3) and (6) are that data are de-identified before they can be shared for research processes, as well as that reasonable steps are taken to minimise disclosure risks within a secure environment, both in the interest of protecting the fundamental rights to privacy and data protection of data subjects. While section 73(2) of the Act excludes information held relating to health and social care functions, the discretionary power established by section 64(1) is now the major source for most research-data-sharing purposes. What happens, however, in cases not covered by explicit statutory language eg, when public authorities are unsure about the nexus.

B. Implied Powers

An answer to the above question may be given by the so-called 'implied powers' of public bodies. The Law Commission maintains that in the absence of an explicit legal gateway, the power may be implied if 'data sharing is *reasonably incidental* to an express power to do something else'.[48] The problem is that there has been very limited discussion on implied powers in the research and innovation context. In fact, one struggles to find a single legal resource or precedent on implied powers as the legal basis for research and innovation data sharing. The 2014 Law Commission report, for example, mentions several examples of implied powers emerging eg, from a duty to co-operate or ensure the proper functioning of a regulatory body; none of them are related to research or innovation.[49]

Similarly unenlightening for research and innovation data sharing is the picture in examples of guidance produced by major stakeholders. The Centre of Excellence for Information Sharing suggests examining whether an activity is 'reasonably associated' with the existing powers of a public body in identifying an implied power to share data.[50] The ICO advises a consideration of: the type of organisation, its relevant functions or powers, the nature of the requested information (eg confidential or not) and any legal obligation to share it.[51] While the above are clearly helpful on a general level, there is no suggestion that 'research'

[48] Law Commission (n 27) [1.35].
[49] ibid 1.41 *et seq*.
[50] Centre of Excellence for Information Sharing, 'Information Governance' https://informationsharing.org.uk/infogovernance/.
[51] Information Commissioner's Office, 'Data Sharing Checklists' https://ico.org.uk/media/for-organisations/documents/1067/data_sharing_checklists.pdf.

or 'innovation' are activities that could be considered relevant to the 'function' or 'type' of specific public bodies.

This lack of precedents and guidance invites an enquiry into the scope of the 'reasonably incidental' norm. Lord Selborne LC defined it in *Great Eastern Railway* as 'whatever may fairly be regarded as incidental to, or consequential upon, those things which the Legislature has authorised'.[52] This interpretation of implied powers has been time and again endorsed by the courts,[53] even in the data sharing context. In *R(W)*, the Administrative Court was asked whether National Health Service (NHS) bodies have the legal power to disclose non-medical information of non-resident debtors for health service charges to the Health Secretary. The latter would later inform the Home Secretary who would apply immigration sanctions. Even though an explicit legal provision was not in place, Mr Justice Silber found that such a legal power existed 'under the general powers of NHS foundation trusts to do anything … necessary or expedient … in connection with their functions' and the Secretary's 'general function of promoting an effective healthcare system'.[54]

Is the above dearth of legal resources on 'implied powers' and research/innovation data sharing, then, merely a coincidence? One is inclined to answer in the negative by looking at the 'reasonably incidental' interpretation by the courts. Specifically, it was ruled in two major Supreme Court judgments, ie in *Ward* and *New London College*,[55] that only considerations which contribute to or emanate from the expressly stated main function of a public body may give rise to an implied power. Their Lordships did not agree on the matter; more restrictive approaches such as the one followed by the majority in *Ward* require that the 'implication has to be *necessary* to make the statutory power effective to achieve its purpose',[56] whereas the minority in *New London College* demanded that 'the source of the incidental power was found in a *specific provision* conferring specific functions'.[57] Even relaxed approaches, however, require a connection between the incidental action and the body's main function.[58] Demonstrating that data sharing for research or innovation is at least related to, if not necessary for, a public body's core function might prove quite challenging for most data providers.[59]

[52] *Attorney General v Great Eastern Railway Co* (1880) 5 App Cas 473.

[53] *D and J Nicol v Dundee Harbour Trustees* 1914 2 SLT 418; *Glasgow Corporation v Flint* 1966 SLT 183.

[54] *R (on the application of W, X, Y, and Z) v The Secretary of State for Health v The Secretary of State for the Home Department* [2014] EWHC 1532 (Admin) (Silber J) at [82].

[55] *Ward v Commissioner of Police of the Metropolis and another* [2005] UKHL 32; *R (New London College Ltd) v Secretary of State for the Home Department* [2013] UKSC 51.

[56] ibid *Ward* (Baroness Hale) at [24]–[27].

[57] *New London College* (n 55) (Lord Carnwath) at [33]–[36].

[58] ibid (Lord Sumption) at [29]: 'If the Secretary of State is entitled to prescribe … rules for the grant of leave … which demand upon the migrant having a suitable sponsor, then she must be also entitled to take administrative measures for identifying sponsors …'; *Ward* (n 55) (Lord Rodger) at [5]: 'those things which are incident to, and may reasonably and properly be done under the main purpose … would not be prohibited'.

[59] Even if, for a few special cases like the Office for National Statistics, whose functions include promoting research, meeting this threshold may be straightforward.

C. Common Law Powers

The 'administrative' common-law powers of the Crown are limited to data providers who are ministerial departments. These providers do not only hold the most comprehensive administrative datasets in the UK but have also mostly pioneered the introduction of research data sharing initiatives in the UK public sector.

The doctrinal legal analysis of common law powers is arguably more straightforward than implied powers. Lord Sumption noted in *New London College* that 'the Crown possesses some general administrative powers … which are not exercises of the royal prerogative and do not require statutory authority'.[60] Perry describes such powers as 'unglamorous, but important', accounting for 'much of the ordinary business of the government'.[61] This category encompasses such powers as the power to form contracts, conveying property, making ex gratia payments, appointing agents and creating policies.[62] While administrative datasets are not 'property' of the public bodies,[63] the latter are, by law, responsible for their use and management. Allowing access based on data sharing arrangements to serve a policy promoting the public interest arguably falls within this ambit. Wade and Forsyth offer another relevant argument; section 1 of the Localism Act 2011 provides local authorities with 'the power to do *anything* that individuals generally may do' (emphasis added).[64] An individual shares data for research lawfully if compliance with specific legal restrictions is satisfied. In case local authorities have this power, then, it would be surprising for central government to lack it.[65] This is a better argument than the contestable contention that the Crown, as a corporation sole, possesses all the legal powers that a natural person does.[66]

There are, however, two caveats to this conclusion. First, many departments, with the Department for Work and Pensions (DWP) being a prime example, claim that their common-law powers have been 'eroded' by the proliferation of statutory legislation.[67] In this view, a ministerial department cannot use common-law powers to cover the gaps of statutory legislation, since the latter exclusively regulates specific areas of decision-making and 'eats away' the common law. While the idea of common-law 'erosion' is indeed well-established,[68] its scope is far from clear. For

[60] *New London College* (n 55) (Lord Sumption) at [28].

[61] A Perry, 'The Crown's Administrative Powers' (2015) *Law Quarterly Review* 652.

[62] ibid 661 citing: *Rederiaktiebolaget Amphitrite v The King* [1921] 3 KB 500 (Rowlatt J) [503]; *Robertson v Minister of Pensions* [1949] 1 KB 227 (Denning J) at [231]; *Crown Lands Commissioner v Page* [1960] 2 QB 274 (Lord Evershed MR) at [287]–[288].

[63] See Chapter 4.

[64] Section 1 of the Localism Act 2011. The Act sought to devolve decision-making powers from the central government in England and Wales to individuals and communities.

[65] W Wade and C Forsyth, *Administrative Law* (Oxford University Press 2014) 180.

[66] Perry (n 61) 658 identifies key deficiencies in this argument.

[67] Law Commission (n 27) at [9.1].

[68] *Attorney General v De Keyser's Royal Hotel Ltd* [1920] AC 508; *R v Secretary of State for the Home Department, ex parte Northumbria Police Authority* [1989] QB 26.

instance, in *Hooper*, the House of Lords refrained from ruling on whether a statutory requirement to make payments to widows 'eroded' the common-law power of the DWP to make payments to widowers.[69] Therefore, public bodies may very well find that they possess such powers contingent on the circumstances. Second, common-law powers must be exercised in conformity with statutory legislation. In this case, the main limitations stem from the right to private life under Article 8 of the European Convention on Human Rights and the requirements of data protection law, found in the Data Protection Act 2018.

D. Prerogative Powers

The final potential source of legal powers discussed here concerns the 'royal prerogative', ie the non-statutory powers of the Crown and its Ministers that were part of its extensive powers over its subjects in earlier times and have not been restricted by legislation.[70] The Law Commission concedes that 'the precise character and extent of the prerogative is a matter of debate'.[71] Endicott argues that a clear articulation of the principles that justify the power of the executive in the British constitution has been undermined by a view of the prerogative as a 'stubborn stain' that would better be 'washed away'.[72]

Nonetheless, when it comes to public sector data sharing for research and innovation, the prerogative does not seem a very good fit for two reasons. First, prerogative powers are usually *constitutional*, ie 'creating the basic institutions of the State and stipulating their powers and relationships with each other',[73] as opposed to administrative, in character. Bradley and others refer to powers relating to the legislature, the judicial system, foreign affairs, treaties, war and armed forces as prerogative examples.[74] Secondly, they are paradigmatically described as the legal powers which 'appertain to the Crown but not to its subjects',[75] which means that they are exclusive. Research and innovation data sharing, however, is much closer to an administrative operation that can also be exercised by natural persons.

[69] *R (Hooper) v Secretary of State for Work and Pensions* [2005] UKHL 29.

[70] Wade and Forsyth (n 65) 179.

[71] Law Commission (n 27) at [1.47].

[72] T Endicott, 'Parliament and the Prerogative: From the Case of Proclamations to Miller' (2016) Judicial Power Project. Available at: http://judicialpowerproject.org.uk/wp-content/uploads/2016/12/Endicott-2016-Parliament-and-the-Prerogative.pdf.

[73] House of Lords Constitution Committee, 'Constitution – First Report' (2000-01). Available at: https://publications.parliament.uk/pa/ld200102/ldselect/ldconst/11/1101.htm ch2.

[74] AW Bradley and others, *Constitutional and Administrative Law* 16th edn (Pearson 2015) 253 *et seq*.

[75] *R v Secretary of State for Health ex p C* [2000] 1 FLR 627 (Hale LJ); *Shrewsbury and Atcham Borough Council v Secretary of State for Communities and Local Government* [2008] EWCA Civ 148.

VI. Legal Limitations to Access Public Sector Information

Legal powers to share data are far from unconstrained; the UK Supreme Court clarified in *Christian Institute* that they are 'conditional upon compliance' with the requirements of data protection and human rights law.[76] The two sources of limitations are discussed, in turn, in this section.

A. Limitations Stemming from Data Protection Law

Data protection law determines whether personal information is processed 'fairly and lawfully'.[77] Public sector datasets, generally, contain information capable of identifying individual citizens. Is it, however, the case that data sharing for research and innovation involves personal data in all cases?

The answer to this question is more elusive than it seems. For example, section 64(3) of the DEA 2017 states that personal data must undergo de-identification, ie removal of any identifying information, before disclosure. The Administrative Data Research Network and other bodies like the SAIL DataBank have been using trusted third parties to de-identify and link the acquired datasets before allowing a researcher access.[78] Data shared under such standards, one might assert, are not personal data, since researchers are not provided with identifying information. Indeed, the House of Lords held in *Common Services Agency* that properly 'barnardised' (a method of de-identification) data are not personal data at the point of becoming available under a Freedom of Information Act 2000 request, as the recipient lacks the information allowing re-identification.[79] The ICO concur in their 'Anonymisation Code of Practice' that 'effective anonymisation' is possible through pseudonymisation (another de-identification method).[80]

Nevertheless, there are salient reasons for discussing data protection law limitations. De-identification is not a uniform legal requirement and there might be public

[76] *Christian Institute v the Lord Advocate* [2016] UKSC 51 (Lady Hale et al) at [58]. The Court also mentioned the common law duty of confidentiality, but this is not applicable in this case because it is not relevant. Administrative data are not confidential information *because* they have been provided within a confider–confidant relationship.

[77] Data Protection Act 2018, s 85.

[78] SAIL Databank, 'The Anonymisation Process'. Available at: htpp://saildatabank.com/saildata/data-privacy-security/#anonymisation-process.

[79] *Common Services Agency v Scottish Information Commissioner* [2008] UKHL 47 (Lord Hope) at [26].

[80] Information Commissioner's Office, 'Anonymisation: managing data protection risk code of practice'. Available at: https://ico.org.uk/media/for-organisations/documents/1061/anonymisation-code.pdf, 21; M Mourby and others, 'Are "Pseudonymised" Data Always Personal Data? Implications of the GDPR for Administrative Data Research in the UK' (2018) 34(2) *Computer Law & Security Review* 222.

sector bodies which do not apply it. In that regard, public bodies in the UK seem to have been treating pseudonymised data as personal data. The National Health Service 'Confidentiality Code of Practice' stresses that pseudonymised information 'differs from anonymised information in that … it allows information about the same individual to be linked in a way that true anonymisation does not'.[81]

The main data protection legal instrument in the UK is currently the DPA 2018 which has, practically, implemented the GDPR into domestic law. Public sector data pose the challenge of containing personal data which were originally collected at a different time and for a different purpose from research or innovation. Three of the data protection principles enshrined in section 85 of the DPA merit particularly careful consideration: lawful basis for processing, purpose limitation and data minimisation. For example, a data provider like the National Health Service interested in providing access to researchers who want to analyse the impact of a government policy on the health and well-being of citizens must ensure that these principles are satisfied. The legitimate aim of processing needs to be carefully defined and an explanation of why specific datasets are necessary to meet this aim needs to be offered.

In Chapter 5, I elaborate on lawful grounds for processing. 'Purpose limitation' comes into play due to tension between Recital 50, Article 5(1)(b) and Article 6(4)(c) of the GDPR. More specifically, Recital 50 stipulates that further processing for a different purpose is allowed only 'where the processing is compatible with the purposes for which the personal data were initially collected', with the exception of, inter alia, 'scientific or historical research purposes' that should be regarded as 'compatible lawful processing operations'.[82] Article 5(1)(b) of the GDPR qualifies this presumption of compatibility by stressing that such further processing 'shall, in accordance with Article 89(1), not be considered to be incompatible with the initial purposes'. This would seem to guarantee compatibility when eg, the initial purpose is routine case management and the further processing takes place for research purposes, provided that the safeguards of Article 89 (including data minimisation) are met. Considering that the European Data Protection Board has recently found the conditions for applying this presumption of compatibility 'horizontal and complex',[83] it is safe to assume that data providers will have to produce a tailor-made policy on the matter. For example, the Justice Data Lab, based in Cardiff, clarifies the precise variables they use to identify sentences and follow-up periods in measuring re-offending, explaining why these are necessary to ensure quality of the analysis.[84]

[81] R Jay, *Data Protection Law and Practice* (Sweet & Maxwell 2012) 596.

[82] GDPR, Recital 50.

[83] European Data Protection Board, 'Opinion 3/2019 concerning the Questions and Answers on the interplay between the Clinical Trials Regulation (CTR) and the General Data Protection Regulation (GDPR) (art. 70.1.b))' (23 January 2019). Available at: http://edpb.europa.eu/sites/edpb/files/files/file1/edpb_opinionctrq_a_final_en.pdf 8.

[84] F Lyon and others, 'Opening Access to Administrative Data for Evaluating Public Services: The Case of the Justice Data Lab' (2015) 21(2) *Evaluation* 232–47.

Finally, yet importantly, research and innovation data sharing raises challenges from a data minimisation perspective, considering that data custodians may be inclined to retain-and-reuse datasets for research to minimise logistical costs related to data extraction.[85] However, under section 90 of the DPA, data minimisation dictates that personal data 'must be kept for no longer than is necessary for the purpose for which it is processed'. The research exemptions established by the GDPR and the DPA mitigate the rigour of these requirements to ensure that they do not 'prevent or seriously impair' the achievement of the purposes of processing,[86] ie in our case the facilitation of data-intensive research in the public interest.

That being said, the research exemptions are far from unconditional. For these exemptions to apply, research purposes must be the *sole* purpose of data processing, the ICO having the power to determine whether this is indeed the case.[87] The processing should always be linked with the publication of academic material[88] and data custodians need to have a reasonable belief that such a publication would be in the public interest.[89] Provided that scientific research is the sole purpose of processing, it is not necessary to set a specific retention period and data can be kept for longer.[90] Therefore, the law allows some scope for accommodating research data sharing but only when it comes to academic research. Human rights law is another significant source of limitations.

B. Limitations Stemming from Human Rights Law

Personal data sharing, especially when done on a massive scale, raises privacy issues. In UK law, breach of a fundamental right is a distinct ground of judicial review in accordance with section 4 of the Human Rights Act (HRA) 1998. The crucial provision here is the right to private life under Article 8 of the European Convention on Human Rights (ECHR), which has been interpreted broadly to encompass numerous privacy interests including the 'fundamental right to protection of personal data' under Article 8.[91] Considering that the UK Supreme Court held in *Christian Institute* that discussing the compatibility of data sharing legislation with Article 8 of the ECHR suffices to determine compatibility with data

[85] P Jackson, 'From "Intruders" to "Partners": The Evolution of the Relationship Between the Research Community and Sources of Official Administrative Data' in N Crato and P Paruolo, *Data-Driven Policy Impact Evaluation* (Springer 2019) 17.

[86] DPA 2018, Sch 2, Pt 6, para 27.

[87] ibid s 174(3)(a).

[88] ibid ss 174(3) & 176(1).

[89] ibid Sch 2, Pt 5, para 26(2)(b).

[90] Information Commissioner's Office, 'Principle (e): Storage limitation'. Available at: https://ico.org.uk/for-organisations/guide-to-data-protection/guide-to-the-general-data-protection-regulation-gdpr/principles/storage-limitation/.

[91] *Satakunnan Markkinapörssi Oy v Finland* [2018] 66 EHRR 8 at 74.

protection,[92] it may very well be the case that human rights limitations will precede data protection considerations in litigation. Does Article 8, however, apply to all scenarios of research and innovation data sharing?

Privacy is a *qualified* right, ie one which lawfully accepts limitations when this is necessary in the pursuit of a legitimate aim. The ECHR adopts a two-staged enquiry: first, the Court considers whether there is an 'interference' with the right and, second, whether this interference is justified after balancing the relevant rights with other rights or interests. The discussion on de-identification and 'identifiability' is again relevant here. Lady Hale held in *South Lanarkshire* that it is difficult to see an interference with subjects' rights in cases where processing does not enable the data recipient or anyone else to identify the data subjects.[93]

Yet, human rights law limitations may be engaged without requiring a definitive legal solution of the identifiability conundrum. This is because, essentially, interfering with a human right covers all cases where the possibility of interference *cannot be precluded*, rather than requiring their positive existence or a rigorous assessment of their likelihood. In our context, in the CJEU case of *Digital Rights Ireland*, Advocate General Cruz Villalón advocated for a broad notion of 'interference', encompassing all cases of storing and collection of personal data by public authorities regardless of the subsequent 'use made of them'.[94] The Advocate General emphasised that for such interference to arise, the data does *not* have to be 'personal data in the traditional sense of the term, relating to specific information concerning the identity of individuals'. It can be data of a more aggregate character. This is often the case with the data held by prominent data custodians in the UK, with large ministerial departments often keeping datasets that do not include identifying variables, being interested in patterns rather than individuals. Similarly, the UK Supreme Court held in *Christian Institute* that the statutory requirement of compliance with the DPA 1998 and the EU directive in section 26(11) of the Children and Young People (Scotland) Act (CYPA) 2014 did not preclude a potential interference with Article 8 of the ECHR.[95]

At the second stage, the European Court of Human Rights adopts a proportionality test under Article 8(2) of the ECHR.[96] Within this test, the 'public' or 'general' interest served by social research may be invoked as a legitimate objective.[97]

[92] *Christian Institute* (n 76) (Lady Hale) at [104].

[93] *South Lanarkshire Council v Scottish Information Commissioner* [2013] UKSC 55 (Lady Hale) at [26].

[94] *Digital Rights Ireland Ltd v Minister for Communications* (ECLI:EU:C:2014:238) Opinion of AG Cruz Villalón [69] citing *Amann v Switzerland* [2000] 30 EHRR 843 [65, 69 and 80] and *Leander v Sweden* [1987] 9 EHRR 433 at [48].

[95] *Christian Institute* (n 76) (Lady Hale et al) at [78–81].

[96] ECHR, art 8(2) states this is: 'necessary in a democratic society in the interests of national security, public safety or the economic well-being of the country (…) or for the protection of the rights and freedoms of others'.

[97] U Kilkelly, 'The Right to Respect for Private and Family Life' (Council of Europe 2003) 30 on the European Court of Human Rights according a wide margin of appreciation to Member States in

Assuming, then, the suitability of data disclosures to attain this objective, there are two issues within proportionality,[98] ie whether data sharing powers are 'in accordance with the law' and whether they are 'necessary' for the achievement of the pursued aim.

Christian Institute shows how challenging both tests can be. The Supreme Court there stroke down major provisions of Part 4 of the CYPA 2014, which obliged or empowered public bodies to share personal data of young persons to a 'named person', when the information was 'likely to be relevant' to their wellbeing. There were two deficiencies in the Act. First, it was not 'in accordance with the law' because it was not sufficiently 'foreseeable and accessible' to prevent arbitrary interferences with privacy rights by public bodies.[99] Secondly, the Act did not establish safeguards that would enable 'the proportionality of an interference to be adequately examined'.[100] In this respect, the Court noted that the ECHR compatibility of the Act could be rescued, had there been legally binding proportionality 'guidance to the information holder'.[101]

Research data sharing legislation is, arguably, a quite different case from CYPA, with research organisations being subject to several constraints. If we consider a few examples, section 253(1)(ca) of the Health and Social Care Act specifically requires that the Health and Social Care Information Centre (the custodian body) consider 'the privacy of recipients of health services and of adult social care' before disclosing data for research. The DEA 2017, while not incorporating such an explicit balancing with privacy, reduces the likelihood of an interference through its requirements of de-identification (section 64(3)) and conformity with the UK Statistics Authority 'Code of Practice' (section 64(10)). The latter is not merely advisory, but legally binding, since it regulates the researcher and project accreditation which is mandatory under sections 64(8)–(9) of the Act. Such accreditation is, under the (current version of) the Code of Practice, strictly dependent on adherence to its legal and ethical principles which, inter alia, cover: data security and confidentiality, proportionality between the disclosure burdens and anticipated benefits, the construction of public interest, data retention, onward disclosure and transparency. Hence, there are salient reasons to believe that existing research data sharing legislation satisfies, in principle, proportionality requirements in human rights law.

identifying a legitimate objective; see O Lynskey, *Foundations of EU Data Protection Law* (Oxford University Press 2015) 135 on the rights and interests balanced with data protection by the Court of Justice of the EU.

98 *R (Daly) v Secretary of State for the Home Department* [2001] UKHL 26 (Lord Steyn) at [27].

99 *Christian Institute* (n 76) (Lady Hale et al) at [79].

100 ibid at [84].

101 ibid at [101].

VII. Conclusion

Enabling access to the treasure troves of data held by governments and public bodies for research and innovation pursuits requires an understanding of the UK legal landscape governing data access and reuse. While 'research' enjoys favourable treatment in data protection law, 'innovation' lacks a clear legal basis to access public sector datasets. The UK's flagship Freedom of Information Act facilitates one-off democratic access to records, but has limitations when tracing impacts of dynamic, automated government processes. If public authorities wish to share data, relying solely on ambiguous 'implied powers' is legally risky. Explicit statutory gateways provide safer ground, but commercial reuse seems handicapped compared to academic research published openly. Though innovations built atop public data can boost productivity and quality of life, data protection principles and privacy rights introduce constraints not faced by university researchers.

While the DEA expands secure access opportunities for accredited researchers, data-intensive innovation seems hindered by uncertainties and risk aversion in the current legal framework governing public sector data. Addressing barriers to commercial reuse while not compromising privacy may require law and policy reforms incentivising accountable data sharing. I will elaborate on this issue in Chapter 5.

5

Commercial Access to Public Sector Data for Research and Innovation

In Chapter 4, I identified the central elements of the legal framework underpinning data access for research and innovation in the UK public sector, stressing that the law allows significant scope for organisational actors to authoritatively interpret the law in a way that fits their interests. Before delving into the empirical analysis of the interactions between these actors in this chapter, I turn to a critical area of legal ambiguity for the purposes of data access for research and innovation: the lawfulness of commercial access.

I examine key challenges surrounding commercial access to public sector data for research and innovation purposes. In doing so, I draw on organisational, economic, legal, and ethical hurdles that can impede data sharing initiatives between government and private sector entities. A central dilemma arises regarding whether private, commercial interests can ever fully align with broader goals of public welfare when accessing government data. In the analysis, I suggest dissociating the notion of 'public interest' from the identity of the organisations involved. Instead, focus should shift towards the contribution of data usage to collective economic or societal wellbeing. This proposed conceptual model facilitates collaborative 'hybrid research' arrangements between public bodies and private entities. Adopting this revised notion of public interest has significant implications. Private companies granted data access must substantiate how their commercial activities, directly or indirectly, support public sector functions or enhance communal prosperity. This places greater accountability on private entities to demonstrate commitment beyond superficial gestures. Additionally, enhanced transparency regarding data governance in public–private partnerships is needed, given previous government secrecy around such arrangements. Realising this conceptual shift requires overcoming key practical barriers. Public bodies must determine appropriate thresholds for private sector contributions to societal interests when handling government data. They need adequate capacity to thoroughly evaluate if partnerships confer greater public or private value. Clear safeguards must be instituted to ensure data usage aligns with communal objectives. Overcoming these obstacles necessitates comprehensive data governance approaches within public sectors.

In this chapter, I highlight economic incentives driving public–private collaborations alongside data governance challenges in reconciling public and private interests. Analysing legal bases and rights protections within the General Data Protection Regulation (GDPR) framework surfaces tensions between access justified through 'public interest' versus 'legitimate interests'. A proposed conceptual model reorientates the discussion, judging the appropriateness of commercial involvement based on its contribution to collective economic or social well-being rather than organisational identity. However, realising this vision requires overcoming barriers related to accountability, transparency, public engagement, and secure data handling.

I. Commercial Access to Government Data for Research and Innovation: Organisational Challenges and Economic Incentives

Previously in this book, I have described the vision of the public sector of the twenty-first century, where data streams, like the lifeblood of an advanced societal organism, continuously flow between public bodies and the citizens they serve. In this public sector, data does not merely inform policy, but transforms it, becoming the cornerstone of a society that values knowledge as the key to solving its most pressing challenges.

Ideally, this vision would be realised by public bodies, inherently aligned with the principles of public welfare and accountability and operating under the mandate of serving the public good. Such bodies would create and manage advanced data sharing infrastructures in the public sector. In practice, however, progress in making better use of public sector data for the purposes of improving public services via research and innovation is unequal among different countries. Some countries seem to be making significant investments in their 'capacity to use data strategically to improve policy making',[1] while other countries are making less progress. Why is that?

There are several recognised obstacles impeding the broader development of data sharing infrastructures within public sectors in Europe and beyond. One such impediment is the absence of a 'data sharing culture' within public sector organisations, which translates to an underappreciation for the potential value derived from data analysis.[2] Similarly, a widespread public distrust towards digital initiatives in the public sector involving personal data reflects a lack of understanding and confidence from citizens.[3] Furthermore, the absence of defined governance

[1] OECD, 'The Path to Becoming a Data-Driven Public Sector'. Available at: www.oecd-ilibrary.org/governance/the-path-to-becoming-a-data-driven-public-sector_059814a7-en 2.

[2] M Micheli, 'Accessing Privately Held Data: Public/Private Sector Relations In Twelve European Cities' (Data for Policy 2020). Available at: https://zenodo.org/record/3967044#.X7as6i0Rry9 2.

[3] High-Level Expert Group, 'Towards a European Strategy on Business-to-Government Data Sharing for the Public Interest. Final report prepared by the High-Level Expert Group on

and legal frameworks for using public-sector data for research significantly contributes to this issue.[4] This deficiency not only hampers data-driven innovation due to prevailing uncertainties but also raises concerns about whether any ongoing data sharing complies with the fundamental rights of the individuals concerned.

The most prevalent challenges faced by European countries, particularly during periods of limited public sector resources like the present, are primarily economic in nature: insufficient funding and expertise. The OECD has highlighted that the push for more effective use of public-sector data frequently encounters a skills gap among public employees,[5] as well as a shortage of necessary hardware and financial support needed to enact a comprehensive strategy for sharing data for research and innovation purposes. For example, the efforts to leverage government data in response to the COVID-19 crisis have been undermined by a lack of established data infrastructures, consistent standards, and interoperability – including scalable tools – as well as clear guidelines on which data should be prioritised for release, alongside the essential technical and operational competencies within government staff.[6]

The inclination for public sectors to share the intricate tasks associated with research and innovation data sharing with private entities becomes apparent upon recognising the nature of this undertaking. Differing fundamentally from the episodic disclosure typical of freedom of information acts,[7] research and innovation data sharing is a long-haul commitment. It encompasses establishing and overseeing data sharing agreements, continuous technical cooperation between data custodians and researchers, and the persistent engagement of numerous stakeholders within the providing organisation. Although the sophistication and technical demands of this process are mirrored in the quality and precision of the resulting evidence and outputs, the investment of resources and time required should not be underestimated. Possessing a valuable resource loses significance if the requisite tools or skilled personnel to fully exploit and 'unlock' its potential are absent. Both a knowledgeable workforce and state-of-the-art hardware are critical to 'ensure the capabilities to use and analyse the data' effectively.[8]

In a comprehensive view of these logistical demands, it's clear that merely obtaining leadership backing for financial investment in technical infrastructure

Business-to-Government Data Sharing' (European Union). Available at: www.euractiv.com/wp-content/uploads/sites/2/2020/02/B2GDataSharingExpertGroupReport-1.pdf 27. As it will be discussed *infra*, such digital experimentation in the public sector has often raised concerns from a privacy, data protection and non-discrimination perspective, with powerful private actors often exercising significant influence over the design of data collection and analysis, as well as governments seeking to develop invasive technologies and predictive analytics.

[4] ibid 7.

[5] OECD (n 1) 2.

[6] C Emilsson and others, 'The interdependency of data governance and open government data: lessons from COVID-19' (Data for Policy 2020) https://zenodo.org/record/3978270#.X7avHS0Rry9 3.

[7] A Savage and R Hyde, 'Using Freedom of Information Requests to Facilitate Research' (2014) 17(3) *International Journal of Social Research Methodology* 303.

[8] A Aral and others, 'Building a Data Ecosystem for Using Telecom Data to Inform the COVID-19 response efforts' (Data for Policy 2020). Available at: https://zenodo.org/record/3992420#.X7auxi0Rry9 6.

or in enhancing civil servants' data literacy is not enough. Public sector organisations, much like their counterparts in the private sector, require a wide-ranging strategic plan that acknowledges the role of data analysis in fulfilling their mission. This informs the development of solid 'business cases' for data infrastructure investments, optimising the use of available funds, whether internally sourced or externally acquired.[9] However, these 'business cases' should not be mistaken for market-driven imperatives. Beyond the gains in government efficacy, the superior utilisation of public-sector data brings a wealth of intangible rewards, such as bolstered accountability, transparency and trust in democratic institutions through independent, evidence-based evaluation of their activities.[10] Yet, without a 'compelling value proposition' that ensures financial viability,[11] the ambitious and enduring venture of establishing a public-sector data infrastructure may confront significant fiscal challenges during its execution.

In response to the complex demands of data management, public sector organisations have increasingly looked to form partnerships with private sector companies to enhance their policy design and implementation strategies.[12] Private entities have historically invested more heavily in data analysis capabilities to bolster business decisions and optimise profits.[13] IT and data analytics firms have often been pioneers in establishing data-centric public–private collaborations. For instance, the global telecom giant Telefónica partnered with the United Nations Food and Agriculture Organization (FAO) to aid Colombian officials in estimating the country's forced migration rates due to extreme drought conditions.[14] Similarly, well before the COVID-19 pandemic, Vodafone had developed a data-driven approach using aggregated anonymous mobile data, aiming to assist governments in monitoring population movement patterns and managing epidemics to thwart widespread disease outbreaks.[15]

These collaborations between public bodies and commercial entities are designed to be more than temporary or sporadic efforts; private companies often pledge long-term involvement to uplift public sector capabilities in data utilisation and to modernise their data infrastructures. In some instances, 'data research and innovation partnerships' are established where both public and private entities work together on projects that serve their mutual interests. Data sharing in such partnerships is quite demanding. A public body aiming to participate would need

[9] S Aidinlis and others, 'Building a Justice Data Infrastructure'. Available at: www.law.ox.ac.uk/news/2020-10-08-building-justice-data-infrastructure 21.

[10] Eg HM Government, 'Open Data White Paper: Unleashing the Potential' (June 2012), Available at: https://assets.publishing.service.gov.uk/government/uploads/system/uploads/attachment_data/file/78946/CM8353_acc.pdf 5: 'Data is the 21st Century's New Raw Material. Its Value is in Holding Governments to Account.'

[11] BC Ubaldi and others, 'Towards a New Data-Driven Service Design and Delivery Model?' (Data for Policy 2020). Available at: https://zenodo.org/record/3978179#.X7auPC0Rry9 3.

[12] ibid 34.

[13] High-Level Expert Group (n 3) 5.

[14] OECD (n 1) 2.

[15] ibid.

to carefully select relevant datasets, ensure the quality of the data (such as minimal missing variables), 'clean' the data to eliminate superfluous details and noise and apply statistical disclosure control methods to reduce any personally identifying information shared with researchers. Additionally, the public entity must draft and enforce data sharing agreements, which include clauses on how long the private party can retain the data. Of course, these data research partnerships do not always involve personal data. For instance, a private company may only need access to anonymised audio data from court hearings to develop a transcription algorithm that can provide written records of trials for litigants.[16] However, as mentioned earlier, technologies like machine learning algorithms often require real personal data, as opposed to synthetic data, to generate analyses that are applicable and beneficial to real-world situations.[17]

The nuanced interplay between public bodies and commercial entities in data research partnerships underscores a symbiotic relationship where each party's contributions and gains are interdependent. Such partnerships, established on the bedrock of shared interests and complementary strengths, pave the way for a critical conversation about the 'public interest' within the realm of commercial access. As we transition from the technicalities and frameworks underpinning these collaborations, it becomes essential to delve into the ethical and societal implications of commercial entities accessing public data. The next section aims to explore how these collaborations, while commercially driven, can align with and serve the broader goals of public welfare, ensuring that the use of public data by private entities contributes positively to society and does not stray from the overarching mission of public good.

II. Finding the 'Public Interest' in Research and Innovation Data Sharing

For some time now, governments in Europe and beyond, including the UK Government, have been channelling resources into leveraging their data for maximum societal benefit. They have been confronted with increasingly complex challenges such as natural disasters, migration, urban congestion, and waste management issues, all of which have outgrown the capabilities of traditional policy instruments.[18] Recognising that population data collected by government

[16] A similar service is performed by JUST: Access, 'JUST: Transcription'. Available at: www.just-access.org/just-transcription.

[17] D Rankin and others, 'Reliability of Supervised Machine Learning Using Synthetic Data in Health Care: Model to Preserve Privacy for Data Sharing' (2020) 8(7) *JMIR Medical Informatics* 2020 e18910: 'A total of 92% of models trained on synthetic data have lower accuracy than those trained on real data.'

[18] M Barbero and others, 'Big Data Analytics for Policy Making' (EU Commission DG DIGIT). Available at: https://joinup.ec.europa.eu/sites/default/files/document/2016-07/dg_digit_study_big_data_analytics_for_policy_making.pdf 2.

agencies in the course of delivering public services can be a powerful catalyst, governments have started to view this information as an essential tool for creating a better society and a more effective public sector. This population data is not just a resource but a beacon guiding the way towards innovative solutions that can enhance the lives of citizens and the operations of government itself.[19]

The OECD identifies three primary activities where analysing public sector data can significantly create public value.[20] Firstly, such analysis enables governments to foresee and shape their policies proactively, staying attuned to the evolving needs of citizens and ready to modify strategies as circumstances change. Secondly, insights gleaned from public sector data empower civil service agencies to implement and deliver policies more effectively, ensuring that efforts are concentrated on citizens who require government assistance the most. Lastly, the evaluation of public sector data is crucial for assessing the tangible effects of government policies on society, facilitating a systematic, thorough, and evidence-based review of the impact that high-level decisions have on individual lives and the community at large.

The considerable scope of public sector data in enhancing public policy development and execution is evident by the expansive and interwoven nature of the three main activities outlined by the OECD. These categories are neither comprehensive nor sharply separated; within them lie numerous specialised applications. For instance, law enforcement agencies are investing in advanced data-driven technologies to boost the situational awareness of officers, improving their understanding of the environments they patrol.[21] Additionally, there's a burgeoning interest in integrating data into AI systems to facilitate automated decision-making processes, which is particularly relevant in the digitisation of the justice system.[22]

The overlap between the three broad categories is notable, with many data analysis efforts serving dual purposes – for example, evaluating the performance of a government initiative while simultaneously guiding strategic policymaking to address specific citizen needs. A pertinent illustration is the 'Fuel Poverty' study funded by the Welsh government, which aims to provide an evidence-based assessment of energy efficiency programs for low-income households by correlating relevant data with hospital admission statistics. This project exemplifies the multifaceted use of government data, demonstrating its capacity to both inform and assess policy impacts in a tangible, beneficial manner.[23]

Governments globally have recognised the transformative potential of big data analytics over the past two decades, actively working to dismantle obstacles to data-centric digital innovation within their operations and services. South Korea,

[19] High-Level Expert Group (n 3) 7.

[20] OECD (n 6) 1.

[21] See the EU H2020-funded project DARLENE. Available at: www.darleneproject.eu on the development of relevant data-driven technologies.

[22] Aidinlis and others (n 9) 1.

[23] Welsh Government, 'The Fuel Poverty Data Linking Project'. Available at: https://gov.wales/fuel-poverty-data-linking-project-impact-health-welsh-government-warm-homes.

for example, has initiated an open contest for 'public sector big data analysis projects', inviting researchers and innovators to assist in harnessing the nation's data to address policy challenges.[24] Singapore has taken to characterising data-driven governmental decision-making as 'entrepreneurship at the national level', positioning it as a cornerstone of the nation's enduring 'competitiveness and liveability'.[25]

During the COVID-19 pandemic, the Qatari government employed data dashboards to collect, visualise, and analyse publicly accessible data, such as 'popular locations' from Google Maps, to monitor adherence to stay-at-home orders and to facilitate detailed assessments of the pandemic's economic impact.[26] Meanwhile, the United States has articulated its commitment through the Federal Data Strategy, aiming to harness the power of government data to support evidence-based policymaking, enhance services, and foster innovation across organisational management.[27]

EU Member States have been swift to engage in the global shift towards data-driven insights and technologies, recognising the geopolitical significance of maintaining a competitive edge in this field. Long before the European Commission's recent proposition for a 'Data Governance Act' aimed at facilitating the reuse of public sector data,[28] member governments were already probing the potential of big data analytics for policymaking. They invested in constructing infrastructures to share research data from the public sector.

For instance, in Germany, government departments have been interlinking data from administrative actions and employment markets, inviting external researchers to assess the effectiveness of federal job policy measures.[29] The Netherlands has seen its Bureau for Economic Policy Analysis offering academic researchers the opportunity to utilise microdata gathered from various government sources to amplify the societal benefits derived from government data.[30] Meanwhile, Greece has launched an open data platform, providing stakeholders with access to anonymised administrative datasets for research and evaluation,[31] further cementing the commitment of EU nations to harness big data for public sector innovation and effectiveness.

[24] OECD (n 1) 3.

[25] Singapore Government, 'Bringing Data into the Heart of Digital Government' (Singapore Civil Service College). Available at: https://knowledge.csc.gov.sg/ethos-issue-21/bring-data-in-the-heart-of-digital-government/.

[26] I Weber and others, 'Real-Time Mobility Analysis Through Google Maps' (Data for Policy 2020). Available at: https://zenodo.org/record/3965386#.X7fmai0RrRZ.

[27] US Government, 'Federal Data Strategy'. Available at: https://strategy.data.gov.

[28] European Commission, 'Proposal for a Regulation of the European Parliament and of the Council on European data governance (Data Governance Act)' (25 November 2020). Available at: https://ec.europa.eu/digital-single-market/en/news/proposal-regulation-european-data-governance-data-governance-act.

[29] D Mueller and J Moeller, 'Giving the International Scientific Community Access to German Labor Market Data: A Success Story' in N Crato and P Paruolo (eds), *Data-Driven Policy Impact Evaluation* (Springer 2018) 101.

[30] R Douven and others, 'Microdata and Policy Evaluation at CPB' in Crato and Paruolo (n 29).

[31] Greek Government, 'data.gov.gr'. Available at: www.data.gov.gr.

In spite of these initiatives, it is still the case that one of the main barriers in realising wider use of public-sector data relates to the lack of appropriate governance frameworks for facilitating and monitoring public–private collaborations in data sharing.[32] More specifically, one of the most salient challenges in that regard is the reconciliation of the 'public interest' and non-public/private interests under lawful grounds for data processing in data protection law and, more specifically, the GDPR. The next section elaborates on this tension.

III. The Lawfulness of Commercial Access: 'Public' and 'Private' Interests in the GDPR

The GDPR presents a complex stance on the governance of commercial access to public sector data for research and innovation purposes. It defines 'research' in broad terms, which readily includes research activities by private enterprises.[33] The European Data Protection Supervisor (EDPS), in their 'Preliminary Opinion on data protection and scientific research' has affirmed that the GDPR's definition of research extends to various research organisations, spanning academic, non-profit, governmental, and for-profit commercial sectors.[34]

However, there is a measure of ambiguity regarding the permissibility of using public sector data in research and innovation by commercial entities, even if when such endeavours aim to benefit the public interest. The following analysis seeks to delve deeper into this matter, examining the principles and conditions under which private actors might access and analyse public-sector data within the framework established by the GDPR.

To elaborate on this ambivalence, the first and the second data protection principles are central, ie lawful basis for data processing under Article 6(1) of the GDPR and purpose limitation under Article 6(3). On the question of lawful basis, considering the difficulties with obtaining consent from data subjects when using such large datasets as the ones held by the public sector,[35] the following two bases are relevant:

- *6(1)(e) Public interest* – processing is necessary for the performance of a task carried out in the public interest or in the exercise of official authority vested in the controller

[32] OECD (n 1) 2; High-Level Expert Group (n 3) 25.

[33] See specifically GDPR Recital 159: '... For the purposes of this Regulation, the processing of personal data for scientific research purposes should be interpreted in a broad manner including for example technological development and demonstration, fundamental research, applied research and privately funded research ...'.

[34] European Data Protection Supervisor, 'A preliminary opinion on data protection and scientific research'. Available at: https://edps.europa.eu/sites/edp/files/publication/20-01-06_opinion_research_en.pdf.

[35] Relying on consent in public sector research and innovation data sharing would be highly impractical considering the need to contact a massive number of individuals and is quite difficult to justify legally due to the imbalance of power between public authorities and individual citizens, see J Bell and others, 'Balancing Data Subjects' Rights and Public Interest Research' (2019) 5 *European Data Protection Law Review* 43.

- *6(1)(f) Legitimate interests* – processing is necessary for the purposes of the legitimate interests pursued by the controller or by a third party, except where such interests are overridden by the interests or fundamental rights and freedoms of the data subject which require protection of personal data, in particular where the data subject is a child

The current consensus in regulatory guidance is that 'public interest' should be called upon by governmental bodies, while 'legitimate interests' are more appropriate for private entities, including businesses. The Article 29 Working Party's Opinion 06/2014 primarily restricted 'public interest' justifications to scenarios involving public sector data sharing, such as instances where governmental agencies or mandated private organisations share data.[36] Post GDPR, this stance is reflected in the guidelines provided by Data Protection Authorities in the UK, Italy, and France.[37]

The interpretation suggests that public and private interests are at odds, implying that addressing one inherently neglects the other. The law appears not to accommodate a mutually beneficial scenario where public and private interests can simultaneously thrive, especially in the context of data processing for research and innovation. Consequently, this has led to a division between government entities, who can share data based on public interest, and private entities, which might not be permitted to use the same legal basis.

Choosing between 'public interest' and 'legitimate interests' as a legal basis for data processing carries considerable legal consequences. 'Public interest' offers data controllers more authority than 'legitimate interests'. For instance, Article 21(6) of the GDPR provides an exception for data processing necessary for tasks in the public interest, exempting it from the data subject's right to object.[38] Similarly, Article 9 of the GDPR gives more flexibility to domestic laws to authorise the processing of sensitive data if it serves the public interest, as opposed to serving a business's 'legitimate interests'.[39] Furthermore, each legal base introduces unique legal considerations that could lead to a patchwork of protections for data subjects' rights, potentially causing confusion. A key distinction is the 'balancing test' required by Article 6(1)(f),[40] which assesses whether 'legitimate interests' outweigh the rights and freedoms of the data subject. This test is not needed when 'public interest' under Article 6(1)(e) justifies data processing, where the mere

[36] Article 29 Working Party, 'Opinion 06/2014 on the "Notion of legitimate interests of the data controller" under Article 7 of Directive 95/46/EC' 21–23.

[37] Information Commissioner's Office, 'Legitimate Interests'; Garante, 'Coronavirus: No do-it-yourself (DIY) data collection, says the Italian DPA'. Available at: www.garanteprivacy.it/web/guest/home/docweb/-/docweb-display/docweb/9282117#1; CNIL, 'Coronavirus (COVID-19): Reminders from the CNIL on the collection of personal data by employers'. Available at: www.cnil.fr/fr/coronavirus-covid-19-les-rappels-de-la-cnil-sur-la-collecte-de-donnees-personnelles-par-les.

[38] GDPR art 21(6).

[39] See GDPR arts 9(2)(g) and (j): 'processing is necessary for reasons of substantial public interest …' and 'processing is necessary for archiving purposes in the public interest, scientific or historical research purposes or statistical purposes in accordance with Article 89(1) based on Union or Member State law which shall be proportionate to the aim pursued'.

[40] Information Commissioner's Office (n 37).

'necessity' of performing a public interest task is enough.[41] This significant difference can have practical implications, especially when considering the legal weight of 'rights' against 'interests'.[42] Therefore, relying on 'legitimate interests' for data processing in research might be inadequate for data handlers and not sufficiently clear for the individuals whose data is being processed.

The issue of divergent lawful bases in data handling might be addressed by clarifying the concept of data 'controllership' as defined in Articles 4(7) and 4(8) of the GDPR. A 'data controller' sets the purpose and means of processing personal data, while a 'data processor' acts on the controller's behalf.[43] This distinction is crucial both for determining the legal basis for processing and for ensuring purpose limitation. Public entities, as data controllers, may invoke 'public interest' to justify processing, and private entities might operate under this legal basis as processors if a robust data sharing agreement is in place. This arrangement is not uncommon in public–private partnerships for law enforcement where data processing aims to protect public and data subjects' vital interests.[44]

However, applying this framework to broader data sharing in research and innovation presents challenges. Research and innovation often involve exploratory work, making it difficult to specify processing scope in advance, as opposed to a business task with a defined outcome like DNA analysis.[45] Therefore, the delineation between 'controllers' and 'processors' becomes blurred in long-term public–private data sharing partnerships, as the nature of the collaboration often evolves over time.

The principle of purpose limitation, which is the second pillar of data protection, presents its own set of challenges within the context of public–private data sharing for research. In some instances, private entities can readily show that their data processing is in line with the initial collection purpose. Take, for example, the scenario where public hospitals in certain countries, lacking the necessary facilities to store a coronavirus vaccine, might pass on patient details to a private firm tasked with refrigeration. The firm would then use this data to arrange vaccination schedules and manage the distribution of vaccines. Here, the link between the public interest-driven task and the private entity's data processing is evident, with both activities aimed at safeguarding public health.[46]

[41] GDPR, art 6(1)(e): 'processing is necessary for the performance of a task carried out in the public interest or in the exercise of official authority vested in the controller'.

[42] G Webber, 'On the Loss of Rights' in G Huscroft and others (eds), *Proportionality and the Rule of Law Rights, Justification, Reasoning* (Cambridge University Press 2014) 123; S Tsakyrakis, 'Proportionality: An Assault on Human Rights?' (2009) 7(3) *International Journal of Constitutional Law* 468.

[43] GDPR, art 4(7).

[44] ibid.

[45] D Erdos, 'Systematically Handicapped? Social Research in the Data Protection Framework' (2011) 20 *Information & Communications Technology Law* 83: pre-determining the scope of processing would be hard to reconcile with the 'fluid and norm-challenging nature of a social science research endeavour' supported by big data analytics.

[46] Note that the private entity is only a data processor in this case, thus this example does not raise difficulties under the first data protection principle.

However, this clear alignment does not always translate neatly into other forms of public sector data sharing for research and innovation. For instance, if a judicial authority shares data on court judgments with a commercial entity for the purpose of identifying technological hurdles in creating natural language processing tools for predictive analytics,[47] the connection between the research activity and practical application becomes more tenuous. While the private entity's processing does theoretically serve the public good by enhancing the justice system's efficiency – for example, by encapsulating a seasoned lawyer's expertise into a technological tool accessible to more clients, fostering competition among legal professionals, and potentially easing the court system's case backlog – the direct effect of such research on the immediate functioning of justice delivery might not be as apparent, especially in the short term.[48]

The implications of this legal analysis for the sharing of public sector data for research and innovation point to 'public interest' being the most reliable and defensible legal ground for data processing. In the absence of a consensus that all parties involved can claim 'public interest', legal issues are apt to arise, potentially hindering smooth operation of public–private partnerships. Practically, this could lead to public entities with limited resources missing out on advanced data-driven insights. Conversely, it might also result in unregulated and potentially problematic public–private data sharing arrangements.

The following section suggests a resolution to these dilemmas: sever the tie between 'public interest' as a legal basis and the organisational identity of the entities involved. Instead, the 'public interest' should be defined in terms of the contribution of research/innovation data sharing to the broader societal or economic well-being. This approach reframes 'public interest' not as an intrinsic attribute of a particular type of organisation, but as a characteristic of the data sharing activity itself, gauged by its potential to benefit the collective welfare.

IV. Reconciling the Public with the Private? A Conceptualisation Based on 'Societal Welfare'

Scholars present several arguments to justify the different treatment of public and private interests. Firstly, a prevalent concept in European data protection and

[47] N Aletras and others, 'Predicting Judicial Decisions of the European Court of Human Rights: A Natural Language Processing Perspective' (2016) *PeerJ Computer Science* 2.

[48] Although note that the legitimate scope of litigation analytics is a controversial issue, with France recently banning the use of such technologies when they use 'identity data' of judges or jurors, see R Tromans, 'France Bans Judge Analytics, 5 Years in Prison for Rule Breakers' (2019). Available at: www.artificiallawyer.com/2019/06/04/france-bans-judge-analytics-5-years-in-prison-for-rule-breakers/.

human rights law is that when pitted against qualified individual rights such as privacy, public interests tend to be given more weight than corporate interests.[49] Secondly, the rise of 'surveillance capitalism'[50] and the consequent concerns over the vast amounts of data accumulated by private entities add to the caution exercised in this area. Thirdly, irrespective of data quantity, advocates for limiting access to government data to public-sector and academic researchers cite studies showing public discomfort with private companies using their data for research.[51] An illustrative case is the Facebook emotional contagion experiment, a collaboration between Cornell University and Facebook. It involved altering users' news feeds to gauge if exposure to negative content would affect their emotions.[52] The experiment led to a public outcry because users were not aware that their news feeds were being manipulated for the study.[53]

While vigilance in the management of public sector data sharing is warranted, and strong protective measures with active oversight from public entities are necessary, it is important not to discount the potential benefits of such collaborations by focusing too narrowly on the nature of the organisations involved. Prioritising organisational identity as the deciding factor in aligning with the 'public interest' may result in missed opportunities for beneficial use of data. Instances like the Cambridge Analytica scandal show that data misuse is not confined to private companies alone.[54]

Moreover, public trust in data sharing initiatives may not be solely dependent on whether a public or private entity is handling the data. Factors like transparency in data usage, clear communication of research benefits, and adequate data protection measures play a more pivotal role. The public wants to see clear, direct benefits from data used by commercial entities, expecting an explicit explanation of how data-driven research will improve public services or the functioning of public bodies.[55] This suggests that the perceived value and

[49] See eg Joined Cases C-293/12 and C-594/12, *Digital Rights Ireland Ltd v Minister for Communications, Marine and Natural Resources and Others and Kärntner Landesregierung and Others* (8 April 2014) paras 44 and 47 about the importance of the 'object pursued by the interference' being 'an objective of general interest'; in the European human rights law area, see *Eweida v United Kingdom* [2013] 57 EHRR 8 para 94: 'too much weight was given by the domestic court to BA's wish to project a certain corporate image and too little to the applicant's desire to manifest her religious belief'.

[50] S Zuboff, *The Age of Surveillance Capitalism* (Public Affairs 2019).

[51] IPSOS Mori, 'Commercial Access to Health Data' (2016). Available at: https://perma.cc/9TK2-JWEB.

[52] A Kramer and others, 'Experimental Evidence of Massive-scale Emotional Contagion through Social Networks' (2014) 111 *The Proceedings of the Natural Academy of Sciences* 8788.

[53] M Murray, 'Users Angered at Facebook Emotion-Manipulation Study'. Available at: www.today.com/tech/users-angered-facebook-emotion-manipulation-study-1D79863049.

[54] P Lewis and others, 'Cambridge Analytica academic's work upset university colleagues' *The Guardian* (2018). Available at: www.theguardian.com/education/2018/mar/24/cambridge-analytica-academics-work-upset-university-colleagues.

[55] E Waind, 'Trust, Security & Public Interest: Striking the Balance. A Review of Previous Literature on Public Attitudes Towards the Sharing, Linking and Use of Administrative Data for Research' (Data for Policy 2020). Available at: https://zenodo.org/record/3971006#.X76I2C0RrRZ 1 on the importance of the public perceiving 'benefits of some sort'.

safeguarding of data can be more influential than the identity of the organisation processing the data.[56]

For these reasons, the currently prevailing approaches to creating and implementing a satisfactory definition of the 'public interest' as a criterion for classifying the users of a public-sector data infrastructure are unduly narrow. One prevalent approach is to use the independent character of research, often associated with academic or civil society/NGO researchers,[57] as a proxy for research in the public interest. Many existing research data sharing initiatives distinguish between academic and commercial researchers,[58] either precluding access to the latter[59] or imposing much stricter requirements on them, eg requiring that their research project is commissioned by a government department[60] or that they demonstrate 'autonomy' and 'independence' in 'formulating scientific conclusions'.[61] A similar approach has been to classify parties requesting access based on their intended use of the data, ie their purpose behind accessing the infrastructure's resources and performing data analysis on them. As with organisational identity, 'commercial' and 'non-commercial' uses are used to delineate which data sharing requests aim to 'generate revenue' as opposed to 'supporting a public good'.[62] In both cases, the realities of multi-stakeholder data sharing for research and innovation may obfuscate a clear delineation of the public good from private interests. Consider the following scenario: A start-up, currently operating as a not-for-profit social enterprise, approaches a public body and proposes a research data sharing partnership. They are interested in developing data-driven insights to improve accessibility of the services offered by the public body to socially excluded citizens. Their mission is to alleviate power imbalances in society and strengthen social cohesion. In the long run, the start-up would consider the marketisation of their data-driven solutions, with governments, international organisations and non-government organisations amongst their potential clientele.[63]

[56] M Oswald, 'Share and Share Alike? An Examination of Trust, Anonymisation and Data Sharing with Particular Reference to an Exploratory Research Project Investigating Attitudes to Sharing Personal Data with the Public Sector' (2014) 11(3) *scripted.*

[57] Eg researchers affiliated with academic organisations or civil society organisations like Privacy International or Amnesty International.

[58] S Price, 'Academic and Commercial Research: Bridging the Gap' (2015) 12(2) *Participations* 168.

[59] Mueller and Moeller (n 29) refer to the example of the Federal Institute for Employment Research in Germany which relies on sections 75 of the German Social Code Book X and 282 of the German Social Code Book III as the legal basis for sharing data only for the purposes of 'independent scientific research'. Also see Research Data Centre of the German Federal Employment Agency, 'Data Access: Background Information'. Available at: https://fdz.iab.de/en/FDZ_Data_Access/background.aspx.

[60] HMRC, 'Research at HMRC'. Available at: https://gov.uk/government/organisations/hm-revenue-customs/about/research.

[61] This is required by Eurostat for access to their 'safe centre' in Luxembourg, see Eurostat, 'How to Apply for Microdata?'. Available at: https://ec.europa.eu/eurostat/documents/203647/771732/How_to_apply_for_microdata_access.pdf.

[62] Eg UK Data Service, 'Registration'. Available at: https://ukdataservice.ac.uk/get-data/how-to-access/registration/commercialusers.aspx.

[63] This scenario is inspired by reference to a similar scenario discussed by Aidinlis and others (n 9) 13.

If the 'public–private' divide were to persist, public bodies would be faced with a harsh dilemma in similar cases: turn down requests that can produce high-quality research in the public interest without overburdening the public purse or interpret the law more creatively, at the risk of severe reputational harm and legal liability in case of data misuse? The very fact of arriving at this dilemma is a problem in itself: with data providers being expected to exercise a certain amount of discretion in deciding access to public data, their decisions are quite likely to suffer from lack of consistency and transparency. To overcome this unsatisfactory situation and dissociate the 'public' interest from the organisational identity of data providers, the following classification is proposed to classify the research users of government data:

- *Public interest research* – when the research project exclusively serves political aims that pursue the collective or societal welfare.
- *Proprietary research* – when the research project exclusively serves private interests of a proprietary nature.
- *Hybrid research* – when the research project serves both the collective welfare and private interests of a proprietary nature.

This framework is founded on the broader objectives of societal or economic prosperity, such as improving the standard of living or other indicators of communal welfare.[64] Importantly, this framework shifts the focus from the nature of the organisation to the contribution that data usage makes to the public good, thereby facilitating the utilisation of public sector data through private sector engagement. This does not imply a blanket application across all public entities or data types, nor does it suggest unrestricted access to public sector data for all research and innovation purposes. Particularly, proprietary research utilising public sector data for private gain would not align with the current data protection regulations. Additionally, agencies responsible for national security or those managing highly sensitive data may need to adapt this framework to suit their specific requirements.

Nevertheless, adopting this conceptual model would facilitate 'hybrid' research data sharing arrangements, such as those between government and business entities, by necessitating that both public and private collaborators affirmatively demonstrate their contributions to the common good. This would mean that private entities with access to government data must prove their engagement in activities that, while possibly commercial in nature, support functions that are public or have traditionally been performed by the public sector by generating valuable analytical insights.[65] However, it's crucial to note that under this model, private entities would not be granted carte blanche to repurpose public-sector data for ongoing commercial activities if such use diverges from serving the public

[64] C Cooper, 'Quantitative Models of Well-Being to Inform Policy: Problems and Opportunities' (2020) 12 *Sustainability* 3180.

[65] E S Savas, *Privatization and Public–Private Partnerships* (Chatham House, New York 2000) 4.

interest. Their use of the data should be confined to the scope of the partnership's objectives. Yet, the model would allow them to leverage aggregate, non-personal insights gleaned from their analyses in their commercial strategies and offerings, provided these insights support their contribution to public-serving activities.

Introducing a requirement for private entities to demonstrate their contribution to the common good would represent progress, particularly in light of the lack of transparency that often characterises public–private data sharing partnerships in Europe and elsewhere. Governments in countries like Greece and the United Kingdom have faced scrutiny from NGOs and the media for not disclosing details of their data sharing arrangements with private entities.[66] Moving forward, it will be necessary for each public sector entity to develop best practices, principles, and guidelines to define and verify contributions to the common good.[67] This endeavour will undoubtedly be complex. The Business-to-Government (B2G) High-Level Expert Group of the European Commission has highlighted the ambiguity surrounding the notion of 'public interest', noting its undefined boundaries and the unresolved question of whether it encompasses the goal of enhancing public services.[68]

While using collective welfare as a measure for public interest does not completely clarify its definition, it does shift the focus from the specific objectives and interests of individual public organisations to a larger framework of societal benefit. This reorientation aligns with broader EU concepts such as 'services of general economic interest',[69] moving the conversation towards the wider political goals of societal advancement.

Adopting the proposed classification for research and innovation data sharing presents several key challenges for public sector bodies. First, public bodies would have to determine the threshold for what constitutes a sufficient contribution to collective or societal welfare by private entities accessing public sector data. This raises critical questions about the extent and nature of the contribution required. How to differentiate between substantial contributions to the common good and superficial, tokenistic efforts designed merely to gain access to valuable public sector data? Identifying the line between genuine public benefit and

[66] N Giannopoulos, 'The Greek Government-CISCO data sharing agreement: the lost Atlantis' (03 October 2020). Available at: www.news247.gr/koinonia/symvasi-cisco-dimosioy-apdpch-tin-zitise-kerameos-den-tin-edose-pote.9005665.html; Privacy International, 'Alexa, what is hidden behind your contract with the NHS?'. Available at: https://privacyinternational.org/node/3298; Naomi Klein, 'How big tech plans to profit from the pandemic', *The Guardian* (13 May 2020). Available at: www.theguardian.com/news/2020/may/13/naomi-klein-how-big-tech-plans-to-profit-from-coronavirus-pandemic.

[67] Eg the UK Office for National Statistics, 'ONS research and data access policy'. Available at: www.ons.gov.uk/aboutus/transparencyandgovernance/datastrategy/datapolicies/onsresearchanddataaccesspolicy.

[68] High-Level Expert Group (n 3) 16.

[69] Ibid citing Cases C-179/90 *Merci convenzionali porto di Genova* [1991] ECR I-5889, para 27; Case C-242/95 *GT-Link A/S* [1997] ECR I-4449, para 53; and Case C-266/96 *Corsica Ferries France SA* [1998] ECR I-3949, para 45: 'services that public authorities of the Member States at national, regional or local level classify as being of general interest and, therefore, subject to specific public-service obligations'.

private gain will be a complex task. Secondly, resource constraints may limit the ability of public bodies to effectively evaluate whether a data sharing partnership is more beneficial to private interests than to the public. The capacity to thoroughly assess the potential impact and benefits of such partnerships is crucial. Public entities need to have the necessary resources, expertise, and frameworks to make informed decisions about the value and appropriateness of data sharing proposals. Thirdly, public bodies must then determine what safeguards are necessary to ensure that data sharing aligns with public interest goals. This involves setting clear guidelines and criteria for private entities to follow, ensuring data security, maintaining privacy, and monitoring usage to confirm that the data is used in ways that contribute positively to societal welfare. Each of these challenges requires careful consideration and the development of robust frameworks and criteria to ensure that research and innovation data sharing serves the broader interests of society, rather than primarily benefiting private companies.

Even if this is a context-specific enquiry, public sector bodies could use the principle of 'public integrity',[70] developed by the OECD with regard to public–private partnerships. Under this principle, public bodies should consistently adhere to 'ethical values, principles and norms for upholding and *prioritising* the public interest over private interests in the public sector' (emphasis added).[71] Guided by this principle, public bodies shall seek to produce and require clear evidence of public benefits as the major and direct output of a relevant research and innovation data sharing partnership, with private benefits only coming as a by-product in the future and under the above-mentioned condition that such benefits rely on non-identifying insights produced via public–private data sharing. To use the previously mentioned example, if a private entity could produce analytical insights that help the public administration of justice reduce accessibility problems to the justice system in a significant and measurable manner, their potential right to marketise their services in the future using non-identifying parts of those data-driven insights would not be barred by the GDPR.

Secondly, for public sector bodies to avoid legal liabilities in research and innovation data sharing, they must rigorously respect the rights of data subjects. This encompasses not only the rights outlined in the General Data Protection Regulation (GDPR), such as the right to object to data processing,[72] but also the fundamental rights to privacy and data protection as guaranteed by the EU Charter of Fundamental Rights and the European Convention on Human Rights. Critical legal principles like proportionality and necessity should be integral to all stages of data sharing processes. This includes data linkage, cleaning, access, and any subsequent data retention or reuse by either party.[73] Public bodies are tasked with the

[70] OECD (n 1).

[71] ibid.

[72] GDPR, art 21(1): 'The data subject shall have the right to object, on grounds relating to his or her particular situation, at any time to processing of personal data concerning him or her which is based on point (e) or (f) of Article 6(1), including profiling based on those provisions.'

[73] Aidinlis and others (n 9) 3.

responsibility to transparently explain the rationale for processing specific datasets within a public--private partnership. This includes providing clear justification for why certain data needs to remain personal, as opposed to being anonymised, and ensuring that the scope of data processing is directly aligned with and necessary for the stated objectives of the data sharing agreement. Each of these steps is vital to uphold the legal rights of data subjects and maintain the integrity of the data sharing process.

Thirdly, it's essential for public bodies to not only consider general data protection principles but also to implement specific data security measures at the operational level. This ensures that public sector data sharing for research and innovation is lawful and adheres to the principles of proportionality and data protection by design. Although such data sharing may not be classified as 'academic' expression,[74] it often falls under 'scientific research' as defined in Article 89 of the GDPR. This article allows for certain research exemptions under domestic law that can make research feasible where it would otherwise be 'impossible or seriously impaired', such as limiting data subjects' rights to rectification (Article 16 GDPR) or to restrict processing (Article 18 GDPR).[75] Article 89(1) of the GDPR mandates 'appropriate safeguards', including technical and organisational measures, to uphold data minimisation.[76] This involves the use of pseudonymisation to reduce the risk of re-identification and safeguard data subjects' rights. For transparency and accountability, public bodies should articulate and publish their approach to such data protection measures. This encompasses both by-design strategies (like pseudonymisation) and by-default tactics (such as processing only essential datasets from the outset). Elaborating on specific methodologies, such as homomorphic encryption or hashing, goes beyond merely asserting a commitment to Article 89 safeguards. It provides a clear, principled stance on how data protection will be integrated into Government-to-Business (G2B) research data sharing initiatives, enhancing the transparency and accountability of these processes.

The experiences of public–private research partnerships using private data can offer valuable insights for public sector data sharing for research and innovation, particularly in the realm of data protection. Although detailed public information on G2B partnerships may be scarce, notable examples from the United States highlight best practice. For instance, Telenor, a major telecommunications company, has partnered with Harvard's Public Health department for research. This collaboration emphasised data minimisation techniques, including hashing, encryption and data aggregation. A key focus was determining the highest level of

[74] To benefit from exemptions that would rely on the 'academic' derogation under GDPR, art 85: '... including processing for journalistic purposes and the purposes of academic, artistic or literary expression'.

[75] M Mourby and others, 'Governance of Academic Research Data Under the GDPR – Lessons from the UK' (2019) 9(3) *International Data Privacy Law* 192, 200.

[76] GDPR, art 5(1)(c): 'Personal data should be ... adequate, relevant and limited to what is necessary in relation to the purposes for which they are processed.'

data aggregation that would minimise re-identification risks while still allowing the academic research objectives to be met.[77] This underscores the importance of effective communication between the legal teams and data scientists of both public bodies and private entities to ensure robust data protection measures. Another example is MasterCard, which provided data to research institutions and universities under stringent conditions.[78] Access to the data was facilitated through remote interfaces, allowing research to be conducted on university premises. The company's privacy and data protection counsel played a crucial role in evaluating re-identification risks prior to data sharing. They also ensured that researchers established a procedure for secure data destruction post-study and developed secure file transfer mechanisms to maintain data security. These cases highlight the importance of meticulous planning and the implementation of stringent data protection measures in public–private research collaborations. They serve as a benchmark for public bodies engaging in G2B research data sharing, illustrating the need for a comprehensive approach to data security, including risk assessment, data minimisation, and secure data handling protocols.

Fourthly, and very importantly, data sharing practice has shown that legal compliance alone is often not sufficient. To avoid jeopardising the operation of a public–private data sharing partnership, public bodies should prioritise public engagement strategies to build societal acceptability for the ethical use of government data within public–private partnerships.[79] The recent case of care.data in the UK is telling: the initiative purported to use primary health care medical records in England, in part for research purposes, unless patients explicitly opted out.[80] Despite being perfectly lawful, the initiative triggered a strong public backlash as health practitioners and patients had not been consulted, resulting in resistance and massive opt-outs. It was subsequently indefinitely suspended. Regardless of whether there is a legal requirement for data subjects' consent, the sustainability of public–private data sharing requires an understanding of what it is that social communities affected by the research or innovation 'perceive as the benefits of the work'.[81] Although there are some great examples of public engagement in the context of data-driven medical research,[82] there is still a lot of progress to be made when it comes to engaging the public.

The common denominator in all these challenges is the need for what has been defined by the OECD as a 'comprehensive model for data governance';[83] it has

[77] C Buckee and K Engø-Monsen, 'Mobile Phone Data for Public Health: Towards Data-sharing Solutions that Protect Individual Privacy and National Security' (2016) arXiv:1606.00864.

[78] J Shkabatur, 'The Global Commons of Data' (2019) 22 *Stanford Technology Law Review* 354, 406.

[79] P Carter and others, 'The Social Licence for Research: Why Care.data Ran into Trouble' (2015) 41 *Journal of Medical Ethics* 404–9. Available at: https://jme.bmj.com/content/41/5/404.

[80] P Vezyridis and S Timmons, 'Understanding the care.data Conundrum: New Information Flows for Economic Growth' (2017) 4(1) *Big Data & Society* 1, 7.

[81] Waind (n 55) 3.

[82] Understanding Patient Data, 'Putting People at the Centre of Decisions about Patient Data'. Available at: https://understandingpatientdata.org.uk/.

[83] OECD (n 1).

urged its member countries to develop a 'cross-government, coherent approach' to data governance that 'reflects the critical elements for achieving system-wide benefits in government'.[84] Governments will need to equip their public-sectors with bespoke and devoted governance structures that will be tasked with addressing both strategic and operational challenges of research and innovation data sharing. These challenges may range from delineating acceptable uses of data to monitoring whether data sharing agreements are complied with. As with the current status quo in trying to make better use of government data, the distance from principle to practice can be quite long, with organisational culture, leadership decisions and resource constraints creating complications. Nonetheless, overcoming barriers to public sector data sharing for research and innovation stemming from the GDPR is certainly a necessary, even if not a sufficient, condition of building a more effective, inclusive and accountable twenty-first century public sector through data analytics.

V. Conclusion

Should private companies access these rich public resources to advance research and innovation that can serve the common good? This chapter has examined key challenges surrounding commercial access to public sector data for research and innovation purposes and has highlighted organisational, economic, legal, and ethical hurdles that can impede data sharing initiatives between government and private sector entities. Public sector data offers invaluable insights about citizen needs and policy impacts. However, governments often lack expertise to fully harness this potential. Commercial partnerships can help plug capability gaps through advanced analytics, but tensions lurk between private profits and public welfare. Ambiguity clouds whether research serving both interests aligns with data protection law. The EU General Data Protection Regulation (GDPR), incorporated in the UK via the Data Protection Act (DPA) 2018, defines research broadly, encompassing commercial entities. However, its legal bases differentiate public and private sector rationales for data processing. This suggests conflicting motives, rather than win-win propositions. Conceptually and legally, notions of 'public' and 'private' appear bifurcated. But collaborative synergies may exist where business applications, while commercially oriented, strengthen public services or social welfare.

Beyond the governance reconsiderations proposed in this chapter, vital too are strategies prioritising public engagement and trust alongside legal compliance. The failure of care.data in the UK highlights sustainability issues when the public has not been consulted correctly. Regardless of lawful data sharing, public scepticism

[84] ibid.

can undermine initiatives. Ongoing societal dialogue regarding the ethical usage of government data in research and innovation is critical. In the following chapters, I further demonstrate the limits of the law in the data access for research and innovation regulatory space, highlighting the centrality of other institutions created by organisational actors in this space for governing data access for research and innovation purposes.

PART 3

Applications

6

Research Data Sharing in the UK Public Sector: Main Phases of Historical Development

> All those involved, from data holders to the general public, (now) have a clearer understanding of the needs of the research community and researchers can plan their research and be confident that access to administrative data will be granted.
>
> Elias, The UK ADRN: Its Genesis, Progress and Future

> The landscape of administrative data … is complex and changeable and is often difficult for researchers to navigate. Problems mainly relate to the length and complexity of the process – making for a challenging research environment.
>
> Iveson and Deary, Navigating the Landscape *of Non-Health Administrative Data in Scotland: A Researcher's Narrative*

The regulatory space lens is apt for understanding power struggles between the actors populating the UK data sharing space for research and innovation. In this chapter, I take stock of the historical development of UK government data sharing during the last four decades (1980–2020). I do so to analyse how processes of 'conflict' and 'bargain' between data managers, researchers (and, in fewer cases, innovators) and intermediary or high-level standard-setting bodies recalibrated this particular space, shifting the goalposts again and again when it comes to appropriate uses of government administrative data. More specifically, in this chapter, I sketch the way in which particular organisations have defined the scope of central issues during the development of this space over the last four decades.

My analysis draws on documentary data, such as legal and policy documents enacting data sharing frameworks, and data from 42 semi-structured interviews with individuals working for organisations with experience in data sharing for research and innovation. Actors in the UK research data sharing space, it is suggested, shaped the historical development of this activity over three, broadly constructed, phases: '*informality*', '*formalisation*' and '*fragmentation*'.

In the first phase, which spans from the 1980s until 2004, there were no formal procedures for requesting parties to be granted access to government data. The success of relevant efforts largely relied on ad hoc bargaining, through the personal relationships between such actors as requesting parties and data managers or government sponsorship of large research projects. In the second phase, from 2004 to 2018, actors on all sides of the playing field invoked strong narratives about widening access to administrative data for research and innovation purposes. These narratives, often voiced in a bold and demanding manner within a conflict between different organisations, triggered the creation of formal procedures and frameworks for allowing data sharing to accredited researchers.

Finally, in the third phase, which has been underway since 2018, it becomes apparent that requesters' struggles to demand a more formalised access to government data have not materialised in consistent and predictable frameworks across the UK. While some formal frameworks exist, it is often the case that many data managers and intermediary bodies do not publicise any or much detail about their data sharing procedures and supported types of projects, leaving researchers and innovators in the dark about their precise requirements or their interpretation of crucial aspects of existing frameworks. A picture of fragmentation emerges, with requesting parties often facing insurmountable barriers to their efforts to get access in a timely and satisfactory manner, contrary to assertions that they can 'plan their research and be confident that access to administrative data will be granted'.[1] Some requesters adopt a more adversarial approach to navigating this landscape, whereas others prefer to bargain with data managers, much like their counterparts in the early phases of UK research data sharing.

Two central narratives stand out and determine who is 'in' and who is 'out' of the data sharing space: '*efficiency*', ie the idea of facilitating data sharing with a view to create an evidence-basis for better policymaking, and '*accountability*', ie the idea of facilitating research data sharing with a view to stimulate critical engagement with the government's policies in the name of transparency and openness. While most actors in the space have paid lip service to the compatibility of the two narratives, the analysis demonstrates that 'accountability' has been gradually eclipsed by 'efficiency'. The role of particular data managers, mostly large ministerial departments like the Department for Work and Pensions (DWP) and the Department for Education (DfE), as well as intermediary bodies like the Administrative Data Research Network (ADRN), has been central in that process. This is not irrelevant to broader, systemic-level changes in the UK public sector over the last four decades. New public management rationales and neoliberal approaches to managing the civil service promote certain solutions prevalent in the UK research data sharing space, eg business-like resource management, contracting-out services like research, cutting down investments to 'do more with less',[2] over traditional

[1] P Elias, 'The UK Administrative Data Research Network: Its Genesis, Progress, and Future' (2018) 675(1) *The Annals of the American Academy of Political and Social Science* 184. This is not to say that there was no fragmentation before the third phase, but this notion is used to convey the patchy landscape after 2018, by contrast to literature claims like the presently cited one about well-structured and transparent routes to data access for researchers.

[2] E Ferlie and others, *The New Public Management in Action* (Oxford University Press 1996) 6; also see E Dove, *Regulatory Stewardship of Health Research: Navigating Participant Protection and Research Promotion* (Edward Elgar 2020) 70 on the 'neoliberal discourse stressing market rationality and economic optimisation' underpinning health research regulatory reform in the UK.

accountability, rule-of-law concerns. I first analyse how actors invoked the two narratives, 'efficiency' and 'accountability', to structure the three historical phases of UK research data sharing and triggered transitions from one to another, before elaborating on the main questions arising for the formation of data sharing institutions for research and innovation in the UK public sector.

I. Informality: Ad Hoc Bargaining to Access Data for Research

The origins of research data sharing in the UK were fraught with technical difficulties and data manager reluctance to take risks. Departments, by and large, commissioned research for their own purposes and, incrementally, started to engage in ad hoc arrangements with trusted external academic researchers for independent research projects.[3] As it will be shown, through adopting both bargaining and conflicting strategies, researchers instigated a transition from the informal governance of data access towards more formalised procedures and data sharing frameworks. It shall be noted that the role of innovators is particularly limited at this stage, as the use of public data for innovation was still considered very controversial.

A. Controlled Access for Researchers and Data Custodian Reluctance

In the 1960s, administrative records were collected for the first time on a massive scale in the UK and information about them was disseminated via official statistical gazettes. At that time, allowing access to these records for research purposes was not deemed legitimate.[4] In the late 1970s, however, the UK Government started to appreciate the 'research value inherent within their large and growing databases'.[5] Departments started producing research in the interests of informing policy delivery, commissioning professional researchers to work on research questions of interest to the department or having in-house statisticians analyse the datasets.[6] The 1980s brought a revolution in computerisation resulting in a more systematic and standardised approach to collecting administrative records and using them for research purposes. In the late 1980s and 1990s, departments started to use administrative data for research purposes on a routine basis.[7]

[3] This is to distinguish commissioned research from independent research, in the sense that commissioned research projects have pre-determined research questions and (often) methods, with the researcher having limited scope as to following a different course of action during the project.

[4] Elias (n 1) 185.

[5] ibid 186.

[6] P Jackson, 'From "Intruders" to "Partners"': The Evolution of the Relationship Between the Research Community and Sources of Official Administrative Data' in N Crato and P Paruolo (eds), *Data-Driven Policy Impact Evaluation* (Springer 2019) 17.

[7] Elias (n 1) 186.

While this time also saw the establishment of the first research data centre for health data in the UK by the Office for National Statistics (ONS) and the Economic and Social Research Council to stimulate the interest of external researchers in analysing government data,[8] similar developments in social-science research data took quite a bit longer to materialise. Access to government data for social research purposes was generally envisaged as *controlled* (or restricted), as opposed to *registered*.[9] In the case of *controlled* access, researchers who satisfy certain technical, legal, and ethical requirements apply for access on a *project-by-project* basis. Their applications, often accompanied by comprehensive research proposals, are reviewed by sector-specific committees or by the data custodians themselves.[10] *Registered* access, on the other hand, envisages the provision of access to users by reference to their *credentials* (eg researchers affiliated with recognised institutions or complying with specific accreditation requirements), rather than requiring a case-by-case decision on the merits of a specifically described research project.[11]

Public bodies have been reluctant to widen access to administrative records for research purposes. With administrative data effectively being treated as the property of public bodies, *controlled* access is the dominant model in the UK public sector for a number of reasons. Firstly, the risks related to the disclosure of identifiable data are deemed as one of the main reasons behind restricted access. Perceptions of such risks were exacerbated due to data breach incidents involving the loss of millions of personal complete data records, putting pressure on data managers to minimise the risk of such leaks in the future.[12] An interviewee who has worked for the DWP recalled the nervousness caused within the department after a massive data breach concerning child benefit data:

> It was always quite difficult to get hold of the benefit data. After the loss, everything came to an absolute standstill for a year and nobody could get access to it. Even by the time I left, you had to be next to God before you could get access to data.[13]

As another interviewee, who has worked for the DfE, explained, such disclosure concerns may be traditionally stronger in departments like the DWP or HM Revenue and Customs (HMRC). In their words, disclosing people's earnings and benefits is a 'tough thing for a government department to do'.[14] Data managers are likely to fight tooth and nail to prevent this from happening. Two interviewees

[8] F Ritchie, 'Secure Access to Confidential Microdata: Four Years of the Virtual Microdata Laboratory' (2008) 2 *Economic & Labour Market Review* 29.

[9] S O Dyke and others, 'Registered Access: Authorizing Data Access' (2018) *European Journal of Human Genetics* (published online) 1.

[10] E M Ramos and others, 'A Mechanism for Controlled Access to GWAS Data: Experience of the GAIN Data Access Committee' (2013) 92 *American Journal of Human Genetics* 479–88.

[11] S O Dyke and others, 'Registered Access: A "Triple-A" Approach' (2016) 24 *European Journal of Human Genetics* 1676–80.

[12] Administrative Data Taskforce, 'The UK Administrative Data Research Network: Improving Access for Research and Policy' (December 2010) 23.

[13] Interview with participant nr 30 (2020, virtual).

[14] Interview with participant nr 33 (2020, virtual).

currently working for the DWP corroborated this assertion. They attributed their department's cautious attitude towards disclosing data to researchers to their need to 'gain assurance that a lot of the things we've got confidence in internally have been applied externally',[15] making sure that requesters do not 'ask for a huge amount of detail'[16] that would exacerbate identifiability risks.

Secondly, government departments allegedly perceive external researchers as less responsible data processors as compared to their own statisticians,[17] preferring to monitor each and every disclosure for research purposes. An interviewee who has worked for the Administrative Data Service, an intermediary body seeking to facilitate wider access to administrative data for academic researchers, recalled that the DWP's 'established processes for receiving requests for data' had to be re-designed before it could facilitate academic requesters.[18] According to them, this necessitates a protracted bargaining process between the requesting party and the data custodian, with the latter insisting on tangible proof that the former are to be trusted as reliable data users. Researchers need to demonstrate not only their skills and competence as professionals, but also their patience and charm as individuals to move things forward.

Thirdly, investing into wider and systematic research access to government data would require significant investment from a logistical perspective.[19] The ONS, for example, has been finding the cost of providing remote access to their Virtual Microdata Laboratory (VML) for the academic community to be 'prohibitively expensive'.[20] Crucially, departments have struggled to see the economic benefit in widening access to their data if they are not the 'beneficiaries of the secondary analysis' since the benefit to the public interest of society as a whole generated by academic social research are 'diffuse … (and) difficult to quantify'.[21] An interviewee doing administrative data research in Scotland suggested that, in many cases, a reluctance to establish a consistent data sharing framework is caused by a high turnover of staff or the lack of resources to recruit a 'decent-size' team.[22] Other interviewees, working for the Economic and Social Research Council and the ONS, confirmed that a reluctance to widen access to administrative data is often related to departments being under-resourced.[23]

[15] Interview with participant nr 8 (2017, Sheffield).
[16] Interview with participant nr 7 (2017, Sheffield).
[17] Jackson (n 6): 'Social and economic research in academia, which had most to gain from using the personal digital information held by public authorities, did not progress in a coherent and deliberate way with reforms that mirrored the changes the official data community were undergoing.'
[18] Interview with participant nr 6 (2018, phone).
[19] T Desai, F Ritchie and R Welpton, 'Five Safes: Designing Data Access for Research' (UWE Economics Working Paper Series) (2016) 3.
[20] F Ritchie, 'UK Release Practices for Official Microdata' (2010) 26(3) *Statistical Journal of the IAOS* 103.
[21] F Ritchie and R Welpton, 'Addressing the Human Factor in Data Access: Incentive Compatibility, Legitimacy and Cost-effectiveness in Public Data Resources' (UWE Economics Working Paper Series) (2014) 4.
[22] Interview with participant nr 29 (2020, phone).
[23] Interviews with participant nr 19 (2018, Swindon) and 28 (2020, London).

Fourthly, and finally, reluctance is often a by-product of organisational inertia, in cases where a type of technology, such as remote data access or data linkage, has not been widespread enough for decision-makers to be familiar and comfortable with it. An interviewee who has worked for the ONS when its VML data infrastructure was established vividly recounted how they convinced the decision-making board to endorse their proposals to establish a novel data-sharing procedure by mentioning another existing application of a similar framework:

> When I first went to the ONS board … presenting the idea for the VML … we were, just, not going anywhere. The board was sitting around and I could see they are unhappy about this stuff and they are not going to sign up for this. And then, someone asks and says, you know, is this the first time this technology has been employed? And I said, no, Denmark's already got this system. And they seemed very happy with it! And that was it. Everyone said, alright, that's ok then. We don't care as long as we are not the first, we don't want to take the risk.[24]

Such delicate bargaining was of the utmost importance to allay custodian worries. With these considerations in mind, it is hardly surprising that public bodies fought hard to confine the first administrative data research projects in the UK public sector within their organisational boundaries.

B. The First Administrative Data Research Projects: Doing Research In-House or Commissioning Academic Researchers

As public bodies started to digitalise government services by collecting and curating new and very large datasets with 'direct relevance to policy issues',[25] both central and local government across the country, explored the potential of administrative data research to inform policymaking. In the late 1980s and the 1990s, government departments started investing in administrative data research either by setting up teams with computer science and statistical expertise to conduct research in-house, or by 'contracting out' research to academic researchers with relevant experience.[26]

Certain public bodies like the Department for the Economy (DfE), the DWP and the ONS were the pioneers in promoting research data sharing initiatives. Two interviewees who have worked for the DfE offer some background on the emergence of research data sharing within their department. According to their recollections, most of the social research was initially happening within the

[24] Interview with participant nr 42 (2020, virtual).

[25] G Smith and others, 'The Value of Linked Administrative Records for Longitudinal Analysis' (ESRC National Longitudinal Strategy Committee) (2004) 5.

[26] Elias (n 1) 186. Non-academic researchers, such as private sector consultants were also contracted out during this period, but this is outside of the scope of this thesis as explained *supra* chapter 2 p 30.

department. The 1990s, however, saw a 'big push to contract out as much as possible' in the public sector, with social research being close to the top of the list of the things that would be contracted out.[27] Beyond political drives to reduce permanently employed public sector staff in the context of austerity and new public management,[28] there were other reasons for contracting out administrative data research. In some cases, such research may involve complex and sophisticated statistical methods, which the department 'wouldn't have the capacity to do'.[29] In other cases, the department would find it more palatable to present particular research findings as carried out by someone 'neutral and independent' rather than by its own statisticians.[30]

When contracting-out a research project, a government department would define the question that would be answered, the variables the researcher would use and the 'hypothesis that they would support'.[31] As an interviewee, who has undertaken commissioned research for the DfE recalled, apart from agreeing on the research objectives, there would be little in terms of data sharing processes at the time:

> If we go back right at the start, there were not really any processes. You just said I want to use the data for this purpose, and it would be sent to you via a CD. Thinking about that now, that's mad, really! But that's how it was. Over time, processes have become more formalised and there are more hurdles to jump over.[32]

As this description suggests, at this stage and at least in some examples of data sharing, it might even have been the case that researchers were able to negotiate the scope of their aspired data use without ruffling too many feathers within public bodies. While departments like the DfE may have occasionally commissioned external researchers to perform analysis on their datasets, the most active department in maximising the use of its administrative data for research purposes in England is certainly the DWP. As an interviewee who has worked for the Administrative Data Service (ADS) explained, the DWP has collaborated with academic researchers 'very closely within specific policy issues'.[33] Beyond contracting academics for the purposes of conducting government research, however, the Department has also invested significantly in building multi-disciplinary teams of data analysts who collaborate with policy officials in the interest of supporting the latter with an evidence-basis for and evaluation of the department's policies.[34]

[27] Interview with participant nr 30 (2020, virtual).

[28] See K McLaughlin and others (eds), *New Public Management: Current Trends and Future Prospects* (Routledge 2005).

[29] Interview with participant nr 33 (2020, virtual).

[30] Interview with participant nr 30 (2020, virtual).

[31] Interview with participant nr 10 (2018, Belfast).

[32] Interview with participant nr 40 (2020, virtual).

[33] Interview with participant nr 5 (2017, Essex).

[34] Department for Work and Pensions, 'Research at DWP'. Available at: www.gov.uk/government/organisations/department-for-work-pensions/about/research.

Major administrative data research projects have been conducted by the DWP. The Work and Pensions Longitudinal Study is an 'unmatched' longitudinal data infrastructure, with complete coverage of unemployment benefit claimants,[35] that has been used for a variety of policy purposes eg counter-fraud or evaluating the success of Jobcentre plus.[36] Through using insights generated from this study, the DWP has been seeking to maximise its 'operational effectiveness' and support its agenda in key policy areas such as child poverty, welfare-to-work and retirement planning by targeting resources to the appropriate people.[37] The 'new deal for lone parent evaluation' is another example of a major research project, within which the DWP contracted experts from the National Centre for Social Research to analyse patterns of participation in the new deal for lone parents and assess the impact of the policy on the socio-economic status of claimants.[38]

The ONS has also been a pioneer in conducting administrative data research. In the late 1990s, it invested resources into developing a linked dataset including data from annual business surveys and data from the manufacturing sector to address research questions, eg about productivity or growth about the characteristics of the UK market.[39] Similarly to the DWP, the ONS hired and supervised within its premises in London academic or research institute experts with a two-fold aim: first, create and curate linked business datasets and, second, produce research outputs that will be published by the Office.[40] These pioneer attempts to use administrative data research for policy-making encouraged other departments in the UK to follow suit. The Ministry of Justice and HMRC collaborated with the DWP to carry out research on employment and benefit outcomes for ex-offenders,[41] whereas the Scottish and Welsh governments invested into developing innovative data linkage studies.[42] Such initiatives as the 'Fuel Poverty' in Wales aimed to link health and social care data (eg hospital admission records) with non-health data resources such as housing support data to assess the impact

[35] P Jones and P Elias, 'Administrative Data as a Research Resource: A Selected Audit' (Report to the ESRC) (2006) 17.

[36] Department for Work and Pensions, 'Work and Pensions Longitudinal Study'. Available at: www.gov.uk/government/statistics/work-and-pensions-longitudinal-study.

[37] Scottish Government, 'Linking Social Care, Housing & Health Data' (2010). Available at: www.gov.scot/binaries/content/documents/govscot/publications/statistics/2019/01/health-community-care-data-linkage/documents/linking-social-care-housing-and-health-data-social-care-clients-and-patients-views/linking-social-care-housing-and-health-data-social-care-clients-and-patients-views/govscot%3Adocument/Linking%2BSocial%2BCare%252C%2BHousing%2Band%2BHealth%2BData%2BSocial%2BCare%2BClients%2527%2Band%2BPatients%2527%2BViews.pdf.

[38] Smith and others (n 26) 16.

[39] F Ritchie, 'Business Data Linking – Recent UK experience' (2004) 33(1–2) *Austrian Journal of Statistics* 89.

[40] ibid 91–92.

[41] Administrative Data Taskforce (n 13) 3.

[42] Scottish Government, 'Data linkage for research in Scotland'. Available at: www.gov.scot/publications/data-linkage-for-research-in-scotland/pages/scottish-government-funded-linkage-projects/; Welsh Government, 'Fuel poverty data linking project: the impact on health of the Welsh Government Warm Homes Schemes'. Available at: https://gov.wales/fuel-poverty-data-linking-project-impact-health-welsh-government-warm-homes.

of the Welsh 'Warm Homes Nest' scheme on health outcomes.[43] In a similar vein, an interviewee working for the Department for the Economy in Northern Ireland confirmed that their department would regularly 'commission research, primarily to be done by economists' on their administrative datasets.[44] What, then, was the impact of these pioneering efforts for the broader regulation of research data sharing in the UK?

As external users started producing valuable and tangible insights for policy-making, data managers understood that had they been able to consistently engage experts from the academic sector to analyse their datasets, the likelihood of their investments paying off would be significantly bigger. To facilitate this, beyond commissioning research in the strict sense to address particular policy questions, departments started supporting 'infrastructure initiatives' that were deemed to be significant enough in terms of policy impact to warrant central government support.[45] Such initiatives were initially introduced in the health data context both in England and the devolved countries, eg the (English) Millennium Cohort Study,[46] the Scottish Longitudinal Study,[47] the Northern Ireland Longitudinal Study[48] and the SAIL Databank in Wales.[49]

The DWP was one of the first departments to proceed with more stable, infrastructural research data sharing initiatives involving external researchers. Within the 'New Deal for the Long Term Unemployed' project, Policy Studies Institute researchers enjoyed full access to DWP records and were allowed to link such records with those from a survey conducted by the British Market Research Bureau International.[50] HMRC, HM Treasury and the DfE facilitated similar initiatives such as the CASE/National Centre Micro-Panel Data Study and the Effective Provision of Pre-School Education study.[51] Does this mean that researchers started seeing in front of them a well-trodden and transparent path towards accessing administrative data?

Not necessarily. The significance of these projects, notwithstanding access to government data for social researchers, was still exceptional and largely driven by

[43] ibid Welsh Government.

[44] Interview with participant nr 16 (2018, phone).

[45] Smith and others (n 26) 5.

[46] ibid 13: 'a major piece of ongoing research examining the health, family, and socio-economic context of children born in the UK in 2000–2001'.

[47] Scottish Longitudinal Study Development & Support Unit, 'Introduction to the Scottish Longitudinal Study'. Available at: https://sls.lscs.ac.uk/about/.

[48] D O'Reilly and others, 'Administrative Data Research Northern Ireland (ADR NI)' (2020) 4(2) *International Journal of Data Population Science* 1148: 'NILS is an ongoing large-scale, representative data-linkage study created by linking data from the Health Card Registration system to the decennial Census returns starting at 1981 and to administrative data for example vital events such as births, deaths and marriages.'

[49] N Richards, 'Introducing the Administrative Data Research Centre Wales (ADRC-W)' (Blogs Wales Institute of Social & Economic Research, Data & Methods): 'themes such as education, health and social mobility data as well as many other long-standing records from different government departments'.

[50] Smith and others (n 26) 16.

[51] ibid 14.

the policy priorities of a data manager and their subsequent appetite to commission or support research that would respond to government-designed research questions. An interviewee working for the Economic and Social Research Council, recalling their earlier experience within an administrative data research project, stressed that data sharing procedures were simplified due to the strong political buy-in from the Treasury that the project enjoyed, as well as the 'good personal relationships with the departments that would help unlock things'.[52] Two analysts working for the Welsh Government concurred that, at this historical time, data managers largely relied on informal relationships and the circumstance of knowing someone within a particular government department, often due to the shared subject matter of interest between academics and policy-makers:

> Wales being a small country … people know their academics. There are teams within Knowledge and Analytical Services who are topic-specific as you might say. They get to know the academics within their field quite well and some would do commissioned work or analysis of linked data sets.[53]

Even though most commissioned research projects would be publicly open for competition under procurement rules, existing relationships between departments and academics shaped the scope of the offered research and, thus, the advantage of specific academics to earn the tender. As an interviewee who has worked for the DfE recalls, such relationships with particular academics would even result, exceptionally, in projects, particularly lower-cost ones, to be informally entrusted to them rather than being available for tender offers.[54] In these circumstances, most academic researchers were often 'put into a class of undesirables … labelled as "intruders" …',[55] with access to data being described as 'unreliable, haphazard and unregulated' from a research perspective.[56]

The fact that public bodies operated by reference to informal relationships unravels the complex processes of bargain and conflict within this phase. The gradual broadening of the space to make external use of government data for research purposes more stable presupposed that requesting researchers would need to negotiate the terms that managers wanted to impose. With specific datasets coming at a premium, as they are uniquely held by specific departments, it is certain that such bargaining happened in parallel with conflict and competition between multiple researcher groups which were interested in the same dataset or datasets. Inevitably, some researchers came out stronger from such conflicts, with the majority of academic social scientists being, at this time, not fully aware of the potential of government datasets, thus, remaining 'at the margins of these developments'.[57] Academics who were interested in conducting their own *independent* research

[52] Interview with participant nr 19 (2018, Swindon).
[53] Interview with participants nrs 25 and 26 (2019, Cardiff).
[54] Interview with participant nr 33 (2020, virtual).
[55] Jackson (n 6) 17.
[56] Elias (n 1) 184.
[57] Smith and others (n 26) 5.

on government datasets would have to 'jump through many hoops' to be granted access, with government departments often relying on legal arguments to reject disclosure.[58] How was, then, independent social-science research on administrative datasets at all made possible?

II. The Origins of 'Independent Research': Demanding Independence, Settling for Informality

Being allowed to analyse government datasets not necessarily to respond to specific policy questions, but to pursue their independent research questions and interests has been one of the consistent claims of researchers within this space. Far from an overnight development, however, the realisation of access to government data for independent social-science research was incremental and context specific. In the absence of a centralised statistical authority within the UK that would provide a more 'regulated' approach,[59] each department had to develop its own data sharing policy in response to requests for various purposes, including research. In the late 1990s, the previously mentioned government initiatives started to yield published outcomes and this stimulated academic interest in using administrative data for social-science research.[60]

The number of requests gradually increased as the research potential of administrative data became clearer to researchers. An interviewee who has worked for the DfE conceded that they were 'quite surprised by the scale of requests' coming from academics, compared to what they were used to seeing at their previous position at the DWP.[61] Compared to previously used data sources like official statistics collated and published by statistical agencies,[62] administrative datasets provided a more comprehensive option for understanding social and economic patterns.

Researchers' interest prompted high-level standard-setters and data custodians to provide more clarity on the possibilities of research data sharing in the UK. With the central government commissioning as part of the UK National Data Strategy a report on the available public-sector data assets for potential research use,[63] specific public bodies like the ONS, excited about the potential benefits for policy-making, started encouraging academics to work on their datasets.[64] An interviewee who has worked for the ONS provided some clarity of its efforts to formalise access to its datasets for independent, external researchers. As they explained, the ONS had already been facilitating access for interested researchers

[58] Ritchie (n 21) 104.
[59] Elias (n 1) 186.
[60] Eg J Ball and M Marland, 'Male Earnings Mobility in the Lifetime Labour Market Database' (1996) (Analytical Services Division, Department of Social Security Working Paper Series).
[61] Interview with participant nr 30 (2020, virtual).
[62] Jackson (n 6) 18.
[63] Elias (n 1) 186.
[64] Ritchie (n 21) 30.

since the 1990s, using a legally controversial method, through which external researchers were nominally appointed to allow them to conduct research on its administrative data. They eloquently recalled how things moved from this state of affairs to formalising data access in the early 2000s:

> When I joined ONS, the person who employed me, the then Chief Economist at ONS … said, we've got this data which is a bit more sensitive, it's all business data, we got a couple of people coming in from different organisations and they physically use our computers or we let them sit on our own computers. It's not a very sustainable model, and we are also not sure about the legal basis for this. Essentially, can you turn this around to something … more than an ad-hoc arrangement?[65]

The same interviewee suggested that a lot of other departments were using similar mechanisms to provide data access to external researchers 'within the spirit of working for the public good'.[66] Increasing academic and policy interest, however, does not necessarily mean that data access for research would be automatically streamlined across the UK public sector. In most cases, procedures for research data sharing did not exist and academic requests often stumbled upon legal concerns about the status of administrative data and technical difficulties with regard to preparing such data for research use.[67]

Bargaining between government departments and academics, within the already existing contractual relationships between them, was crucial in overcoming these barriers. Some research groups managed to gain consistent access to specific datasets for the purposes of producing their own independent research.[68] As part of the agreement, researchers would, in turn, commit to disseminate the results of their work to improve knowledge of the general public, as well as feed back to the government analysts with a view to strengthening the existing evidence-basis for evaluating government policy.

This idea of 'partnership' between the academic research community and the government was embraced by key data managers in England.[69] The DWP granted academics access to some of its datasets to study issues relating to labour market transitions and earnings,[70] particularly when requests for projects corresponded to its key areas of research interest. Significant administrative data research projects were conducted in this period. Elias, an established administrative data researcher, led a couple of these projects: he used Higher Education Statistics Agency data to create a longitudinal sample of graduate students to track their entry into the labour market, as well as the DWP's JUVOS database to assess the impact of the Employment Zones programme on unemployed individuals.[71] Hales, another

[65] Interview with participant nr 42 (2020, virtual).
[66] ibid.
[67] Ritchie (n 21) 29.
[68] Smith and others (n 26) 5.
[69] Jackson (n 6) 25.
[70] Jones and Elias (n 36) 21.
[71] Smith and others (n 26) 19.

leading researcher, and his team contributed to the evaluation of the Employment Zones programme by using another DWP dataset, JSA, to identify potentially eligible participants who had failed to make use of the programme to get out of unemployment.[72] DWP data was also used by other academics for projects focused on analysing individual level claimant dynamics in the context of housing benefits.[73] Beyond the DWP, not many partnerships between academics and government departments are recorded from this period, although the DfE is also reported to have facilitated access to its National Pupil Database for researchers to work on pupil microdata.[74]

The language of 'partnership', also popular within public management drives for public–private partnerships in general,[75] naturally, obfuscates power imbalances in public bodies-researchers' relationships. In the previously mentioned cases, there was no established and publicly documented process or 'access route' for interested academic researchers.[76] Very much like commissioned research, academics who worked in a particular research area would be better positioned to make contact with data managers in quite an '*ad personam* way, rather than a necessarily open or transparent way'.[77] As a result, the availability of certain datasets was communicated to a 'limited circle of researchers' who 'knew the correct people to speak to' within the relevant departments.[78] Processes of conflict and bargaining, between researchers and managers and between researchers and other researchers, shine through their absence when these 'partnerships' are seen from a distance.

Coming closer to the intricacies of such partnerships, however, one sees a very different picture. An interviewee who has worked for the DfE conceded that data disclosures at this time 'wouldn't be to some random individual – it would only be with someone we've worked with before'.[79] Administrative data researchers working in Scotland corroborated this picture, reflecting on how their personal relationships with individuals working for the data managers enabled them to get access:

> I mentioned the informal there and I think that actually was crucial in moving forward the work … through individuals within National Records of Scotland, we were really able to start moving forward, thinking how we would enable the data to be made available for linkage and later for analysis.[80]

[72] J Hales and others, 'Evaluation of Employment Zones: Report on a Cohort Study of Long-Term Unemployed people in the Zones and a Matched Set of Comparison Areas' (2003) (National Centre for Social Research).

[73] M White, 'Macro Evaluation of the New Deal for Young People' (2000) (PSI briefing note).

[74] Jones and Elias (n 36) 4.

[75] McLaughlin and others (n 29).

[76] A Sexton and others, 'A Balance of Trust in the Use of Government Administrative Data' (2017) 17(4) *Archival Science* 305.

[77] Interview with participant nr 20 (2018, phone).

[78] Sexton and others (n 77) 313.

[79] Interview with participant nr 33 (2020, virtual).

[80] Interview with participant nr 34 (2020, virtual).

> My PI had actually negotiated access beforehand. I think it was an easier task for him, because he was part of the research team that conducted the PSE survey (for the DWP).[81]

> Because of the funding, I already got to know them from the very first day of my PhD. They had the best available data. Not brilliant, but the best available for national linkage. ... Other people had to change their PhD basically. I suppose because of the funding and the will to share this data, this was more feasible.[82]

As a result, access to government data for social-science research in the late 1990s and early 2000s was far from transparent, predictable and equally feasible for less well-connected academics, and more of a 'patchy landscape' with researchers being unable to predict whether and when they would be granted access.[83] Nonetheless, studies like those mentioned in this section, which were made possible on the basis of informal and ad hoc arrangements, yielded significant policy benefits, elucidating the socio-economic impact of particular policies on target populations and throwing light on questions which were previously obscured by high non-response rates to government surveys.[84] This fuelled the appetite of high-level standard-setters such as the central government to explore how academic data access for social-science research could be consistently widened and formalised.

III. Widening Research Data Access: The View from the High Level

In 2002, the Cabinet Office published a set of recommendations about making use of government data more 'widespread and coordinated'.[85] These recommendations reflected an increasingly held appreciation that administrative data are a 'largely untapped source of information for research and policy evaluation in the UK', the potential of which can only be fully realised if departments become more transparent about their data sharing policies.[86] In the light of statistical research methodologies also becoming more sophisticated in the early 2000s, central government encouraged public-sector data managers to consider facilitating 'general research not directed by the department' in a more streamlined and systematic way.[87] An interviewee who has worked for HMRC provided some background on their department's motivation to set a 'uniform data sharing strategy':

> So there were two reasons driving towards the data sharing strategy – one was ... a recognised risk that HMRC wasn't making the best use of the business intelligence

[81] Interview with participant nr 38 (2020, virtual).
[82] Interview with participant nr 37 (2020, virtual).
[83] Interview with participant nr 21 (2019, Swansea).
[84] Smith and others (n 26) 13.
[85] Jones and Elias (n 36) 69.
[86] Administrative Data Taskforce (n 13) ii.
[87] F Ritchie and R Welpton, 'Sharing Risks, Sharing Benefits: Data as a Public Good' (Conference Paper) (2011 Eurostat) 4.

> it had – that translates as it was not exploiting data as best or as effectively as it could do. … And then there is a stated objective from the HMRC strategy that HMRC will use its assets across government for public benefit or benefit of other departments.[88]

This was, certainly, not only in the minds of HMRC officials. The central government was generally keen on seeing more policy-relevant social-science research on government data in areas such as evaluating the long-term impact of drugs or health policies, school performance, the connection between re-offending and unemployment or between tax cuts and social benefit provision.[89] The research data sharing arrangements of the time, ie informal and ad hoc procedures governing access based on pre-existing relationships between a small number of academics and public officials, were hardly satisfactory in that regard. Access to government data for social-science research purposes had to become more predictable, organised and reliable, in the interest of attracting the interest of expert researchers who can, at a low cost for the government, contribute to the production of a robust evidence-basis for UK policymaking. This was also in line with a shift to more technocratic methods of managing the civil service to boost efficiency, prevalent within the new public management approach.[90] What were, however, the major factors driving the production of such an evidence basis by the actors within the research data sharing space?

IV. Formalisation: Creating Formal Frameworks to Streamline Research Data Sharing in the UK

The process of formalising access to administrative data for social-science research purposes was motivated by two major narratives, co-constructed and employed by not only central government and data custodians, but also academic researchers and funding bodies or research consortia. I elaborate on these two narratives, 'efficiency' and 'accountability', before presenting the first examples of formalised research data sharing frameworks in the UK public sector.[91] Then, I discuss the major effort to expand formalisation across the public sector furthered by the ADRN investment, as well as the resulting crystallisation of specific stages of research data access. The final section will interrogate whether this crystallisation corresponds to the adoption of transparent and predictable data sharing frameworks by data custodians across the UK public-sector *in practice*.

[88] Interview with participant nr 32 (2020, Oxford).
[89] Administrative Data Taskforce (n 13) 1.
[90] McLaughlin and others (n 29).
[91] It will be noted that, from an innovator's perspective, 'efficiency' is a more likely aim compared to 'accountability'.

A. 'Independent' Research Data Access, 'Efficiency' and 'Accountability'

While improving collective knowledge about social and economic behaviour can be seen as an end in itself, coordinating individual and organisational behaviour to streamline data access for social-science research purposes required a commitment to some greater underlying aim. Why should government departments be carrying out this function at the risk of incurring logistical and reputational costs?[92] Two major narratives emerged to promote the production of better knowledge through streamlining research data access thus, facilitating more administrative data research in this space: achieving higher levels of government 'efficiency' and strengthening government 'accountability' to its citizens and organised political stakeholders. Although both relate to the operation of government, these narratives have been strategically employed, as it will be shown, by various actors populating the research data sharing space, eg researchers, funding bodies and data custodians.

The idea of 'efficiency' hints at both strictly construed financial gains in delivering public services and the broader aim of policy improvement. In the advent of long-term austerity measures and constant grappling to find adequate resources for public service, many departments aimed to harness the potential of administrative data research to inform resource allocation.[93] The potential of administrative data research to yield financial gains was not only adopted by departments with the remit to produce statistical research in the first place,[94] but more generally by departments keen to maximise 'the returns on the resources they invest in data collection by exploiting administrative data to the full'.[95]

Crucially, such departments saw the formalisation of research data access as a necessary step to stabilise requester expectations and thus guarantee consistent analytical interest in their data in the long term. These departments did not see data sharing as an one-off activity, but invested into the 're-use' of their data by external researchers.[96] An interviewee who has worked for HMRC highlighted better debt management and the reduction of debt as the key incentives behind the establishment of data sharing procedures in their department.[97] Another interviewee working for the ONS clarified that one of the primary purposes behind sharing data to external researchers was the aim of 'measuring the effects of policies and ensure that … government … spends money in a more effective way'.[98]

[92] Ritchie (n 21) 105.
[93] Scottish Government (n 43).
[94] Ritchie and Welpton (n 22) 4.
[95] R Welpton and M Wright, 'HMRC Datalab: Engaging with the External Research Community' (2011) (ESRC) 1.
[96] Administrative Data Taskforce (n 13) ii.
[97] Interview with participant nr 32 (2020, Oxford).
[98] Interview with participant nr 2 (2017, Titchfield).

The fact that academics are willing to conduct such research 'for free' made this type of data sharing even more appealing.[99]

Beyond financial or 'monetary' gains,[100] departments aspired to become more 'efficient' in tackling complex policy issues, the root causes of which had hitherto not been well-researched. Both in respect of challenging or triangulating existing knowledge, research and statistics produced by the government,[101] increased access to administrative data promised to enable decision-makers to gain novel insight into multi-layered policy questions by linking large-scale administrative datasets belonging to various public bodies.[102] For example, the Welsh Government has sought to explore the relationship between social care, health and housing support within their 'Fuel Poverty' project.[103] More 'efficient' and accurate interventions on behalf of the government can, the narrative goes, stimulate economic growth and improve the health and well-being of the British people.[104] Within the 'Fuel Poverty' data linkage project, the Welsh Government measured the extent to which a fuel benefit policy actually led into an improvement of the health of vulnerable Welsh citizens.[105] One of this study's interviewees, who worked in this project, stressed that making clear the 'big evidence gap' that existed and the 'health impact' that their project would have was crucial to establish and implement a process for data sharing.[106] With evidence-based policymaking increasingly regarded as an 'essential part of good governance',[107] commentators have gone as far as suggesting that policy improvement is a prerequisite for the legality of granting researchers access to administrative data.[108]

However, the notion of 'accountability' draws on ideals of transparency and openness in governmental decision-making, with a view to consolidating public trust in the executive.[109] The UK Government has repeatedly committed over the

[99] Interview with participant nr 30 (2020, virtual).

[100] Interview with participant nr 21 (2019, Swansea).

[101] C Allsopp, 'Review of Statistics for Economic Policymaking: Final Report to the Chancellor of the Exchequer, the Governor of the Bank of England and the National Statistician' (2003) 40.

[102] Jones and Elias (n 36) 76.

[103] Scottish Government, 'Linking social care, housing support & health data for statistics: Project Plan and Privacy Impact Assessment (PIA)'. Available at: www.gov.scot/binaries/content/documents/govscot/publications/statistics/2019/01/health-community-care-data-linkage/documents/linking-social-care-housing-support--health-data---privacy-impact-assessment/linking-social-care-housing-support--health-data---privacy-impact-assessment/govscot%3Adocument/Linking%2Bsocial%2Bcare%252C%2Bhousing%2Bsupport%2B%2526%2Bhealth%2Bdata%2B-%2BPrivacy%2BImpact%2BAssessment.pdf.

[104] Administrative Data Taskforce (n 13) 2.

[105] Welsh Government (n 43).

[106] Interview with participant nr 25 (2019, Cardiff).

[107] HM Government, 'Open Data White Paper: Unleashing the Potential' (June 2012) 41: 'It is increasingly clear that evidence-based research and policy are fundamental to understanding and responding effectively to the challenge of assuring the health and social and economic wellbeing of people.'

[108] Jackson (n 6) 22: 'It follows that the necessity test is met best when a research project is complementary to the analysis of the department. Interference with the privacy of the department's clients may be necessary if the outcome is evidence that fills a knowledge gap in the department or provides elaboration or greater context and insight to the evidence the department already has.'

[109] HM Government (n 108) 5: 'Data is the 21st century's new raw material. Its value is in holding governments to account.'

last few decades to 'empowering citizens' with information that will allow them to 'challenge government if they see inefficiencies'.[110] Independent' research on government data, ie research conducted by a neutral individual or group, ideally when the latter subscribes to recognised standards of professional and ethical integrity as in the case of academic researchers, has been regarded as integral to realising this commitment.[111] This aspiration stemmed from a broader policy agenda on 'greater openness' as part of a 'global movement towards transparency' and 'open policy making',[112] premised on the idea that factual evidence underpinning policy decisions shall be made public to allow citizens 'scrutinise the work of those they elect'.[113] Hence, by streamlining access to government data for independent social-science research, the government aspired to realise the value of data 'in holding governments to account … (and) driving choice and improvements in public services'.[114]

An interviewee working for the ONS argued that there is 'public benefit' in external researchers using its data to 'prove that our statistics are incorrect' or to 'produce a better measure of inflation', even if there is no 'direct use' of these findings for public policy.[115] Another interviewee working for the Honest Broker Service in Northern Ireland drew a connection between the idea of accountability and the professional identity of 'statisticians', shared by many individuals working for data managers:

> I don't know whether this is simply a Northern Irish Statistics and Research Agency culture, we are statisticians, we like things to be open, completely clear and transparent to everybody. This is part of our independence as statisticians … putting all the information in the public domain about what research is this, when it is happening, what it is about, when the application came in etc.[116]

Research output, produced from research on administrative data, is to be treated as a 'public good' under this narrative.[117] As one of the interviewees mentioned, this is also reflected in the ONS requirements that all outputs from administrative data research are published on open-access websites because:

> A lot of the projects evaluate Government's policies, evaluate government delivery. That is very important for democratic debate, for the public to actually know how effective the government is. Ensuring that transparency and accountability exist.[118]

[110] ibid 12.

[111] M Woolard, 'Administrative Data: Problems and Benefits. A Perspective from the United Kingdom' in A Dusa and others (eds), *Facing the Future: European Research Infrastructures for the Humanities and Social Sciences* (Scivero 2014) 49.

[112] HM Government (n 108) 5; HM Government, 'Open Government'. Available at: www.gov.uk/government/collections/open-government.

[113] Department for Digital, Culture, Media & Sport, 'UK National Action Plan for Open Government 2019–2021' (2019).

[114] HM Government (n 108) 5.

[115] Interview with participant nr 1 (2017, Titchfield).

[116] Interview with participant nr 12 (2018, Belfast).

[117] Ritchie and Welpton (n 22).

[118] Interview with participant nr 3 (2017, Titchfield).

An interviewee who has worked for the ONS argued that the Statistics and Research Service Act 2007 rebutted the previous presumption that data is not available for research unless the public bodies provide them for this purpose. Essentially, this is to make a bold claim that all data are 'fair game' for researchers unless custodians can justify withholding them.[119] Another interviewee working as an administrative data researcher in Northern Ireland expressed the same ideal in the following words:

> There has to be an aspiration … that this is public data and … if you have an ethically approved, methodologically sound project that addresses something that has public benefits, then we should be advocating for this project to be supported.[120]

Following this line of thought, various organisations have explicitly committed to realise the potential of 'independent' administrative data research to make government policymaking not only more efficient, but also more accountable. One of the first research data infrastructures in the UK public sector to facilitate streamlined access of external researchers, the HMRC DataLab, was established in fulfilment of HMRC's commitment to the government's 'Transparency Agenda'.[121] The benefits of transparency were associated by the HMRC with both the aim of 'promoting social and economic growth' and that of promoting 'public understanding of its work, … accountability and public confidence'.[122]

More recently, in the context of digitalising the UK justice system, the CEO of HM Courts and Tribunals Service (HMCTS) committed to making data, 'in a suitably anonymised way', available for researchers and academics to use.[123] This commitment was elaborated upon in later HMCTS publications, where it was clarified that 'independent research' on the reform programme is integral to establishing accountability and transparency.[124] Both HMRC and HMCTS have acknowledged the need to improve the way they share data with external researchers, who are facing a number of difficulties in accessing their data.[125] Such researcher organisations as the Education Policy Institute have also pledged their commitment to use administrative data research to 'hold government … to

[119] Interview with participant nr 42 (2020, virtual).

[120] Interview with participant nr 10 (2018, Belfast).

[121] D Bega, 'The HMRC Datalab: Sharing Administrative and Survey Data on Taxation with the Research Community' in Dusa and others (eds) (n 112) 61.

[122] ibid 64.

[123] HMCTS Chief Executive, 'Modernising the Courts and Tribunals Service: Future of Justice Conference' (14 May 2018). Available at: www.ucl. ac.uk/laws/sites/laws/files/ucl_ foj_01_03_acland-hood.pdf.

[124] Ministry of Justice, 'Evaluating Our Reforms: Response to PAC Recommendation 4, January 2019'. Available at: www.gov.uk/government/news/moj-response-to-public-accounts-committee-transforming-courts-and-tribunals.

[125] N Byrom, 'Digital Justice: HMCTS Data Strategy and Delivering Access to Justice Report and Recommendations' (October 2019). Available at: https://research.thelegaleducationfoundation.org/blog/digital-justice-hmcts-data-strategy-and-delivering-access-to-justice 31; M Almunia and others, 'Expanding Access to Administrative Data: The Case of Tax Authorities in Finland and the UK' (2019) 26 *International Tax Public Finance* 661–76.

account for their performance' and help improve policy-making.[126] These aspirations materialised through both public demands and bargaining in the creation of the first formalised data sharing frameworks and infrastructures for external researchers in the UK public sector.

B. Formalising 'Independent' Research Data Access: Trailblazers and the Ambition for Wider Formalisation

Very much like its role in pioneering government-led administrative data research, the ONS established the first data infrastructure for independent research on government data in 2004, the Virtual Microdata Laboratory (VML).[127] Driven by the central government's interest to better understand the productivity of UK manufacturing,[128] the VML was launched to provide a 'secure facility for access to confidential business micro data across all ONS sites'.[129] In its first few years of operation, the VML significantly streamlined external researcher access to ONS data. It started by supporting six research projects in 2004, reaching 89 by 2008 and more than 230 by 2017.[130] Research outputs on such issues as the impact of innovation to productivity or the calculation of labour cost assessments for the National Health Service were published and 'influenced policymaking at all levels'.[131]

Such stellar research outputs were instrumentalised by the research community in their efforts to convince the ONS to make data access even more transparent and predictable. Indeed, beyond the particular research projects, the VML has gradually come to be widely regarded as a 'model of best practice … emulated across the UK and world-wide'[132] and a 'major resource for academic researchers'[133] due to its establishment of fundamental governance principles for external researcher data access to government data. The ONS has published comprehensive guidance on its decision-making procedure and interpretation of its governance requirements, as well as a four-week timescale within which researchers will normally receive a response to their request.[134] More specifically, the ONS created a specific governance infrastructure, the Micro-Data Release Panel (MRP), and entrusted it with responsibilities to manage the strategic and operational aspects of research data access to the

[126] Education Policy Institute, 'About Us'. Available at: https://epi.org.uk/our-mission-and-purpose/.
[127] Jones and Elias (n 36) 39.
[128] Welpton and Wright (n 96) 11.
[129] Jones and Elias (n 36) 39.
[130] Ritchie (n 21) 31; interview with participant nr 1 (2017, Titchfield).
[131] Ritchie ibid 29; F Ritchie, 'Access to business microdata in the UK: dealing with the irreducible risk' in Eurostat, *Monographs of Official Statistics: Work Session on Statistical Data Confidentiality* (2005) 239.
[132] Welpton and Wright (n 96) 12.
[133] Ritchie (n 21) 29.
[134] ibid.

VML. External researchers interested in using ONS datasets must apply to the MRP to convince the panel that their request is 'related to a viable and relevant research topic' and that they themselves are able to undertake high-quality research that will 'add significant value to existing research in that area'.[135]

Crucially, the ONS has not only published guidance but has also consulted the research community about the appropriateness of its criteria in July 2016. As an interviewee working for the Office explained, the data managers themselves were not satisfied with the previous criteria because they were 'a lot vaguer and gave us a lot more room for manoeuvre', aiming instead for a 'set of criteria that could then be applied consistently throughout'.[136] Another interviewee working for the ONS highlighted the significance of formalisation for external researchers by referring to the function of access decisions as precedents for other researchers:

> Over the years, we built up a system of precedent decisions ... we decided we had to rework the whole process and formalise it a lot more. ... So now we have a written set of precedents, which allow us to make decisions and the understanding is this is a lot more formal and transparent procedure ... We want to make sure that everybody understands the precedents and we apply them consistently and correctly.[137]

The ONS is, then, a clear example of widening the scope of appropriate access to administrative data for research purposes through collaborative modes of dialogue and bargaining through invoking tangible outcomes. This example inspired the Economic and Social Research Council (ESRC) to invest resources into the creation of a similar to the VML research data infrastructure to facilitate access to broader public-sector data assets. In 2009, the Secure Data Service (SDS) was launched within the ESRC-supported UK Data Archive, allowing for the first time in the UK remote access for academic researchers via their accredited institution's 'safe room'.[138] As an interviewee who has worked for both the ONS and the SDS recalled, the latter's data sharing policy was largely influenced by the need to demonstrate conformity with the VML framework, in the interest of enhancing data sharing collaboration and technical compatibility between the two infrastructures.[139] The same interviewee highlighted the significance of remote access for attempts to formalise access for the majority of the external research community, noting that previous models like the VML unavoidably privileged researchers who happened to live closer to their secure research environments ('safe settings').[140]

Nonetheless, infrastructures are not used unless more data managers have the appetite to grant access to their datasets. In 2011, HMRC were one of the first major ministerial departments in the UK to formalise access to their datasets for

[135] Jones and Elias (n 36) 51.
[136] Interview with participant nr 1 (2017, Titchfield).
[137] Interview with participant nr 2 (2017, Titchfield).
[138] Welpton and Wright (n 96) 12.
[139] Interview with participant nr 28 (2020, London).
[140] ibid.

academic researchers ‘working independently’ through the ‘HMRC DataLab’.[141] Only allowing access onsite, HMRC sought to establish a secure research environment within which researchers would access ‘anonymised taxpayer and customs data for research and analysis purposes’,[142] with a view to producing high-quality research that would benefit both HMRC and the academic community. Mirroring the ONS governance procedures, HMRC created their own Microdata Release Panel. This handles operational aspects of data sharing, reviewing research proposals and performing output validation and disclosure control checks to assess identifiability risks.[143] Researchers applying for access to the HMRC DataLab have to demonstrate that their proposed research will ‘deliver a public benefit to society’.[144] As an interviewee who has worked for HMRC explained, the latter would be interpreted by reference to HMRC functions, covering such areas as ‘understanding compliance, taxation or commercial activity’.[145] This demonstrates that researchers’ bargaining does not always have the same results, with HMRC adopting a narrower criterion to govern data access compared to the Office for National Statistics.

Formalisation gradually expanded to other public bodies, in the interest of attracting more researchers by reassuring them that they will no longer ‘have to know the right person’ to access data in a predictable timescale.[146] For example, the DfE established its own Data Sharing Approval Panel and approval process, providing guidance to researchers interested in accessing such datasets as the National Pupil Database and the Individualised Learner Record.[147] An interviewee who has worked for the DfE recalled that the Panel would assess whether the requester is a trusted organisation and the data will be used appropriately, often engaging in communication with them to clarify the scope of the data use.[148] Furthermore, the DfE funds a National Pupil Database User Group, hosted at the University of Bristol, to encourage better communication between academics using the Database and communicate to them the availability of new data extracts.[149]

Beyond England, the Honest Broker Service (HBS), part of the Business Services Organisation within the Health and Social Care department of the Northern Irish government, is one of the luminary bodies in formalising external researcher access to its resources.[150] The HBS created ‘safe havens’ for secure data linkage and de-identification, allowing access to anonymised data for researchers

[141] Bega (n 122) 68.
[142] ibid 66.
[143] ibid.
[144] Welpton and Wright (n 96) 7.
[145] Interview with participant nr 32 (2020, Oxford).
[146] Sexton and others (n 77) 313.
[147] HM Government, ‘How to access Department for Education (DfE) data extracts’ (2018). Available at: www.gov.uk/guidance/how-to-access-department-for-education-dfe-data-extracts.
[148] Interview with participant nr 33 (2020, virtual).
[149] Centre for Market and Public Organisation, ‘NPD User Group’. Available at: www.bristol.ac.uk/cmpo/npd-user-group/.
[150] G Robinson and others, ‘Public Attitudes to Data Sharing in Northern Ireland: Findings from the 2015 Northern Ireland Life and Times survey’ (2018) (ADRC-Northern Ireland) 4.

interested in the social dimensions of health and social care.[151] An interviewee working for the HBS confirmed that they have established their own Governance Board and follow a similar decision-making procedure with other departments:

> So, we have our discussion, an in-depth discussion, about what their intentions are, what the aims of the project are, perhaps tease out a bit more the variables they are interested in, … mindful of the requirements of the Governance Board, what they will be looking to see in that application, and there are some sets of criteria that it must meet.[152]

How widespread were such initiatives across the UK public sector? Despite this gradual expansion, the truth is that the majority of the UK public-sector bodies remained somewhat cryptic and inconsistent as to the ways in which they handled access to their data for independent research purposes, let alone for innovation purposes. To encourage broader consistency and transparency through widespread formalisation of research data sharing, the central government, through the Economic and Social Research Council, funded in 2011 the establishment of the Administrative Data Taskforce (ADT).[153] The taskforce brought together all the major actors of this space: senior academic researchers, representatives from funding bodies, data managers, as well as government policy-makers.[154] ADT's organisational mission was to provide recommendations for widening the use of administrative data by independent researchers, with a view to creating a 'robust UK-wide evidence base' that would both improve policy making and inform 'evaluation of government policy' by the academic community.[155]

In this direction, the taskforce recommended the establishment of a UK-wide ADRN, accompanied by one Administrative Data Research Centre.[156] Through this network, the taskforce suggested, researcher access to administrative data would become much more uniform and streamlined. This would be assisted by establishing common training and accreditation processes, as well as common approval requirements. Crucially, especially for the latter aim, the central government relied on the collaboration between departments (or other data managers) and the UK research community.[157] How did this collaboration work out in practice?

V. The ADRN (2013–2018) as an Agent of Systematic Formalisation

Since its establishment and funding by the Economic and Social Research Council (ESRC) in 2013, the ADRN has worked towards extending the formalisation

[151] ibid.
[152] Interview with participant nr 14 (2018, Belfast).
[153] Administrative Data Taskforce (n 13); interview with participant nr 19 (2018, Swindon).
[154] Elias (n 1) 188.
[155] Administrative Data Taskforce (n 13) ii.
[156] Woolard (n 112) 50.
[157] Administrative Data Taskforce (n 13) ii.

of research data sharing processes from a handful of pioneer data managers to the vast number of public-sector bodies in the UK.[158] In the words of an interviewee working for the ESRC, the aim of the Network was to use 'the wealth of the UK's administrative data for the purpose of scientific research, in social science and economics'.[159] With 'independent' – understood as 'original' and 'non-commissioned'[160] – research at the heart of its mandate, the network established a clear and transparent process to handle data sharing requests, assisting academics in preparing their applications. In that sense, the ADRN was the first intermediary body to go beyond general advice and guidance to personalised support in this space. The ADRN's Approvals Panel would take into account a set of key considerations: the feasibility of the proposed study, its ethical acceptability (considering the lack of consent), its scientific merit and potential for yielding benefits to the public, as well as the risks from a privacy and data protection perspective.[161] Applicants, supported by ADRN officers, would submit their research proposals, often receiving feedback and required amendments by the Approvals Panel.

The network aspired to promote these criteria as core elements of a research data sharing process across the public sector through its commissioning panel (the 'ADRN Board').[162] The panel, which was chaired by a senior academic, comprised of government statisticians and ESRC representatives, as well as of representatives from major data managers such as the DWP, the HMRC and the governments of the devolved countries.[163] The existence of the four Administrative Data Research Centres in the UK countries served both as a reflection of the devolved nature of government functions in the UK and as a way of developing consistent data sharing standards across different jurisdictions.[164]

Through this collaboration between academics and government departments in the four countries, the network aspired to 'leverage' the expertise of its members and supported researchers to trigger wider formalisation of researcher data access and streamline the production of independent administrative data research.[165] Viewed from the perspective of regulatory space, this might be seen as a more adversarial and blunt approach compared to previous organisations in this space that might have tried to negotiate wider access to administrative data through more incremental steps. As the following section will explain, this effort might have been overambitious in respect of maximising actual data acquisition

[158] Elias (n 1) 185.
[159] Interview with participant nr 19 (2018, Swindon).
[160] Administrative Data Taskforce (n 13) 6.
[161] UK Statistics Authority, 'First Meeting of the Administrative Data Research Network Board' (2014). Available at: https://uksa.statisticsauthority.gov.uk/wp-content/uploads/2015/12/images-minutesandpapersfromadrnboardon14april201_tcm97-43879.pdf.
[162] UK Statistics Authority, 'Meet the ADRN Board'. Available at: https://uksa.statisticsauthority.gov.uk/about-the-authority/committees/adrn/meet-the-adrn-board/.
[163] Elias (n 1) 190.
[164] ibid 185.
[165] Interview with participant nr 19 (2018, Swindon).

from government departments. The Network faced barriers that made access to government-held administrative data very difficult and, at times, impossible.[166]

Does this mean that the ADRN was a failure? Regardless of actual data access, the Network was a resounding success in terms of making the demand for wider formalisation of research data sharing much more mainstream in the UK public sector. By sponsoring more than 120 independent research projects by academics and negotiating access with a vast number of data providers across the UK,[167] the ADRN contributed significantly to the crystallisation of specific research data access procedures. These procedures and their accompanying guidance, covering legal, ethical and information security aspects of data sharing, are now recognised as best practice and adopted by many data custodians in the UK.[168] Broadly formulated, these aspects relate to four 'stages' of data sharing: de-identification of the data to mitigate disclosure risks from a data protection and privacy perspective,[169] public benefit and ethical review of the research proposal, accreditation and training of the individuals that will be accessing the data and data security of the working environment within which the research will be conducted.[170] In developing this data sharing framework, the Network largely drew on pre-existing practice in the context of health data sharing for research and the '5 safes' framework developed by the ONS.[171]

By simplifying the 'complex discussion around data access into a set of related but independent questions',[172] the ADRN facilitated the adoption of consistent and formalised research data sharing standards by various public bodies in the UK.[173] These standards have been endorsed by the ICO[174] and were recently enacted, to a significant extent according to some interviewees who have worked for the ONS,[175] into formal UK legislation. Sections 64 and 70 of the Digital Economy Act 2017 empower all public authorities to disclose data for research in accordance with operational requirements and accreditation criteria published by the

[166] In its fourth year of operation, the Network had managed to get the data for circa 19% of the ADRN-approved projects it had been facilitating.

[167] ibid.

[168] D Hand, 'The Role of the ADRN Governing Board' (2013). Available at: https://esrc.ukri.org/files/research/administrative-data-taskforce-adt/the-role-of-the-adrn-governing-board-david-hand/.

[169] On the meaning of de-identification as 'a process which reduces the risk of direct identification, but which does not produce anonymous data', see M Mourby and others, 'Are "Pseudonymised" Data Always Personal Data? Implications of the GDPR for Administrative Data Research in the UK' (2018) 34(2) *Computer Law & Security Review* 222, 224.

[170] Jackson (n 6) 22.

[171] C Brett and I Deary, 'Realising Health Data Linkage from a Researcher's Perspective: Following up the 6-Day Sample of the Scottish Mental Survey 1947' (2014) 5(3) *Longitudinal Life Course Studies* 283; Desai, Welpton and Ritchie (n 20) 5: 'safe people, safe projects, safe data, safe settings, safe outputs'.

[172] ibid.

[173] See O'Reilly and others (n 49) on the Northern Irish Statistics and Research Agency: 'NISRA hosts the Secure Environment where accredited researchers access data for ADR NI research projects. This operates under the "Five Safes" principles which have been endorsed by the Information Commissioner's Office'.

[174] ibid.

[175] Interviews with participants nrs 1 and 4 (2017, Titchfield), 42 (2020, virtual).

UK Statistics Authority,[176] largely mirroring the standards adopted by the ADRN. There is, still, significant way to go until a similar legislative commitment about broader innovation purposes comes into fruition.

In the light of these developments, the former ADRN Director has claimed that administrative data researchers in the UK 'can plan their research and be confident that access to administrative data will be granted'.[177] Does this claim, however, reflect adequately the realities of implementing research data sharing frameworks in the UK public sector today? A discussion of the following, and last, historical phase within which actors shaped the development of research data sharing in the UK indicates the existence of significant limitations to the formalisation of this activity across the public sector, with ideals of 'accountability' often giving rise to 'efficiency'-driven priorities.

VI. Fragmentation: Unequal Access of Researchers to Administrative Data in the UK

Contemporary research data sharing realities in the UK indicate that formalisation is rather a work in progress than a widely applied reality. With 'accountability' reasons for consistent and predictable data access for independent researchers gradually being eclipsed by 'efficiency' rationales, a fragmented and unequal picture arises as an outcome of the processes of conflict and bargaining between the actors of this space. I sketch the contours of this fragmentation, identifying the amount of existing uncertainty about the data sharing practices of major data custodians, before reflecting on the impact of such fragmentation on independent researcher access. Finally, I will be concluding with the implications of this analysis for studying the formation of 'research data sharing institutions' in the UK public sector.

A. After the Administrative Data Research Network: Fragmentation and the Limits of Formalisation

After its first years of operation, the ADRN was particularly struggling in facilitating access to ministerial department UK-wide data in areas such as social security, licensing and tax records.[178] In 2016, its Mid-Term review report noted that despite spending £25.3m (66% of its overall budget) it was 'behind its intended schedule for linked data projects, and far behind schedule for projects that made use of linked UK-wide data'.[179] ADRN's funding finished in 2018, as originally foreseen

[176] UK Statistics Authority (n 162).
[177] Elias (n 1) 185.
[178] ibid 200.
[179] Research Project Management, 'Administrative Data Research Network (ADRN) Mid-Term Review Report' (8 November 2016). Available at: https://esrc.ukri.org/files/research/research-and-impact-evaluation/adrn-mid-term-review-report-8-november-2016/ 8.

by the Economic and Social Research Council (ESRC), and its successor body, Administrative Data Research (ADR) UK, received ESRC funding on the condition that it would adopt a more effective approach than the ADRN in securing access to government data. During the last phases of its funding, the ADRN sought to demonstrate how its sponsored research can be more useful for government departments through so-called *thematic partnerships*, ie long-term relationships between the Network and specific public bodies in the interest of prioritising research on datasets and policy questions of central interest to government policy-makers.[180] The fundamental redirection of the Network's acquisition policy did pay off during the last year of its operation. Relationships between key government departments and the Network improved and data finally started becoming available for use by more ADRN-approved projects aiming to access government data.[181]

The ADRN story is, arguably, a lesson in humility for 'pressurising constituents'[182] that seek to overcome established power imbalances through robust strategies of conflict. 'Efficiency', in the sense of satisfying data managers that independent research can be of benefit to them as organisations, eventually mattered more than 'accountability' amidst increasing uncertainty about the requirements and procedures followed by data managers in disclosing administrative data. Nonetheless, the ADRN, while it existed, played a significant role in extending research data sharing standards in the outer limits of the UK public sector. As a result, it is true that many transparent and formalised data sharing frameworks have been established, making 'the journey to obtaining data clearer and smoother' for independent researchers.[183] Indeed, an interviewee, who has worked for the ONS, observed with satisfaction that:

> For a lot of the UK now, the idea that we should be default open is taken for granted, in a lots of places. Certainly, compared to what we started with many years ago, it's an awful lot easier to get access to data now.[184]

Indeed, in some cases, the ADRN has contributed to some public bodies being more 'friendly' to independent researchers, adopting open-ended definitions of the public good, allowing methodological studies without a clearly demonstrable policy impact[185] and responding to requests within strict timescales.[186] Such

[180] P Jackson, 'The Route to Better Knowledge for a Better Society' (2017). Available at: https://prezi.com/6pe-8m2u9ad0/the-route-to-better-knowledge-for-a-better-society/?utm_campaign=share&utm_medium=copy – these cover: children, world of work, ageing, productive society, and health and society.

[181] Strategic Data Negotiator, 'April 2018 Data Acquisition Project Report' (not published, on file with the author as part of his affiliation with the Administrative Data Service) 3.

[182] N Chowdury and R Wessel, 'Conceptualizing Multilevel Regulation in the EU: A Legal Translation of Multilevel Governance?' (2012) 18(3) *European Law Journal* 335.

[183] M Iveson and I Deary, 'Navigating the Landscape of Administrative Data in Scotland' (2019) 4 *Wellcome Open Research* 9797.

[184] Interview with participant nr 42 (2020, virtual).

[185] Ritchie (n 21) 31.

[186] Jones and Elias (n 36) 51.

bodies, eg the ONS in England or the Honest Broker Service in Northern Ireland, may also be more explicit about the availability of their datasets,[187] as well as less stringent in respect of their disclosure and confidentiality controls to maximise the usefulness of data for research.[188]

This is not to say that existent data sharing frameworks are always relaxed in granting access when it comes to assessing the appropriateness of the applicant researchers or the contribution of a proposed research to the public benefit. Some bodies may be more likely to err on the side of caution, interpreting their published requirements narrowly and applying strict controls and safeguards. Custodians like the HMRC or the DfE, for example, restrict access or 'treat more sympathetically'[189] to requests for research that 'serves one of their functions'.[190] An interviewee who has worked for HMRC conceded that this essentially confines the HMRC DataLab to things that are 'more akin to what the HMRC themselves would do'.[191] The Scottish government stipulates that it is 'crucial' for the facilitation of data access that a senior civil service manager or a minister endorses a project for its potential contribution to a 'national outcome'.[192] This means that certain bargaining and negotiation skills are still critical to securing access. Interested researchers, in these cases, should demonstrate how their outputs will benefit the manager's understanding in specific policy areas eg modelling the effects of tax reforms or optimising economic efficiency in designing tax operations.[193] Even if that is the case, many frameworks are now formalised and, to an extent, transparent, allowing researchers to manage their expectations in respect of data access.

Are these 'many' frameworks enough to speak about a widespread formalisation of research data sharing in the UK public sector? While significant progress has been made, this is hardly the case. For a vast number of public bodies, a fragmented picture emerges when seeking to identify the data sharing frameworks they are actively operating, with both major ministerial departments and 'smaller' public bodies or local authorities remaining silent about their preferable standards and procedures. A researcher working in Scotland conceded that major data managers like the National Records of Scotland do not have 'any discoverability for their datasets'.[194] Another interviewee, who has worked for the DfE in England and is now working for the National Foundation for Education Research (an independent research organisation), conceded that while they are

[187] Health and Social Care Northern Ireland, 'Honest Broker Service'. Available at: www.hscbusiness.hscni.net/services/2454.htm.
[188] Ritchie (n 21).
[189] Jones and Elias (n 36) 8.
[190] Bega (n 122) 62.
[191] Interview with participant nr. 32 (2020, Oxford).
[192] Scottish Government (n 104).
[193] Welpton and Wright (n 96) 7.
[194] Interview with participant nr 29 (2020, phone).

familiar with the DfE's data sharing procedures, the same can hardly be said about other departments:

> Do I know how to do this with the Department for Work and Pensions? No ... I don't know how long other government departments take ... We have applied for data from Wales and Scotland while I'm here – that was hard work, very hard work, especially Scotland.[195]

Another interviewee with a similar background, ie first a DfE analyst and now working for the Education Policy Institute (an independent research organisation), complained about lack of clarity in the DfE's own procedures. Especially in the beginning of their interactions with the DfE as external researchers, they found its guidance to be 'quite limited' and 'information does not really flow appropriately many times'.[196] Interviewees with experience in negotiating data access across the UK corroborated this impression of uncertainty. A researcher working in Scotland found the approval procedures in the Scottish public sector to be 'extremely messy' and 'very bumpy',[197] whereas an interviewee working for an intermediary body in Scotland claimed that 'disparity among data providers and how they do things' is even greater when trying to access central government data.[198] Another interviewee working as an administrative data researcher in Scotland associated lack of clarity with lack of experience in developing data sharing policies. In their view, transparency around data sharing is 'hit and miss' with smaller organisations.[199] An interviewee who has worked for the ONS made a counterargument, stressing that officials in large data custodians are 'strongly incentivised' to refrain from establishing and enabling transparent data sharing procedures.[200]

Other interviewees cautioned against the meaningfulness of this distinction, highlighting that, with larger organisations, there is a lot of internal disparity in how data sharing works. Departments like the DfE are 'complex organisations, with lots of different parts'.[201] An interviewee working for the Welsh government made this point eloquently when referring to their own department:

> The thing about Welsh Government is that even Welsh Government is not a homogenous whole ... parts that came in from the wider public sector had a different perspective, a different history. ... surely, there are still pockets of Welsh Government that would not know data linking if you kicked them on the head.[202]

Nonetheless, the lack of procedural clarity becomes more striking when thinking about the major ministerial departments with significant organisational capacities

[195] Interview with participant nr 30 (2020, virtual).
[196] Interview with participant nr 33 (2020, virtual).
[197] Interview with participant nr 34 (2020, virtual).
[198] Interview with participant nr 36 (2020, virtual).
[199] Interview with participant nr 37 (2020, virtual).
[200] interview with participant nr 42 (2020, virtual).
[201] interview with participant nr 40 (2020, virtual).
[202] interview with participant nr 25 (2019, Cardiff).

and a wealth of administrative datasets at their disposal. For example, HM Courts and Tribunals, while in the midst of an ambitious digitalisation reform that will generate a wealth of novel justice-related datasets, delegate their research data sharing decision-making to an informal data access panel which communicates via e-mail and does not record or publicise minutes of meetings or particular access requirements.[203] The DWP, one of the pioneering bodies in government-led administrative data research,[204] is also laconic about its research data sharing procedure, encouraging researchers to submit a written application to the department and avoiding to publish information about the progress of applications online.[205] Transparent and formalised data sharing frameworks, similarly, shine through their absence on the websites of most local authorities or other public bodies.

As described by an interviewee with work experience in the Administrative Data Research Centre in Northern Ireland, its efforts to formalise research data sharing was intended as a '*push factor*' but was perceived by many departments as a '*fear factor*'.[206] Beyond merely neglecting to disclose information about their data sharing practices, some data custodians actively resist providing any relevant information to the general public. The DWP recently rejected a Freedom of Information Act (FOIA) 2000 request to disclose information about their use of their customers' data.[207] HMRC responded to a similar request by providing only partial information about its external data sharing for research purposes and refusing to disclose information about its internal procedures. As a result, despite the significant progress in formalising independent research access to government data, it currently seems 'unlikely that a standard pattern of use for researchers in general would emerge across government'.[208] In many cases, data access seemingly remains 'unregulated, unreliable and haphazard',[209] with researchers facing the tall task of navigating a complex landscape without a reliable compass in their possession. This seems to sketch a picture that is often present in power struggles: both conflict and bargaining is helpful to ameliorate power imbalances, yet this is often not enough to radically eradicate such imbalances, at least for a long time. Who are, then, the 'authors' of the applicable data sharing standards and practices within this uncertain and fragmented picture?

[203] Byrom (n 126) 6; HMCTS (n 124).

[204] Department for Work and Pensions, 'DWP Open Data: Case Studies' (2013). Available at: https://assets.publishing.service.gov.uk/government/uploads/system/uploads/attachment_data/file/221159/dwp-open-data-case-studies.pdf; National Archives, 'Information Management Assessment: Department for Work and Pensions' (2015) https://www.nationalarchives.gov.uk/documents/information-management/dwp-ima-report-2015.pdf.

[205] ibid.

[206] Interview with participant nr 10 (2018, Belfast).

[207] R Booth, 'Benefits system automation could plunge claimants deeper into poverty' (The Guardian) 14 October 2019. Available at: www.theguardian.com/technology/2019/oct/14/fears-rise-in-benefits-system-automation-could-plunge-claimants-deeper-into-poverty.

[208] Smith and others (n 26) 28.

[209] Elias (n 1) 184.

B. The Eclipse of 'Accountability' and the Complications for Independent Researchers

While elements of a popular narrative throughout the development of this space, 'accountability' and transparency of data sharing procedures seemingly waver in practice. In the absence of comprehensive knowledge about the data sharing standards and procedures that are applied by most data custodians in the UK public sector,[210] commentators and stakeholders have drawn on anecdotal information or individual researcher narratives to reflect on the governing forces of data access.[211] According to Elias, most public bodies prioritise such factors as the legality of the request, the public interest, the resources they will need to allocate in meeting the request and the risks they would be exposed to if they grant access.[212]

As resources and disclosure risks become increasingly pertinent, the ideal of bolstering the 'accountability' of government towards its citizens through independent research on administrative datasets breaks down, with more efficiency-driven rationales becoming more prominent. With data managers being likely to approve requests which do not generate risks of portraying them negatively or critically,[213] Administrative Data Research (ADR) UK, the Administrative Data Research Network's successor, has opted to facilitate research that can 'predominantly help inform … government policy decisions … ensuring that decision making is evidence based'.[214] Researchers are called to 'compromise on the detail of the data' and potentially 'bundle together a number of projects' in the interest of satisfying the appetite of government departments.[215] Access to administrative data is often regarded as a 'privilege, not a right'.[216]

Various interviewees shed light on the prevalence of 'efficiency' within custodians' data sharing policies. An interviewee working for the DWP noted that their internal review board, called the External Data Sharing and Access Committee, assesses the 'usefulness … (ie) the practical use' of the proposed research within their definition of the 'public benefit'.[217] An interviewee who has worked for HMRC also noted that, when defining their 'prioritisation' criteria within the HMRC data sharing policy, the main considerations would relate to 'higher priority and better

[210] Smith and others (n 26) 39: 'there are no consistent patterns or always clear reasons for the different levels of access that different groups have obtained'; Iveson and Deary (n 184): 'without single points of administrative data permissions, researchers must negotiate with and complete the governance procedures of all concerned data controllers, resulting in a complex and often unclear process'.

[211] Eg Iveson and Deary *ibid*.

[212] Elias (n 1) 194.

[213] ibid 196.

[214] O'Reilly and others (n 49).

[215] Jackson (n 6) 24.

[216] J Lane, 'Building an Infrastructure to Support the Use of Government Administrative Data for Program Performance and Social Science Research' (2017) 1 *The ANNALS of the American Academy of Political and Social Science* 240, 246.

[217] Interview with participant nr 8 (2017, Sheffield).

fit with HMRC objectives', as well as 'ease to deliver'.[218] Another interviewee working for the ONS attributed this imbalance between 'efficiency' and 'accountability' to the fact that many policy-making departments feel that 'the more they would allow the public to see, the harder it is going to be for them to actually put policies in place'.[219] Where does this leave independent administrative data researchers?

Power imbalances between researchers and data managers are as clear as ever. Much like the first phase of administrative data sharing for social-science research, researchers have to grapple with a 'complex and changeable' landscape within which they are unable to predict how long they will need to access data and how they should fulfil data provider requirements.[220] Such requirements are often communicated in a way that is not helpful to researchers or relate to technical and legal information governance issues that they are not necessarily able to comprehend.[221] A researcher working in Scotland recalled their surprise when, after an initial approval from the data custodians, they were asked to undergo a 'whole new process' of 'negotiating the contracts (and) … the particular conditions of access etc'.[222] Another interviewee who has worked for the DfE conceded that the expansion of data sharing policies to novel areas may take really long and make the lives of researchers very difficult:

> If you do it for the first time, then good luck, I don't think you will necessarily navigate this, at least not after a long time.[223]

The task is even taller for researchers who are interested in linking datasets managed by more than one data manager. Without sufficient clarity on the compatibility between the respective data sharing frameworks, researchers are often expected to conform with conflicting rules and guidance on meeting various data sharing requirements.[224] An interviewee who has been attempting to link datasets between different parts of the Scottish government reflected on their so-far unsuccessful efforts over the last six (6) years:

> To be honest, it's been such a long time, I'm not entirely sure what the roadblock was other than the fact that we had to have the right sign-off from … as part of their internal sub-linkage things.[225]

Under these circumstances, access becomes a time-demanding and herculean task, whereas disclosure decisions are hardly consistent across government departments in respect of the application of access rules. As a result, fewer researchers are inclined to embark on administrative data research, observing that many of their

[218] Interview with participant nr 32 (2020, Oxford).
[219] Interview with participant nr 3 (2017, Titchfield).
[220] Iveson and Deary (n 184).
[221] ibid.
[222] Interview with participant nr 29 (2020, phone).
[223] Interview with participant nr 33 (2020, virtual).
[224] G Laurie and N Sethi, 'Information Governance of Use of Health-Related Data in Medical Research in Scotland: Current Practices and Future Scenarios' (SHIP Core Programme 2 Working Paper No 1) 9.
[225] Interview with participant nr 35 (2020, virtual).

colleagues had to abandon existing plans and funding due to the data not arriving in time (or at all). An interviewee working in Scotland went as far as conceding that they actually amended their research agenda in the light of data sharing considerations:

> Let's say that it was not the original focus we were interested in, it was part of a wider research program … In the course of the applications process, we had to … change the focus.[226]

The secondary literature is also awash with researcher narratives of struggles in getting access to administrative data. Iveson and Deary report long delays and uncertainty in trying to use data from the Scottish Census and link it to health data.[227] While they found health data permissions and access procedures in Scotland much more streamlined, they faced various complications such as a change in the legal interpretation of the power to share data by the Scottish Government or an unpredictably long queue to have their request considered.[228] Eventually, they had to wait more than three years to acquire access to linked data, also opting for a more modest choice of datasets than originally envisaged.[229] Morris and colleagues offer a lucid account of similar difficulties while trying to link datasets belonging to the Department of Education (the National Pupil Database) and the National Health Service Digital (Hospital Episode Statistics).[230] The research team negotiated access with data custodians over three years and 11 months, conducting six meetings and with 108 email exchanges and phone calls with the managers before an agreement on linkage of datasets could be reached.[231]

Other researchers corroborated that they faced a 'complex landscape, unclear and conflicting guidelines',[232] lamenting the 'extraordinarily disturbing' impact on the careers of academics, particularly early career researchers who will produce a reduced research output as a result.[233] These narratives are telling of power imbalances between researchers and data custodians. They are indicative of the strategic changes the ADRN had to implement to increase the likelihood of satisfying data custodian requirements and achieving greater progress in data acquisition. The last sub-section takes stock of the central lessons learned from the historical development of this space for the purposes of empirically studying the formation of research data sharing institutions in the following chapters.

[226] Interview with participant nr 38 (2020, virtual).
[227] Iveson and Deary (n 184).
[228] ibid.
[229] ibid.
[230] H Morris and others al, 'Challenges of administrative data linkages: experiences of Administrative Data Research Centre for England (ADRC-E) researchers' (2018) 3(2) *International Journal of Population Data Science* 97; the time mentioned here does not include the additional time within which technical challenges of data linkage were dealt with.
[231] ibid.
[232] Brett and Deary (n 172).
[233] Iveson and Deary (n 184): 'the current situation essentially prohibits researchers, particularly early-stage researchers from conducting projects involving linked administrative data unless permissions are sought well in advance'; Sexton and others (n 77).

VII. Conclusion

This chapter has analysed how the continuous employment of both conflict and bargaining strategic approaches between researchers and data custodians has been recalibrating the UK research data sharing space in the last four decades. From the dawn of 1980s to the dusk of the 2010s, the governance of administrative data sharing for research purposes in the UK public sector seems to have come full circle. It started as an ad hoc, informal activity, initially led and conducted within the confines of public authorities and gradually expanding to a closed circle of entrusted academics until the 2000s. With various actors in the data sharing space evangelising about the importance of widening access to independent social-science researchers for 'efficiency' and 'accountability' purposes, formal data sharing frameworks with concrete requirements and approval stages were established and their use became more widespread due to initiatives like the ADRN. Yet, as we are moving forward, the process of data sharing remains fraught with significant uncertainty, with major public-sector data managers avoiding or actively resisting publicising their criteria and requirements for granting access. With this analysis of the actors of the space in mind, a few central questions arise for the formation of the 'rules of the game' that filter access to government data for social-science research purposes. These questions emanate from the overarching view of the space provided in this chapter and seek to address more specific issues that relate to the other two dimensions of the presently adopted analytical framework, ie institutions and interactions. First, to what extent do such research data sharing institutions as the complex technicalities and legalities of data sharing determine the creation and application of transparent and predictable frameworks in practice? Second, how do the interactions between the actors of this space, mainly government departments, researchers, and intermediary bodies, shape the requirements and processes for data access that actually apply? The next two chapters will elaborate on these questions and articulate empirically informed and context-specific arguments about the shaping of data access frameworks for research and innovation in the UK public sector.

7

Rise of Different Data Sharing Cultures

> From first-hand experience of being in a meeting, asking them to provide data for specific purposes, being told that they could not see where there was any value for them. I think it's very much in the front of their mind in terms of 'what's in it for us'
>
> [Interviewee 31]

> We can see that it can be of interest in a general sense, but truly in the public interest as would the taxpayers expect us to be putting our efforts into this, that's a different thing. We describe this as the 'so what?' questions. We can sometimes see requests for data sharing for something that demonstrates a very interesting methodological question, but of no practical use whatsoever and we must legitimately ask the question: is that in the public interest?
>
> [Interviewee 8]

How do the attitudes, beliefs, and values of government data managers influence the application of data access frameworks? The answer to this question has far-reaching implications for public policy, scientific and innovation advancement, and the very nature of democratic governance in the digital age.

Through extensive interviews with key stakeholders across the UK public sector, I uncover, in this chapter, two central elements that form what I term 'research data sharing cultures'. The first is the 'perception of government data ownership': How do data managers view the data they hold? Is it a public good to be shared for the greater benefit of society, or is it the property of their department to be closely guarded? The second element concerns assumptions about the appropriateness of policy-relevant research: How do data custodians evaluate the alignment of proposed research with their organisational priorities? What role do they believe they should play in shaping research questions and methodologies? Views as to the ownership of administrative data, or as to the desired alignment between independent research and a custodian's policy aims, are often shared collectively. Such views are associated, as it will be shown, with certain tendencies in the application of data sharing frameworks. At times, the result is the establishment of transparent data sharing procedures, whereas, at other times, transparency gives way to entitlement and discretion, resulting in researchers being kept in the dark by data managers. In other cases, these views result in the establishment of particular powers of data managers, such as their right to intervene and co-design the questions that will be posed to the data by the independent researchers.

These cultural factors often operate beneath the surface, yet they wield significant influence over who gets access to data, for what purposes, and under what conditions. They can either facilitate transparent and collaborative research practices or create opaque barriers that hinder scientific inquiry and public scrutiny of government actions. By unpacking these cultural dynamics, I offer crucial insights into the often-invisible forces that shape the production of knowledge in our data-driven society and highlight the need for a more nuanced understanding of the human factors at play in data governance. As we navigate the opportunities and challenges of the big data era, understanding these research data sharing cultures is not just an academic exercise – it is essential for ensuring that the vast troves of government data are leveraged effectively and ethically for the public good. The findings presented here have profound implications for how we design data sharing frameworks, foster trust between government and researchers, and ultimately harness the power of data to address pressing societal challenges. In this chapter, I explore these themes in depth, drawing on real-world examples and experiences from across the UK public sector. The two central elements of 'research data sharing cultures', as well as their influence on the application of data sharing frameworks for research and innovation in the UK public sector, are analysed in turn.

I. Perceptions of Administrative Data 'Ownership': Sharing whose Data?

Some data managers treat government data as a 'public good', much like other types of public infrastructure like roads or parks,[1] that should be used to produce research in the public interest. On the other hand, others treat such data as belonging to them. This division is clearly reflected in the divergent practices in applying data sharing frameworks: managers who view government data as a public good are more likely to establish specific procedures and criteria, becoming accountable to researchers, and the broader public about their data sharing decisions. Managers who treat data as their ownership are more likely to resist accountability, thus avoiding committing themselves to particular data sharing criteria and processes.

A. Data as a 'Public Good': Enabling Research and Scrutinising the Government

There is a growing aspiration among researchers to ensure that government data are to be treated as a common resource. These actors have sought, time and again,

[1] House of Commons Science and Technology Committee, 'The Big Data Dilemma: Fourth Report of Session 2015–16'. Available at: https://publications.parliament.uk/pa/cm201516/cmselect/cmsctech/468/468.pdf.

to negotiate with data managers, with a view to making their view more influential and widespread in the UK public sector. As the following discussion will illustrate, there are two main ideals behind viewing government data as a public good. First, since such data belongs to the public, it should be used in research that will improve our collective knowledge about pressing social and economic challenges. Second, since such data belongs to the public, it should be used to scrutinise the validity of government decisions, as well as the evidence based on which these decisions were taken. A researcher, working with administrative datasets in Scotland, associated this view with communitarian political ideals, originally expressed regarding public-sector data in Scandinavian countries:

> Denmark and Norway are much more oriented around the idea of social communities. The whole thing about the rights of the individual versus the rights of the general public, and getting that balance right. In those countries, more social-minded countries, the balance is geared towards the public.[2]

The Office for National Statistics (ONS) in England has been the torchbearer of this aspiration in the UK. An interviewee, having significant background as both a data analyst and a policymaker for the ONS in England, explained that it is important to think of data availability for research purposes as the *default*, not the aim of a data sharing policy. For them, convincing their colleagues at the Office about this through constant bargaining has been one of their key 'achievements'. After quite a few internal discussions, they recalled that they managed to convince the data managers within the ONS that the data is 'fair game for researchers … if you could come up with a valid reason for using it'.[3] In their view, this was a significant departure from the previous position within the Office, under which researchers had to 'ask the various data holders and then get sign-off from the information asset owners'.[4] They recounted vividly the process of negotiating this change of policy with their colleagues who were responsible for managing the datasets:

> Going around in the department, to the Information Asset Owners … and saying, basically, you have all of this data under your control – how about this, we work on the assumption that all the data is available for research use. Rather than me having to justify use of it, we want you to justify why you can't share it.[5]

Even before the ONS pioneering initiatives, researchers have been going to great lengths to support the broader adoption of this understanding of government data as a shared resource. In some cases, convincing government data managers about the merits of this view may necessitate the adoption of a more conflict-orientated approach from researchers. An interviewee, working as a data analyst for an independent research organisation and with significant experience in negotiating access to Department for Education (DfE) data, admitted that they often aim

[2] Interview with participant nr 41 (2020, virtual).
[3] Interview with participant nr 42 (2020, virtual).
[4] ibid.
[5] ibid.

to 'be hard and vocal' in their critique of education policies.[6] Interestingly, they explained that they would often find an unlikely ally in this effort in the face of DfE officials who were keen on seeing external scrutiny of their policies:

> Actually, many from the department may be welcoming criticism, because it's easier for us to do, rather than carry it out as an internal project.[7]

Another interviewee, having a very similar background, explained that data managers might prefer external use of their data in scrutinising their policies because 'neutral' and 'independent' criticisms of government work often have 'more currency' than internal research.[8] An interviewee, working as a data analyst for the Department for the Economy in Northern Ireland, expressed a similar view. In her view, research data sharing bears great potential in 're-examining' government policies and data custodians should not be afraid of it.[9]

In a similar vein, a policymaker working for the Health and Social Care Department in Wales noted with approval that in recent years people within their organisation have been appreciating the value of government data for public service delivery as a whole.[10] An interviewee, working for the Honest Broker Service (HBS) in Northern Ireland in an information governance capacity, explained that their organisation charges researchers for access to data solely because there is no funding available to 'provide the service free of charge',[11] not as a *quid pro quo*. Another interviewee, working as a data analyst for the Administrative Data Research Centre (ADRC) – Wales and having experience in negotiating access to data in Wales, largely concurred. They characterised Welsh data custodians as 'incredibly open' and receptive to criticism:

> They just want to know what the single version of the truth is. If it shows things are problematic, they will look to see how they can make it better. And they are interested in what can the data tell them.[12]

The data presented here from the four countries of the UK demonstrates that perceiving government data as a 'public good' and a shared resource facilitates widening access to data for research purposes, even if, *or precisely because*, it allows criticism of government policies. As the next sub-section (ii) will show, there are concrete repercussions for the regulation of research data sharing decisions, ie, the establishment of transparent procedures and mechanisms of accountability by data managers who espouse the perception of government data as a common good.

[6] Interview with participant nr 33 (2020, virtual).
[7] ibid.
[8] Interview with participant nr 30 (2020, virtual).
[9] Interview with participant nr 16 (2018, phone).
[10] Interview with participant nr 24 (2019, phone).
[11] Interview with participants nrs 11, 12 and 13 (2018, Belfast).
[12] Interview with participant nr 22 (2019, Swansea).

B. Data as a 'Public Good': Establishing Mechanisms of Accountability

When data managers view government data as a public good, they will often follow a consistent and transparent data sharing procedure. For example, they will set up a precedent system, enable appeals against their decisions and delegate decision-making powers to colleagues or other parties with experience in government data research and innovation.

Interviewees who are currently working, or have worked in the past, for the Office for National Statistics (ONS) elaborated on the Office's steadfast commitment to becoming an accountable data manager. Consistency in decision-making is highly valued to ensure that the same standards are applied to different research applications. In the words of an information governance official, it would 'cause us a problem' if similar project requests were treated in a different manner:

> Say if we had a project that wants to use labour force survey data … and we said yes, and then a year later we had another project request and said no to it, the second researcher would know that we had approved the other one a year ago because it's published on our website, so what's changed?[13]

Another interviewee, working as a data analyst for the ONS, identified consistency as the central driver behind 'centralising and formalising' the decision-making process through the establishment of a 'panel of people from around the organisation' (ie the Microdata Release Panel).[14] To properly observe consistency and streamline decision-making, the ONS, after careful considerations and lengthy internal deliberations, started developing a system of precedent decisions:

> So, over the years, we built up a system of precedent decisions, where we would probably end up about 10% of the requests that were coming in to us actually being considered by the Panel … now we have a written set of precedents, which allow us to make decisions and the understanding is that we can make it as a team, make decisions based on those precedents that the panel had agreed.[15]

There is a two-fold function of this precedent system. First, internally, it allows better co-ordination and application of data sharing decisions, especially when requests are similar to previous requests to use the Office's data. With around. 250 projects currently facilitated within the ONS Virtual Microdata Laboratory,[16] the precedent system facilitates a more expedient approval process:

> We have a lot of these projects, the first one of them gets approved in the full proper process: talking to data owners, going through the panel. Then … when the next

[13] Interview with participant nr 1 (2017, Titchfield).
[14] Interview with participant nr 2 (2017, Titchfield).
[15] ibid.
[16] Interview with participant nr 1 (2017, Titchfield).

> project comes up, my team says we can use these precedents and I then say yes … So, it streamlines the process.[17]

Second, externally, it is a practical illustration of the Office's commitment to transparent decision-making, enabling requesting parties to assess whether the ONS's research data sharing criteria are consistently applied in practice. Transparency and clarity also allow for better negotiations between the ONS and researchers, who are better placed to understand the purpose behind the Office's requirements and potentially even challenge them when it comes to eg methodological preferences or limitations to the allowed data uses.[18]

Apart from establishing a precedent system, the Office's commitment to accountability has been realised through its receptiveness to feedback from the research community, as well as through granting the right to appeal a data manager decision to requesting researchers. Currently, the ONS adopts an informal approach to allowing appeals against its custodians' decisions. The same interviewee mentioned before, working as a data analyst for the ONS, explained that both their own recommendations and the formal decisions of the Microdata Release Panel can be challenged by requesting parties:

> If it was, let's say, my decision, the obvious thing is that the Panel can then reassess my decision. If it is a decision the Panel had already made … they would probably wish to reconsider that if there was more evidence that could be provided … or maybe a clarification on sth … I'm sure that would come back to the Panel and the Panel would just reconsider it.[19]

Essentially, this is less of a hostile appeals process and more of a collaborative, constructive effort to exchange views between the researcher and the decision-maker to improve a project request and increase its chances of approval.[20] As the aspiration for widening access to administrative data for research purposes grows, the Office intends to formalise this appeals process to guarantee that requesting parties will be able to effectively challenge managers' decisions. As an interviewee working as an information governance official mentioned, the Office aspires to have a sophisticated, two-tier system of appeals in place, with researchers being able to first challenge a decision before the ONS's data governance committee and, ultimately, before the National Statistician (who is the head of the ONS).[21] They even considered the possibility of judicial review after that stage, although they admitted that it would be really rare for a project request to reach that stage.

Finally, yet importantly, a critical indication of the ONS's commitment to accountability is the readiness of its data managers to delegate decision-making responsibilities to colleagues who are closer to using the data for research purposes as data analysts. In other words, policymakers, who are the ones formally responsible

[17] Interview with participant nr 1 (2017, Titchfield).
[18] Interview with participant nr 42 (2020, virtual).
[19] Interview with participant nr 2 (2017, Titchfield).
[20] Interview with participant nr 1 (2017, Titchfield).
[21] ibid.

for approval decisions, may delegate such decisions to the technical experts, the data analysts, despite the latter being lower in the organisational hierarchy. Delegation, of course, did not happen overnight, but it took quite a lot of bargaining to be established as a practice. An interviewee, who has worked both as a data analyst and a policymaker for the Office, vividly recounted their experience in negotiating such a delegation of decision-making capacity. They recalled the example of a particular data manager and their efforts in allowing the Office's analysts to perform critical data security assessments with regard to research data sharing:

> Because we know what the research is, what we want to get out of this, we said to the (redacted) team, why don't we do this disclosure control? We could make these decisions quickly – we'll send you what we've done, our decisions, and you can check it. You can keep an eye on this, but, basically, we will do the work … and the responsibility of signing-off something which you don't really necessarily understand.[22]

As the same interviewee recalled, the data managers agreed to this arrangement and, in fact, exercised a light-touch review over the disclosure control reports submitted to them by the Office's analysts.[23] Although this may look like a minor delegation of technical responsibility, the interviewee found it very significant from a symbolic perspective: it brought a 'change in culture' by gaining acceptance of the position that 'the people who are responsible for the research are the best-placed to sign-off the outputs'.[24] If, however, the ONS is the luminary example of establishing accountability mechanisms in the name of maximising the benefits of government data for the common good, how common are such mechanisms in the broader UK public sector?

An interviewee, who has worked as a data analyst for the Department for Education (DfE) in England, hailed the achievement of the Welsh government to be consistent in their data sharing standards, as opposed to England where 'you have different departments, everyone has their own separate arrangements and legislation'.[25] They expressed their hope that England will manage to achieve a similar level of consistency in the future, drawing inspiration from the DfE itself. The DfE takes great pride in being very consistent and transparent in its research data sharing decision-making and it is, arguably, the ministerial department which publishes the most information about its external data shares.[26] This is admitted by another interviewee, who works for an independent research organisation and has worked in the past for the DfE as a data analyst. In their view, the data like the National Pupil Database and the information about the data provided by the DfE to interested researchers is a 'resource like no other in the public sector'.[27]

[22] Interview with participant nr 42 (2020, virtual).
[23] ibid.
[24] ibid.
[25] Interview with participant nr 30 (2020, virtual).
[26] Department for Education, 'DfE external data shares' (18 July 2019). Available at: https://gov.uk/government/publications/dfe-external-data-shares.
[27] Interview with participant nr 33 (2020, virtual).

Beyond being consistent and transparent about their research data sharing decisions, the DfE have been willing to delegate its research data access arrangements to other organisations in recent years.[28] In other words, the DfE have authorised another public body to decide on their behalf about whether particular data sharing requests for research and innovation purposes should be granted. More specifically, they have delegated the responsibility to handle access requests to the Secure Research Service, owned by the ONS.[29] According to an interviewee, many other government departments are considering following DfE's footsteps and delegating decision-making responsibilities to trusted third parties.[30] The image of delegation of data manager responsibilities is corroborated by an administrative data researcher with experience in negotiating data access in Scotland. As they mentioned, the Scottish Government has been aiming to centralise data by handling access to datasets it curates on behalf of its various departments.[31]

Interviewees from the devolved UK countries elaborated on how the mechanism of delegating the responsibility to make data access decisions has been always prevalent in respect of access to health data, which is paradigmatically considered as a common good.[32] An interviewee, working in an information governance capacity for the NHS Wales Informatics Service (NWIS), explained that they have been handling access to research requests 'on behalf and under the instruction of the data custodians'.[33] NWIS, by virtue of their expertise in health data management, are making access decisions on behalf of such data managers as National Health Service Trusts and Hospitals in Wales. When asked whether a research data sharing request would necessitate going back to the data custodians and asking for their approval, they responded in the negative:

> No, not necessarily. We are given that element of control in some respects … For instance, for any research request, we would look at that request, see if it has been through the normal ethics approval and … what are the legal aspects that ensure appropriateness of the data sharing.[34]

A policy-maker for the Health and Social Care Department in Wales added that the existence of 'secure locations' like the SAIL databank are integral to convince organisations to sign-off and delegate their management duties to decide about

[28] Interview with participant nr 30 (2020, virtual).
[29] ibid.
[30] Interview with participant nr 30 (2020, virtual).
[31] Interview with participant nr 35 (2020, virtual).
[32] Understanding Patient Data, 'Putting people at the centre of decisions about patient data'. Available at: https://understandingpatientdata.org.uk/; KH Jones and others, 'The Good, the Bad, the Clunky: Addressing Challenges in Using Administrative Data for Research' (2019) 4(1) *International Journal of Data Population Science* 587.
[33] Interview with participant nr 23 (2019, Cardiff).
[34] ibid.

access.[35] In the Welsh context a data analyst for the Knowledge and Analytical Services (KAS) of the Welsh government noted that such delegation has expanded from health data sharing to statistical research, with the statisticians of the KAS convincing their equivalents within data managers to 'delegate the permission to share data for statistical research purposes'.[36]

An information governance official, working for the Electronic Data and Research Information Service in Scotland, clarified that it is the Scottish Government's aspiration to adopt a similar rationale (ie delegating access decisions) in the interest of streamlining access to government data in the broader public sector. They mentioned Scottish education data as one of the first examples where this has been made possible, advocating for a 'graded approach in terms of the governance' when it comes to data managers that may be more reticent to delegate responsibilities.[37] Another interviewee, working in an information governance capacity for the HBS in Northern Ireland, noticed a similar trend of delegating management responsibilities to other trusted organisations. They pointed out that they are currently exploring their options with a view to expanding the delegation of access decisions, from health data sharing where it already happens in Northern Ireland as in Wales (with NWIS), to broader government data research.[38]

Beyond the examples mentioned here, information is scarcer about the employment of similar accountability mechanisms within the public sector, although it seems that several public bodies are likely to rely on precedent systems and allow appeals of their decisions, even if not formally. A policymaker for the Economic and Social Research Council pointed out that many data managers often rely on their previous decisions, in the interest of 'simplifying the complex requirements of the legislative landscape'.[39] Another interviewee, working for the KAS of the Welsh government, suggested that they aim to organise their previous decisions so that they can 'build on them' when a new request is submitted.[40]

The data presented here illustrate a strong association between viewing government data as the 'public good' and establishing accountability mechanisms to ensure that research data sharing decisions will be consistent and transparent. Bodies like the Office for National Statistics in England, as well as others in the devolved countries, have been mentioned here as examples of this type of, facilitative for research and innovation, data sharing culture. Nonetheless, as it has been shown, this perception is by no means unrivalled. As the following sub-sections will demonstrate, a conflicting perception of government data ownership is also very salient in influencing the regulation of data sharing decisions.

[35] Interview with participant nr 24 (2019, phone).
[36] Interview with participant nr 26 (2019, Cardiff).
[37] Interview with participant nr 36 (2020, virtual).
[38] Interview with participant nr 12 (2018, Belfast).
[39] Interview with participant nr 19 (2018, Swindon).
[40] Interview with participant nr 26 (2019, Cardiff).

II. Data as 'Property': 'Our' Data and 'Their' Research

Not all data managers share a perception of government data as a shared, common resource that should be utilised for the broader public benefit. To many, government data is 'owned' by the body responsible for its collection and management. Such bodies often express strong ownership attitudes, treating researchers as external parties who are interested in benefiting from their property. As it will be shown, strong perceptions of government data ownership are contingent on context and organisational mission, with large ministerial departments like the Department for Work and Pensions (DWP) or the Department for Education (DfE) being paradigmatic examples.

An interviewee, who has worked for the DfE in England as a data analyst, provided some background to perceptions of government data as the property of the department. To them, the nature of the data is really important; education data may be seen more naturally as public record compared to data related to income or taxes:

> In education, people's data are almost public record, whereas eg DWP or HMRC data, it's a far more sensitive thing for a department to be releasing people's earnings data … People expect that if they are reporting their incomes to HMRC, then the HMRC would hold on to that data and not go anywhere else.[41]

One common strategy of data managers, with a view to ensure that they fully determine the uses of data by researchers, is to reserve the right to unilaterally revoke their consent to the data sharing agreement and, thus, block data access at any time. An interviewee, working for the ADRC – Northern Ireland as a data analyst, recalled that already agreed upon projects often see delays due to last-minute objections by data managers. Sometimes, these objections are whimsical rather than comprehensively explained, reflecting a strong attitude of entitlement on behalf of the custodians:

> In this project, we still don't have a data sharing agreement signed, because there was a change of staff … and the new guy didn't agree with the older guy's policy and was much more conservative and saying 'you are not having it'. And he is still saying 'you are not having it'.[42]

The same interviewee attributed this attitude to the tendency to see government data as 'the property of the Department', noting that it is the exception to find data managers who 'really like research and think it's worth doing'.[43]

Another interviewee, working as a data analyst for the DfE in Northern Ireland, conceded that a data sharing agreement 'does not necessarily guarantee access to

[41] Interview with participant nr 33 (2020, virtual).
[42] Interview with participant nr 15 (2018, virtual).
[43] ibid.

data'.[44] Data managers may very well revoke their consent to a research data sharing process, without necessarily providing a justification for their withdrawal. This is corroborated by an interviewee, working in an information governance capacity for the Northern Irish Statistics and Research Agency (NISRA). They clarified that a data sharing agreement does not preclude custodians from 'vetoing' projects or particular variables that researchers were interested in accessing.[45] The picture is not different in other UK countries: the DfE in England still reserves the right to refuse access even after having outsourced their data access arrangements to the ONS,[46] Welsh data custodians retain the right to 'review any proposal to use the data'[47] and Scottish data managers 'can potentially turn around and say "no, we are not going to provide the data".'[48]

To what extent can we hope for change in these attitudes? An interviewee, working for the Welcome Trust (WT) as a policy officer, expressed some scepticism about the progress towards viewing government data as a 'public good':

> There is definitely further to go before reaching the point where data will be viewed as a public good and shared resource. There is definitely a dominant view that data is something on which departments have rights on to allow them get credit.[49]

Viewing administrative data as their own property, data managers are more likely to feel entitled to provide fewer justifications when deciding whether to grant access or not for research and innovation purposes. What practical implications does this have for the regulation of data sharing decisions? As the following sub-section will demonstrate, the particular perception of government data as 'property' is associated with organisational resistance to accountability mechanisms such as the ones established by data managers who view government data as a 'shared resource' and a common good.

A. Data as 'Property': Resisting Accountability

Managers who feel strongly entitled to decide how 'their' data will be used by researchers tend to prefer informal data sharing arrangements over formalised procedures, avoiding binding themselves to publicly available decision-making steps. Informality encourages researchers to bargain with data custodians to achieve access to data. During such bargaining processes, however, the power often lies with the one holding the resource under negotiation, ie, the data.

One of the most common indicators of entitlement is when managers are not inclined to grant the right to appeal an access decision to requesting parties.

[44] Interview with participant nr 16 (2018, phone).
[45] Interview with participant nr 9 (2018, Belfast).
[46] Interview with participant nr 30 (2020, virtual).
[47] Interview with participant nr 21 (2019, Swansea).
[48] Interview with participant nr 36 (2020, virtual).
[49] Interview with participant nr 17 (2018, London).

An interviewee, working for the DWP as a policymaker, conceded that there is no appeals process available to researchers:

> Nothing in place at the moment … there's not really anyone to which you could really appeal and say could you just have a look what they've decided.[50]

To what extent does this reluctance to provide an appeals process reflect broader practices in the UK public sector? This is often the case, according to another interviewee, who works for HM Revenue and Customs (HMRC) (custodian body) in a policy-making capacity. They associated this reluctance with ministerial departments, which often require the ministers to approve before granting access to their data. In such cases, allowing an appeal against a ministerial decision would provide scope for proving that government ministers judged erroneously a particular request. This turns the question of appeals into a political issue, which 'makes it a bit more complicated and whimsical'.[51] An interviewee, who works in an information governance capacity for the Northern Irish Statistics Research Agency in Northern Ireland, noted that 'nobody has tried to formally appeal or complain against an owner decision'.[52] Another interviewee, who works as a data analyst for an independent research organisation and having experience in negotiating access to DfE data, concurred. Asked whether she has ever challenged a data manager decision, they admitted that:

> Mostly you have to conform to what is being asked … I don't think we could not find a way to work around some things (in doing the research), there's always been a solution.[53]

Researchers with experience in negotiating access with Scottish data managers corroborated the widespread lack of appeals processes. Three researchers who are affiliated with the ADRC – Scotland conceded that:

> To challenge a data custodian decision would be very difficult – they are data controllers, they are really all powerful.[54]
>
> They [data custodians] are really powerful – we would pretty much agree to whatever they said, because we wanted the data.[55]
>
> I don't know how you would ever come back on that, if someone said we aren't going to give you the data … You wouldn't really have a choice I guess.[56]

Refusing researchers the right to appeal a decision is indicative of the entitlement a data manager feels over 'their' data. It is not, however, the only indication of this entitlement. Many managers express their ownership entitlement by refraining from publishing any or sufficient information about their data sharing procedures,

[50] Interview with participant nr 8 (2017, Sheffield).
[51] Interview with participant nr 32 (2020, virtual).
[52] Interview with participant nr 9 (2018, Belfast).
[53] Interview with participant nr 40 (2020, virtual).
[54] Interview with participant nr 34 (2020, virtual).
[55] Interview with participant nr 35 (2020, virtual).
[56] Interview with participant nr 29 (2020, phone).

effectively keeping requesting parties in the dark. An interviewee, who currently works for an independent research organisation and has worked for the DfE as a data analyst in the past, admitted that they are able to navigate the Department's data access requirements because of their experience working for it:

> When we started applying, it was a little bit like having to guess … The advice from DfE would be quite limited on that and we had to guess … The information would not really flow appropriately many times … If you do it for the first time, then good luck, I don't think you will necessarily navigate this, at least not after a long time.[57]

An interviewee, who works for an independent research organisation as a data analyst, agreed. They complained that the DfE's data sharing process is 'not at all predictable'.[58] As they explained, the default position is that the decision-makers do not provide much information about the decision-making process, with the researchers having to 'chase it along'.[59] Even after two decades of experience in negotiating access to DfE data, the interviewee conceded that they still have 'no idea' about the different roles of the officials making data access decisions on the DfE's behalf.[60]

In a similar vein, a researcher, who is affiliated with the ADRC – Scotland, reflected on their experience in negotiating access to DWP data. They recalled that, during negotiations, they were 'not so clear' on the Department's requirements and the progress of the request, even though they had regular meetings with DWP officials. Interestingly, the interviewee did not attribute responsibility for the lack of transparency to the DWP analysts which were present in the meetings: these analysts were found to be 'very helpful and progressive'.[61] Delays seemingly 'had to do with other dependencies … it was difficult to gauge what the priorities were'.[62] The problem, from the interviewee's perspective, was that data managers were only 'disclosing information partially' about the request's progress,[63] making it very challenging for her to estimate why things are not moving forward:

> I still haven't got the full picture of how many (decision-making) layers are there, because … there was only partial information that was disclosed … When we were lifting the first barrier, we didn't know how many barriers we would have until we reached that point.[64]

DWP decisions, in this interviewee's narration, resemble a Russian doll: the more barriers researchers were overcoming, the more they were faced with novel

[57] Interview with participant nr 33 (2020, virtual).
[58] Interview with participant nr 40 (2020, virtual).
[59] ibid.
[60] ibid.
[61] Interview with participant nr 38 (2020, virtual).
[62] ibid.
[63] ibid.
[64] ibid.

challenges and unknown difficulties. The same interviewee clarified that this is far from exclusive in the case of the DWP. In their broader experience in the UK, there were many cases were there was 'no information from the data *owners*, no interaction' (emphasis added).[65]

Another researcher with experience in negotiating data access with Scottish data managers, recounted their own difficulties in understanding what is required from them:

> We kind of assumed that once everybody said yes and signed some contracts, that was going to be it. We did not realise it would be a whole process of negotiating the contracts, negotiating the particular conditions of access etc. There was a whole kind of middle section that we were not aware of.[66]

They complained that most (non-health) data managers in Scotland do not have 'any discoverability for their datasets',[67] making it essential that interested parties engage in a relationship with specific persons within the data managing body in the interest of understanding the requirements and, ultimately, getting access. This relationship often requires delicate balancing between the priorities of researchers vis à vis the priorities of managers, an exercise that is not always facilitated by the information provided to researchers by managers. An interviewee, working for the Economic and Social Research Council (ESRC) in a policy-making capacity confirmed that the most common complaint they get from their funded researchers is that the latter 'never get a clear answer back' from data managers with regard to the status of their access request.[68]

Considering the 'perceptions of government data ownership' on the whole, the data from the four countries of the UK presented in this section illustrate the association between particular attitudes and the establishment of accountability mechanisms and procedures, or lack thereof. Managers who are committed to viewing government data as a shared resource are very likely to introduce transparent data sharing procedures and accountability mechanisms. They will do so in the interest of achieving transparency and consistency in the way in which they manage access to a public good. By contrast, managers who feel that government data belongs to their organisations are much more likely to express their strong feelings of entitlement by refusing to provide reasons behind their decisions, as well as relying on more informal and less accountable data sharing processes. While perceptions of data ownership are very strong in influencing the application of data sharing frameworks in the UK public sector, there is another significant constituent of the dominant research data sharing culture: policy relevance of research using government data.

[65] ibid; even the word 'data owners' used by the interviewee is indicative of the attitudes of entitlement expressed by data custodians in this relationship.

[66] Interview with participant nr 29 (2020, phone).

[67] ibid.

[68] Interview with participant nr 19 (2018, Swindon).

B. Policy Relevance of Government Data Research: 'What is in it for Us'?

Although there are some notable exceptions like the ONS in England, whose very organisational mission is to promote data-driven research and knowledge, most data managers evaluate the alignment of a proposed request for research and innovation data access with their policy priorities and their capacity to deliver them.

When managers are satisfied that research is compatible with their policy aims, they are more likely to set up a data sharing process, even committing themselves to specific decision-making steps. When, however, they are unclear as to the relevance or the compatibility of a proposed research request with their policy agendas, inertia, reluctance, and caution are likely to emerge, hampering progress in the establishment or the transparent implementation of data sharing frameworks. This section unpacks the ways in which policy relevance to research concretely accelerates or hampers the establishment of data sharing procedures.

C. Policy-Relevance within Data Sharing Frameworks: Brigading Research Projects

The superiority of policy-relevant research has increasingly been reflected in the application of data sharing frameworks, shaping the conditions under which data managers allow access to government data. With researchers increasingly grasping the need to incentivise data managers by demonstrating the policy relevance of their projects, two main strategies to facilitate 'appropriate' and 'legitimate' research that have emerged. First, data managers have been *brigading* research projects, organising requests around certain themes that align well with their policy priorities. These themes operate as proxies for the notion of the 'public interest' and effectively filter access to government data for research and innovation purposes. Second, data managers have been *co-designing* research projects, demanding that they are involved in the construction of the research questions and, in many cases, the research methodology. Alluding to popular catchphrases like 'research co-production' and 'research with impact', also perceived as important for high-quality research outputs, data sharing frameworks, by requiring co-design, seek to steer independent research projects in a direction that is beneficial for data managers.

To start with brigading research projects, data sharing frameworks are structured around a few key areas of policy interest to the particular data manager. An interviewee, working for the DWP, explained that, in their department, it is considered really 'wasteful' to supply data for 'individual, isolated' research projects.[69]

[69] Interview with participant nr 7 (2017, Sheffield).

If the data sharing policy is focused, instead, on some key themes, then future requests will require 'very similar datasets, a little bit further down the line' and the DWP's analysts will be able to provide them easily by just 'rerunning the code and producing a slightly updated dataset'.[70] Another interviewee, who has negotiated access with the DWP, confirmed that the department has communicated to her a document with 'areas of research interest',[71] within which she had to frame her research project. An interviewee, who has worked for the Office for National Statistics (ONS) as a data analyst, explained that not brigading projects around certain key areas means that 'you're going to have a large cost for one project and that project is not clearly going to be of benefit to the organisation that is spending the money on that'.[72]

Where do these 'key areas' come from? The same interviewee provided some background on the construction of the key themes around which a data sharing framework is developed. They clarified that a data manager's 'list of strategic objectives' is an essential point of reference for developing such key areas of research interest.[73] These objectives may include boosting productivity and welfare, combatting inequality and unemployment etc. From these broad goals, the data managing body would develop some distinct directions of a research agenda, potentially adding some concrete research questions that are of interest to the department – eg inquiring into what the relationship between unemployment and reoffending is.[74] The researchers would, then, have to make a compelling case for how their projects are well-aligned with the data manager's main areas of interest. Will this be assessed very rigorously? According to the interviewee, yes and no. On the one hand, it is important to clearly explain the relevance of research to policymaking. On the other hand, it may very well be the case that indirect evidence of serving the relevant policy aims will suffice. In their words:

> It's not necessarily that you will directly prove that you will raise productivity, but it's to show awareness that you know this is what they have been trying to achieve … I can't tell you that this piece of work has changed your goal, but it's clearly contributing to the strategic goal as a body of work.[75]

Another interviewee, who has worked for HMRC as a policymaker, reflected on the creation of their department's 'data sharing strategy' and the need to concentrate focus on specific areas of policy interest. They remembered that the production of this strategy was the product of lengthy internal organisational deliberations, which often involved delicate balancing of the interests of the different parts of

[70] ibid.

[71] Interview with participant nr 38 (2020, virtual); it is quite striking that this document was not available in the public domain until 2018.

[72] Interview with participant nr 42 (2020, virtual).

[73] ibid.

[74] P Jones and P Elias, 'Administrative Data as a Research Resource: A Selected Audit' (Report to the ESRC) (2006) 17.

[75] Interview with participant nr 42 (2020, virtual).

the organisation. As they recalled, the Executive Committee of the HMRC had identified a risk in the department 'not exploiting data as best or as effectively as it could do',[76] due to different lines of duty within the HMRC adopting different priorities when sharing data. The strategy was devised to ensure 'a more strategic approach from a departmental view' with regard to using the HMRC's data assets and produce 'genuine public benefit for the department and other departments'.[77] Compliance with tax regulations, managing debt and counter-fraud were some of the key areas of interest, with researchers having to make the case about how their proposed projects will contribute to the HMRC's understanding of these policy issues.

Data managers in the three other UK countries seem to be even more familiar than English managers with the practice of requiring conformity with specific research 'themes' within their data sharing frameworks. An interviewee, working for the ADRC – Northern Ireland, clarified that their organisation had reached 'agreements in principle' around specific areas of research interest with Northern Irish data custodians, requiring that researchers who want to access data are 'interested in that kind of data'.[78] Another interviewee, who has worked for the same body in a policy-making capacity, explained that such a thematic approach to research data sharing has been a constant element of the data sharing landscape in Northern Ireland. They explained that there were four main, broadly conceived, areas of interest for the Northern Irish Government (as a data manager): 'migration', 'education', 'benefits' and 'health'.[79] As another interviewee, explained, research requests would have to fall under these broad areas, even if meaning that 'researchers are not going to have as free a hand in determining what kinds of projects must be taken forward'.[80] The idea has traditionally been, as another interviewee noted, that independent researchers will 'make do' with what is available:

> Once the dataset is available, researchers will find something to do with it. They will find a corner that hasn't been looked at. If the datasets are curated and kept, they will do something with it.[81]

Like their Northern Irish counterparts, Welsh data sharing participants do seem privy to the significance of brigading research projects around certain key areas of policy interests. An interviewee, who works in a policy-making capacity for the SAIL Databank, provided some background to the historical establishment of the databank back in 2005. They recalled that the Welsh Government was really keen to promote 'thematic research areas', through 'infrastructure support services' that will be able to stimulate ongoing engagement with these areas.[82] The SAIL

[76] Interview with participant nr 32 (2020, Oxford).
[77] ibid.
[78] Interview with participant nr 9 (2018, Belfast).
[79] Interview with participant nr 10 (2018, Belfast).
[80] Interview with participant nr 14 (2018, Belfast).
[81] Interview with participant nr 15 (2018, virtual).
[82] Interview with participant nr 21 (2019, Swansea).

Databank was funded by such an infrastructure. As the interviewee explained, a similar 'themed' approach is currently followed by the ADRC – Wales around the following areas of policy interest: 'housing', 'homelessness', 'mental health' and 'children'.[83] They explained that the thematic approach allows Welsh data managers to see that research can produce 'clear benefits' for them, in the sense of a 'return of their investment' in putting in resources to enable such data sharing to happen.[84] An interviewee, working for the ADRC – Wales as a data analyst, confirmed that it would be the 'standard research approach' to:

> Undertake a thematic research project, produce a research paper and … then take that paper to a policy area and say are you interested.[85]

Welsh data managers, the data analyst explained, see this as 'very much a quid pro quo':

> I am approaching you, you are a government department, I want to know what projects would benefit you. I will work with you on those projects, you will share data with me to do those projects and at the end we will establish a relationship where you are happy to provide data in the future.[86]

Making certain areas of policy interest public enables this research data sharing collaboration to happen. Interviewees working for the Welsh government provided further justifications for this approach. An interviewee, working for the Health and Social Care department of the Welsh Government as a policymaker, claimed that 'themes' provide the necessary accountability to evaluate 'how a good system needs to run and support research and innovation in the long term rather than on a project-by-project basis'.[87] Themes provide the necessary coherence and overarching logic, by reference to which the contribution of individual research projects to collective knowledge will be assessed. A data analyst who works for the Knowledge and Analytical Services (custodian body) of the Welsh Government, added that this coherence is really integral to make research seem 'serious' and appeal more to all stakeholders, including higher-ups in the government.[88] They noted that this ability of government datasets to be organised around certain themes and then be curated, retained and reused in future research is their greatest strength compared to other sources of data like surveys. As they explained:

> Ministers are more likely to fund something if there is an ongoing admin infrastructure underneath it than just a one-off survey or even repeated surveys after certain intervals. They can see the benefit of having an admin data source underpinning all of that that you could then model the survey on.[89]

[83] ibid.
[84] ibid.
[85] Interview with participant nr 22 (2019, Swansea).
[86] ibid.
[87] Interview with participant nr 24 (2019, phone).
[88] Interview with participant nr 25 (2019, Cardiff).
[89] ibid.

Scottish data sharing participants sketched a substantially similar picture. An interviewee, working for the ADRC (intermediary body) – Scotland as a policy-maker, explained that introducing the thematic approach to research was one of the key changes from the Administrative Data Research Network (ADRN) to its successor investment, the Administrative Data Research (ADR) UK:

> Under ADRN, you went to the research centre with your project, and if it's accepted it came back to be implemented as a project, but nothing is working like that under ADR UK. Under ADR UK, we need to specify the projects first, and get funding for those, and the projects are run by the researchers who have been brought on board across Scotland.[90]

Another interviewee, who has worked in a consulting role for the ADRC – Scotland, a body which aims to facilitate government data access for research, expressed relief over this change and the introduction of the thematic approach. She welcomed the Scottish Government's 'greater role in terms of data acquisition and research focus', stressing that it was a 'real struggle' when researchers asked the ADRC to establish on its own initiative a data sharing procedure with the government.[91]

Brigading research projects around specific themes that are of policy interest is, to use the words of a policymaker working for the Economic and Social Research Council, an effective way to 'steer researchers towards the big questions that the government departments would have'.[92] The perception of policy-relevant research as more appropriate, however, would not only be satisfied with a delineation of the research topic. To make sure that research addresses their worries and interests appropriately, data managers have sought to co-design the research projects to which they would provide data.

D. Policy-Relevance within Data Sharing Frameworks: Co-Designing Research Projects

Research 'co-design' or 'co-production' has been a buzzword in the social-science academic discourse for some time.[93] It hints at the involvement of real-world stakeholders, about whom the research is, in developing the scope and the parameters of the project.[94] Research evaluation frameworks, like the UK's Research Excellence Framework, recognise 'co-production' as a way of demonstrating the

[90] Interview with participant nr 31 (2020, virtual).
[91] Interview with participant nr 34 (2020, virtual).
[92] Interview with participant nr 19 (2018, Swindon).
[93] T Zamenopoulos and K Alexiou, 'Co-design As Collaborative Research' (2018) (Connected Communities Foundation Series, Bristol). Available at: http://oro.open.ac.uk/58301/1/Co-Design_CCFoundationSeries_PUBLISHED.pdf.
[94] R White and H van Koten, 'Co-designing for Sustainability: Strategizing Community Carbon Emission Reduction Through Socio-ecological Innovation' (2016) 19(1) *The Design Journal* 25.

'real-world impact' of research.[95] Data managers are not blind to the appeal of impact to researchers, especially academic ones, and often invoke it to enshrine a right to co-determine the research questions and the methodology used by the researchers within their data sharing frameworks.

The DWP is a prime example of a data manager who seeks to co-design research projects before allowing access to its data. The department's input may, in some cases, go as far as minimise the researchers' own contribution to the substantive content of the project. An interviewee, who has worked in the past for the ONS and is currently in academia, elaborated on the process of co-designing a research project with both departments. Worried that they would struggle to access government data, they explained that they first approached the ONS and the DWP, before having a concrete idea about their research questions.[96] After getting the buy-in of the departments, the researchers established a 'government stakeholder group', essentially deferring the research questions to the data custodians:

> What we're going to do is develop this and have the government departments tell us where they want to go … sometimes you're concentrating too much on the academic goals, and the small-level – 'wouldn't this be really interesting as a research project?', whereas we started by saying 'what are you interested in? what do you need to know? what is your constraint?'[97]

The interviewee described this experience of getting feedback from the data custodians as 'really useful', even if they conceded that they must now 'put in place a clearer goal':

> The thing is we got all these government departments to sign up for this, but we didn't actually think very much about the research goals. We said, basically, help us support this, we are going to put all of this data together and then we can do all these fantastic things. We haven't actually said we are going to do a particular thing! We hadn't thought about that![98]

Another interviewee, who has also negotiated access to DWP data as a researcher, reported another radical intervention to the substance of the proposed research. More specifically, the DWP convinced the researchers to redesign the substantive focus of the project, making the health impact of benefit sanctions a central part of the research questions instead of the original focus, which was on educational outcomes for children whose parents had received sanctions. The interviewee confirmed that this 'was not the original focus we were interested in',[99] yet admitted that changing their original focus was required to align their interests with those of the department. They downplayed the importance of this change by

[95] G Chowdhury and others, 'Measuring the Impact of Research: Lessons from the UK's Research Excellence Framework 2014' (2016) 11(6) Public Library of Science ONE.

[96] Interview with participant nr 42 (2020, virtual).

[97] ibid.

[98] ibid.

[99] Interview with participant nr 38 (2020, virtual).

mentioning that health impact 'was part of the wider research programme, it was ok'.[100] Nonetheless, the promises of smooth data access have not been fulfilled in this particular case, with the researchers still waiting for the necessary permissions by the department for over a year:

> It's a set of research questions that DWP analysts themselves have committed to address, but, somehow, I don't know what happened, we are still waiting for their support. It was supposed to be a quick win ….[101]

A data analyst for an independent research organisation, conceded that they often have 'no say' about the scope of the research questions.[102] Although they claimed that their organisation still pursues their independent research aims, they admitted that accessing data for an independent project is often really difficult, and using 'whatever is available' as part of an agreement with the DWP is common practice and, often, the only option if they are to do research using government data.[103] A similar experience is recounted by a data analyst who works for the ADRC – Northern Ireland. As they explained, in response to data managers' attempts to shape the research questions, researchers have had to 'come back and completely rework their applications'.[104] This would, in some cases, mean that the projects would change substantively:

> Maybe (they would then) answer research questions that aren't as specific as they would have liked. Some researchers … have gone back and reframed their proposal as a Northern Ireland Longitudinal study … with a view to branch out to a larger, ADRN study.[105]

An interviewee, working for the ADRC in Northern Ireland as a policy official, described a similar state of affairs:

> We have experiences of projects being changed and tweaked, because the data provider is like, no, no, you can ask this, but you can't ask that. You can set this hypothesis, but you can't check this one. An independent researcher will feel, you've changed my whole research question, this is not what I wanted to ask, how is that independent?[106]

This is not to say that data managers will always be available to accommodate requests from researchers. In some cases, such requests may not be feasible from a technical perspective. Still, the interviewee implied that it will often be the custodians' policy priorities, rather than objective technical difficulties, behind the rejection of a particular disclosure. Even when data managers do not go as far as writing the research questions from scratch or making researchers change their focus, they may still influence the construction of the proposed research projects

[100] ibid.
[101] ibid.
[102] Interview with participant nr 40 (2020, virtual).
[103] ibid.
[104] Interview with participant nr 14 (2018, Belfast).
[105] ibid.
[106] Interview with participant nr 10 (2018, Belfast).

and seek to 'co-design' them. Another interviewee, who has negotiated access with the Scottish Government, noted that their colleagues have received nudges to 'target this other population or this subset of population', despite their research initially selecting different variables.[107] A similar practice in Northern Ireland is to hold meetings between the researchers and the data managers, where the latter advise the former on 'issues of disclosure and data security … as well as on what they would be interested in in terms of policy impact'.[108]

Coming back to Scotland, a researcher, who has negotiated access with Police Scotland, reflected on their experience. They referred to a project, which originated in a 'roundtable meeting' of academics with data managers from the Scottish National Crime Agency and Police Scotland. The interviewee acknowledged that the data managers respected the researchers' independence, but there were indirect ways of steering them towards their preferred way of designing the project. For example, they would be less enthusiastic and keen on moving things forward, unless the researchers would come closer to their view about the way the research would be undertaken. When the researchers remained firm to their views, the project came to a standstill:

> I think this project was not quite what they wanted, and not quite what we wanted, but it would make us both happy enough for people to share data. And, in the end, it all sort of fell apart because we couldn't agree what specifically our research questions were.[109]

Speaking about the same data custodian, ie Police Scotland, another interviewee, who works as a policy official for the ADRC – Scotland, reported similar difficulties. They mention that one of the researchers, who is affiliated with the ADRC, tried to engage with them over a long time to access their data. It took quite some time to reach this agreement, which was conditioned upon the data manager's right to 'co-produce' the research:

> There have been 35 meetings over 4 years and the result is that now Police Scotland are going to work with us on the co-production of projects … At this moment, as we speak, they are setting up a couple of cautious projects to test the water.[110]

The same interviewee mentioned that the Ministry of Defence was also very keen to co-design with ADRC – Scotland a project using veteran data. In this case, it was not only the data custodians who participated in this process, but also other stakeholders and 'representatives of the veterans' community'.[111] The ADRC policy-maker explained that after agreeing on some 'very simple questions' with the custodians and the stakeholders, it will now be for the researchers to make the questions 'more academic' so as to satisfy 'fundamental academic rigour' for

[107] Interview with participant nr 29 (2020, phone).
[108] Interview with participant nr 14 (2018, Belfast).
[109] Interview with participant nr 35 (2020, virtual).
[110] Interview with participant nr 31 (2020, virtual).
[111] ibid.

publication purposes.[112] In other words, instead of starting with an independent research question and then seeking to clarify its policy impact, administrative data researchers often have to start with a policy question and then seek to clarify its interest as an academic research question and the scientific rigour they should apply to its study to meet academic standards.

Like perceptions of government data ownership and their related entitlement attitudes, conventional assumptions about the policy relevance of research on government data effectively filter access to data for researchers. Researchers can try to oppose this or to bargain their way out of too many interventions to their research project. Nonetheless, if they want to get data access, researchers may eventually have to respect interventions as a legitimate aspect of the data sharing procedure.

III. Conclusion: The Salience of 'Research Data Sharing Cultures' for Regulating Decisions

In the UK public sector, access to data for researchers is a privilege, not a right and, as such, it is subject to the unwritten, cultural forces which were presented in this chapter. Although there is a sophisticated legal framework governing access to public-sector data by independent researchers, presented in the previous chapters, the rules that effectively regulate this conduct are non-legal and non-codified. As it has been shown, such rules are not necessarily the outcome of democratic processes, as is normally the case with legislative law-making, but are often produced by the organisations who bargain and clash with one another in the day-to-day workings of the research data sharing space.

Data managers take advantage of the interpretative latitude afforded to them by a legal framework which does not regulate either government data ownership, or government data access in a prescriptive manner, filling the gaps in the way they see fit. Not all data managers subscribe to the same conventions and assumptions, as I have demonstrated in this chapter, nor do their data sharing practices form a uniform response to the novel challenge of utilising government data to create evidence-based research. Nonetheless, I have presented how their cultural approaches to research data sharing are very effective in shaping the way in which they will apply data sharing frameworks. These cultural approaches may be interlinked: eg it is reasonable to assume that managers with strong perceptions of data ownership are also very likely to demand clear relevance of research to their policy priorities, resisting accountability and exercising sovereign rights to shape research questions. In any case, there are numerous ways in which the constituents of the 'research data sharing culture' are associated with the application of specific research data sharing frameworks, enhancing or confining the powers of specific actors.

[112] ibid.

8

Low-level Interactions and Communicative Possibilities

> The political situation at the time was also more sensitive. That naturally makes any minister more cautious. On occasion, getting stuff out was less about 'Is this good research?' and more about 'What's the politics going on now?'. Nothing is unaffected by the political side.
>
> [Interviewee 33]
>
> I mentioned the informal there and I think that actually was crucial in moving forward the work. Lots of things just happened to align … Through individuals …, we were really able to start moving forward, thinking how we would enable the data to be made available for linkage and later for analysis.
>
> [Interviewee 34]

In the complex world of government data sharing for research and innovation, the most pivotal decisions are often made not in boardrooms or legislative chambers, but in the day-to-day interactions of those on the front lines. I now turn to a critical yet often overlooked aspect of data governance: the role of low-level interactions and informal communications in shaping the landscape of data access. In doing so, the analysis peels back the curtain to reveal the hidden mechanisms that truly drive change. High-level policymakers may not be, ultimately, the primary architects of data sharing frameworks. Instead, the work of data analysts and other ground-level actors can have profound implications for the accessibility and utilisation of government data.

Through extensive interviews with 42 data sharing participants across the UK, I uncover key insights that reshape our understanding of data governance. I present the central role of data analysts as expert mediators and de facto decision-makers, often wielding more influence than their formal positions might suggest. The research highlights the power of informal, relationship-based communications in overcoming bureaucratic hurdles that might otherwise stymie data sharing initiatives. Furthermore, the iterative, small-scale nature of interactions that incrementally shape data sharing policies, often far removed from official channels, is sketched.

These findings have far-reaching implications for how we conceptualize and implement data sharing initiatives. They suggest that effective data governance requires not just top-down policies, but also bottom-up approaches that empower and leverage the expertise of those closest to the data. This realisation challenges policymakers and organisational leaders to rethink their strategies for fostering innovation and collaboration in the data ecosystem. Moreover, important questions about transparency, accountability, and democratic oversight in the age of big data are raised. If crucial decisions about data access are being made through informal channels, how can we ensure that public interest is being served? How might we redesign governance structures to better reflect the reality of how data sharing occurs? These are not merely academic questions but pressing concerns for anyone involved in the creation or implementation of data policies. Readers are invited to reconsider their assumptions about how data governance works in practice. As we continue to grapple with the immense potential and challenges of big data, the lessons gleaned from this research will be useful in shaping a more effective, equitable, and innovative data sharing landscape. I proceed from unpacking the role of data analysts as the prominent network behind these interactions, before discussing the nature of the interactions themselves.

I. The Central Role of Data Analysts in Data Access Regulation for Research and Innovation

In terms of organisational hierarchy, *analysts* are the lowest-ranked officials in the process of data sharing for research and innovation. They perform technical tasks and facilitate the actual execution of data disclosure, yet they do not really decide if such a disclosure will happen. *Policymakers* are those who weigh the risks and the benefits related to a proposed data share and ultimately give the green light, provided they have received assurances from *information governance officials* that the disclosure is consistent with legal and other governance (eg ethical) requirements. Perhaps understandably, then, data analysts are not celebrated enough in the public-sector data sharing literature. The academic literature,[1] as well as reviews of the data sharing practices of public bodies in the UK by the government or by civil society bodies,[2] mainly discuss the role of higher-level officials within data managers and other data sharing participants. Data analysts are often perceived as merely the technical executors of the policy directions around enabling or constraining data sharing for research and innovation.

[1] Eg G Laurie and L Stevens, 'Developing a Public Interest Mandate for the Governance and Use of Administrative Data in the United Kingdom' (2016) 43 *Journal of Law & Society* 360; P Jackson, 'From ''Intruders' to 'Partners'': The Evolution of the Relationship Between the Research Community and Sources of Official Administrative Data' in N Crato and P Paruolo (eds), *Data-Driven Policy Impact Evaluation* (Springer 2019) 17; MJ Taylor, 'Legal Bases for Disclosing Confidential Patient Information for Public Health: Distinguishing between Health Protection and Health Improvement' (2015) 23(3) *Medical Law Review* 348.

[2] Law Commission, `Data Sharing Between Public Bodies: A Scoping Report' (2014). Available at: www.lawcom.gov.uk/app/uploads/2015/03/lc351_data-sharing.pdf; R Thomas and M Walport, `Data Sharing Review Report' (2008). Available at: https://webarchive.nationalarchives.gov.uk/+/http:/www.justice.gov.uk/docs/data-sharing-review.pdf; REFORM, 'Sharing the Benefits: How to Use Data Effectively in The Public Sector'. Available at: https://reform.uk/research/sharing-benefits-how-use-data-effectively-public-sector.

Yet, analysts are those who actually manage the datasets, as well as being well-placed to identify what needs to happen before data access can be granted to external parties. They normally represent data managers in their relationships with requesting parties and intermediary bodies. Relationships that, often, involve the participation of multiple parties and necessitate long-term engagement and constructive collaboration. Analysts, it will be shown, are crucial 'nodes' of the network of interactions that shape the boundaries of the data sharing space due to their expertise: being administrative data experts, they are uniquely placed to streamline processes by solving problems that are not even visible to other actors. Often coming from a data science or similar research background themselves, they are also keen on enabling more data to be used by researchers. The crucial role of data analysts as mediators within data sharing interactions is contrasted here with the more high-level, detached role of the two other main groups, ie policymakers and information governance officials.

A. Analysts as Experts: Knowing the Data, Shaping the Process

Do all analysts perform the same type of duties? According to an interviewee, who has worked as a data analyst for the Department for Education (DfE) there are 'three different types of data people':

> Those who are responsible for the data collection, those that put out the basic headline statistics for publication and then those who are working with policy specialists to develop how the government operates.[3]

This third type of 'policy-facing analysts' are mainly of interest within the present study, as they are able to evaluate whether a dataset can be used for research and innovation purposes.[4] To provide some background on the pivotal role of data analysts in the data sharing space, one needs to associate their authority with their expertise. There are two reasons why their expertise makes them integral to making things happen in the context of data sharing for research and innovation. First, analysts are the only ones who really understand the data in respect of the contents of administrative datasets. As the technical experts who have been tasked by public bodies with collecting and curating the very datasets that relate to an organisation's functions, they know very well the substance of the data and, thus, its utility for research or innovation. Second, analysts possess the necessary statistical and methodological knowledge to envision solutions to limitations or barriers that arise during a data sharing relationship. Both skills are necessary in creating and implementing data sharing frameworks for research and innovation.

[3] Interview with participant nr 33 (2020, virtual).
[4] ibid.

Although not all data analysts are statisticians,[5] most share some fundamental knowledge about statistical research and advanced quantitative methods. For example, most analysts come from studying degrees with some, often significant, mathematical components, as well as normally have experienced in using data for research or analysis. An information governance official, who works for the Office for National Statistics (ONS) explains that the Office requires a particular level of competence to hire someone as a data analyst: an 'undergraduate degree with a significant component of mathematics, stats, economics, something numeric effectively',[6] or, alternatively three years of research experience using quantitative data. An interviewee, who has worked as a data analyst for the ONS, claimed that the UK Government is considering establishing a distinct 'track of professional development' for government data analysts, to boost the government's expertise in that field.[7] A policymaker, working for ADRC – Scotland, welcomed this idea, observing that the lack of statistical-methodological expertise is one of the main reasons behind the inability of Scottish local authorities 'to benefit from the data they collect'.[8] Considering the technical complexity of data-driven research and innovation,[9] such expertise is integral to envisage solutions to data sharing challenges, regardless of the subject matter that the data's contents relate to.

Because of their expertise, data analysts are playing a central role in four key moments of the data sharing lifecycle:[10] *identifying* the types of data that are of interest for research or innovation purposes; *establishing consistent standards* in terms of organising and classifying datasets and variables within datasets to enable data linkages between different organisations; *cleaning and curating* the datasets so that they can be used by researchers and innovators and *establishing safeguards* to reconcile the need for more data that will allow engagement with more or broader research questions or innovation purposes with data protection and minimisation requirements. The functions that the data custodian bodies exercise within these four key moments are, to a significant extent, carried out by data analysts, even if the latter are not formally seen as making the final decisions.

To start with the *identification* of the appropriate administrative dataset for research or innovation purposes, this might in some cases necessitate the creation

[5] Eg at the electronic Data Research and Information Service Scotland, interview with participant nr 36 (2020, virtual): 'We've got a bit of a mix, we've got people on the team who have come through analytical roles in the NHS … We've got a couple of researchers … We've got people who were managing data rather than IT within the NHS.'

[6] Interview with participant nr 1 (2017, Titchfield).

[7] Interview with participant nr 28 (2020, London). This track of professional development would essentially encourage government officials to invest into gaining statistical skills by establishing relevant incentive structures in the public sector.

[8] Interview with participant nr 31 (2020, virtual).

[9] Administrative Data Taskforce, 'The UK Administrative Data Research Network: Improving Access for Research and Policy' (December 2012).

[10] S Aidinlis and others, 'Building a Justice Data Infrastructure Opportunities and Constraints' (2020) (AI for English Law UKRI Grant). Available at: www.law.ox.ac.uk/sites/files/oxlaw/ukri_justice_data_report_fv_0.pdf.

of a dataset anew and in other cases the identification of a dataset among existing datasets. In the first case, creating datasets for the first time might necessitate the very heavy task, from an administrative perspective, of having to register the content of the dataset for the first time. Even if this process is to an important extent automated,[11] it is still a considerable challenge in terms of understanding the key parameters that need to be satisfied for a high-quality dataset to be built. As an administrative data researcher with experience in negotiating access to health data in Scotland explained, the role of data analysts is critical because 'everyone wants to harvest databases, but no one wants to input the data'.[12] Data analysts are the ones with the crucial task to ensure good quality of input data, or to 'clean the data up a bit' when the input data are not of ideal quality.[13] Another policy-maker, who has worked for HMRC, identified internal disparities in ways to register data as a real obstacle in creating a uniform dataset:

> There are 30 or 40 different lines of duty in HMRC – stamp duties, tax credits, different things – they all have different data systems and within them there are different strands of recording data developed by different IT contractors.[14]

Even if the dataset exists, however, it might still be quite a challenging task to identify which one of the many datasets that data custodians hold is appropriate for research use. In respect of achieving this, sound knowledge of the strengths and the limitations of the datasets is necessary, particularly in the case of large ministerial departments that hold a massive wealth of information.[15] Many interviewees acknowledged the significance of this skill. An interviewee who works for the ONS as a policymaker explained that data analysts are their first port of call when they receive a data sharing request:

> They are the experts in the data, they are very much giving advice, guidance to us on the feasibility of a research proposal … they would advise for instance that oh, that is the annual population survey that is your most useful dataset for that.[16]

Including data analysts in all stages of the decision-making process, as the interviewee explained, is necessary to ensure that any questions that policymakers might have about a request can be addressed.

This exercise of identification is often hampered by the lack of *consistent standards* among datasets and variables, so that data managers, either within their own organisation or in collaboration with another data manager, have compatible data resources that can be linked together to produce a valuable analytical resource. In many cases, the lack of such standards has to do with how vast and fragmented

[11] SAIL Databank, 'The Anonymisation Process'. Available at: httpp://saildatabank.com/saildata/data-privacy-security/#anonymisation-process.
[12] Interview with participant nr 39 (2020, virtual).
[13] ibid.
[14] Interview with participant nr 32 (2020, Oxford).
[15] Law Commission (n 2) 10.8.
[16] Interview with participant nr 4 (2017, Titchfield).

in terms of standardisation administrative datasets are. Since such datasets are primarily collected to serve the primary functions of public bodies, they are far from consistently organised to be used by researchers and innovators. Data analysts are integral to overcoming this barrier and turning datasets into consistent resources. A policymaker, who works for the DWP expressed their gratitude for the department analysts who help them to make sense of DWP datasets. They highlighted that this is an incredibly complex process, as the datasets are 'incredibly messy' and no external user could understand how to use them if they are not first organised in a more standardised way:

> There are some datasets where, if were to release it tomorrow … you just know that anybody would look at it and say 'What on earth is this? '… there is that task which should not be underestimated of turning the data which we use every day, which can be quite messy into something which is more readily understood by an external user.[17]

Data analysts, possessing sound knowledge about the datasets, can 'tie the data together' and provide such consistency.[18] This is corroborated by two interviewees working for the DWP. A policy-maker working for the department explained that they find it impossible to understand what exactly can be done with it, particularly when there is 'such a wealth of data covering such a range of topics'.[19] According to them, even the analysts need to collaborate closely, since 'there isn't anybody who actually understands it all'.[20] This is why the department has established a sophisticated network of 'Lead Analysts', responsible for distinct areas of DWP data, employing 'around 20 of those' at the time of writing.[21] An information governance official working for the department concurred that these expert analysts 'really do know these bits better' and have a 'very deep knowledge of the research that's happened in their area and knowledge gaps in their area'.[22]

The same rationale of relying on data experts to achieve consistency between datasets applies, when it comes to linking datasets with the those belonging to another body. For example, a researcher may be interested in linking health data belonging to the National Health Service with DWP benefit sanctions data to assess the health impact of DWP's enforcement policies.[23] An information governance official, who works for the Honest Broker Service in Northern Ireland (HBS), explained that, in such cases, the linkage is facilitated by another organisation (an intermediary body), which provides the secure environment to ensure that identification risks created by the aggregation of data will be minimised.[24] As the

[17] Interview with participant nr 7 (2017, Sheffield).
[18] ibid.
[19] ibid.
[20] ibid.
[21] ibid.
[22] Interview with participant nr 8 (2017, Sheffield).
[23] S Pattaro and others, 'Labour Market and Wider Impacts of Benefit Sanctions: A Scoping Review' (2019) 17th Annual ESPAnet Conference, Stockholm, Sweden, 5–7 Sept 2019.
[24] K Harron and others, 'Challenges in Administrative Data Linkage for Research' (2017) 4(2) *Big Data & Society* 1134.

interviewee explained, the presence of the data analysts working for this 'trusted' intermediary is necessary in all meetings concerning the provision of access to linked data as they have the 'expertise over the secondary care data'.[25] In a similar vein, an interviewee, who has worked for HMRC as a policymaker, recalled how important the contribution of the department's data analysts was in developing consistent data quality and interoperability standards.[26] Had these standards not been established, HMRS's entire aspiration to create a data lab that allows access for external researchers would have been put to rest due to financial concerns:

> A major obstacle arises around simply tracing and matching between data sets which can dramatically increase cost and expense for data sharing – sometime terminally. Having common data standards and better data quality addressed this.[27]

Having identified and consistently organised the appropriate datasets for research or innovation uses, data managers also need to ensure that the data are *curated* and *cleaned* for use by external parties.[28] While this sounds an extremely technical and, arguably, mundane task, the truth is that it is as necessary a step for a data sharing initiative as any other. Sharing datasets with irrelevant out-of-date variables may yield unsatisfactory results, both from the perspective of heightened data protection risks (ie lack of conformity with the requirement to process as little data as necessary) and reduced utility (ie using data points that are not updated and, thus, less useful). A start-up founder, with experience in the Scottish data sharing landscape, described data analysts as those who 'curate the dataset' and clarified that they are normally the first point of contact if someone is interested in gaining access.[29] As an ex-DfE data analyst explained, analysts would be sitting on an internal Approvals Panel within the department to 'ensure that the data have been prepared appropriately' and that the requesting party will be able to make sense of them.[30]

Beyond cleaning and curating datasets, however, the role of data analysts is generally critical in *establishing safeguards* to facilitate access to the data. After the datasets have been prepared, there are still many challenges around ensuring that access strikes a balance between maximising utility and complying with legal and ethical safeguards.[31] Analysts are well-placed to help public bodies to strike this balance by advising on the 'kind of methods' that can be applied to particular datasets in the interest of addressing particular research questions or innovation purposes.[32] Thanks to their expertise, they understand a lot about 'statistical disclosure and security', while at the same time ensuring that 'the research questions are

[25] Interview with participant nr 11 (2018, Belfast).
[26] Aidinlis and others (n 10) 24.
[27] Interview with participant nr 32 (2020, Oxford).
[28] SAIL Databank (n 11).
[29] Interview with participant nr 35 (2020, virtual).
[30] ibid.
[31] Aidinlis et al (n 10) 31.
[32] Interview with participant nr 14 (2018, Belfast).

still being answered and are not being compromised'.[33] In some cases, analysts may help by performing a particularly challenging statistical technique to enable meaningful data sharing that can allow researchers tackle their research questions without compromising the protection of sensitive data. A policymaker for the DWP recalled such an example:

> Potentially, depending on the nature of the work, there may also be a need to do some fuzzy matching of an external dataset against a DWP data. And there is a separate team that does that, because there are very few analysts in DWP who have access to data with names, addresses and all that, so you can do this kind of matching.[34]

A data analyst for the Knowledge and Analytical Services of the Welsh Government, went as far as to imply that the data analysts' recommendations with regard to methods and project particulars should receive deference from the policymakers:

> You know, a policy maker actually shouldn't know the methods whereby we deliver that evidence. They should tell us what their evidence need is. It's our job to tell them the best way to deliver that.[35]

Some interviewees reflected on scenarios where data analysts used their statistical and methodological expertise to break an impasse in data sharing negotiations by providing assurances that sufficient safeguards have been applied to the procedure. For example, the Welsh Health Trusts were very concerned with the potential risks of the re-identification of individual patients if the SAIL databank collected huge amounts of health data and linked it with administrative datasets belonging to the Welsh Government.[36] It was not a political assurance or a high-level declaration that allowed the SAIL databank to allay these worries and proceed with establishing their data sharing framework, now considered an example of international best practice. It was the ingenuity of a team of data analysts:

> There were people there who were in a position who could create this algorithm that allowed the de-identification of the data, so that the data, when they were analysed, were only used in de-identified form. … Them developing the algorithm was really crucial, actually, for good data quality'.[37]

A similar function is operated by the data analysts of the National Records of Scotland (NRS) when it comes to linking their data with National Health Service (NHS) data. The NRS team apply a technique called 'probability matching' to produce unique identifiers as a way of encrypting the datasets before providing access to researchers.[38] Through such techniques, analysts effectively facilitate the compliance of data sharing with the principles of data minimisation and security

[33] ibid.
[34] Interview with participant nr 7 (2017, Sheffield).
[35] Interview with participant nr 26 (2019, Cardiff).
[36] SAIL Databank (n 11).
[37] Interview with participant nr 21 (2019, Swansea).
[38] Interview with participant nr 36 (2020, virtual).

in data protection law,[39] ensuring that researchers are only accessing data they strictly need for their projects. It will often be the case that advanced statistical expertise is needed to achieve this:

> We would discuss issues like do they want what we call a long or a wide dataset, do they want one row per item … and we need to be re-assured that the researcher is comfortable with linking a long dataset to a wide *dataset because it is quite a challenging process. You need some good STATA skills.*[40]

The analysts' central role in establishing data sharing safeguards is acknowledged, in practice, by intermediary bodies or researcher groups employ data analysts with a view to making communication more efficient with data custodians. As a data analyst who works for the Knowledge and Analytical Services of the Welsh Government explained, they do not feel that they can negotiate data access efficiently with people who do not have the skills required to understand it:

> This is a definite weakness … people who negotiate are often divorced from the uses of the data. Sometimes we have research questions and requesting parties might have been able to say – if you give us the data, we will use the data for this purpose, and you will see these benefits.[41]

Some intermediary bodies have, indeed, heeded this call and have hired data analysts to ensure that their requests are communicated to the data custodians in the right manner. The Administrative Data Research Centre (ADRC) – Northern Ireland is a particularly interesting case-study in that regard. As an interviewee, who has worked as a policymaker there, explained, the ADRC has appointed two 'expert administrative data researchers' with data analyst skills as 'Statistical Methodological Officers (SMOs)'.[42] The role of the SMOs is scope the feasibility of requests, based on their knowledge of the data that are available for research use in the Northern Irish public sector. Another interviewee working for the same body as an information governance official concurred that it is really important to use people with statistical expertise when trying to 'establish a good working relationship' with data analysts working for data custodians'.[43] As another policymaker, who works for the Economic and Social Research Council (intermediary body), eloquently put it: 'If you do not know the dataset, how are you supposed to know what to ask for?'[44]

Using their expertise in managing data, as well as their knowledge of particular datasets, analysts have been instrumental in the development of data sharing processes. Through this role, they have often authoritatively interpreted data sharing criteria and requirements, shaping the formation of data access frameworks in

[39] Under GDPR, arts 89 and 32.
[40] Interview with participant nr 12 (2018, Belfast).
[41] Interview with participant nr 25 (2019, Cardiff).
[42] Interview with participant nr 10 (2018, Belfast).
[43] Interview with participant nr 9 (2018, Belfast).
[44] Interview with participant nr 19 (2018, Swindon).

this space. Crucially, even if this is not formally required, they have as mediators between data managers and other data sharing participants, seeking to facilitate research and innovation data sharing processes in a number of ways.

B. Analysts as Mediators: Helping Requesting Parties, Streamlining Data Sharing Processes

Data analysts, while often under the supervision of higher-level colleagues such as information governance officials, are central in the data sharing space not only because of their expertise, but also because they tend to bridge the distance between public bodies and other actors.

As mentioned, analysts are often first to assess a data access request received by a data manager, which means they set the terms of the discussion for the remainder of the data access negotiation. An information governance official, working for the ONS, explained that they supervise a team, consisting of a number of data analysts. These analysts take it upon themselves to clarify the scope and the requirements that the researchers will need to meet for the access to be granted:

> The researcher's application comes to my team. We, then reflect within the team … do you agree that this data is appropriate for this research? Can their research goals be met by using this data?[45]

There are various ways in which analysts seek to help requesters negotiate data access with public bodies, assist researchers and innovators in understanding data access requirements and streamline data sharing processes. A common requirement is that data sharing requests are precise enough to allow managers to assess whether the requested disclosure conforms with the principles of proportionality and data minimisation. Analysts are those officials who assist requesters in turning a broad interest in some administrative datasets into a concrete request that will satisfy custodian requirements. A data analyst who works for the ADRC – Northern Ireland, described the main steps of this process. First, they receive queries via email and seek to clarify what the requesting party's analytical interest, seeking to determine whether this is 'the right thing for them'.[46] After this is established, they would meet with the requesters and 'talk through all the different processes to access the data',[47] helping them understand how they will satisfy the various governance requirements, either examined directly by the custodians or by other bodies such as ethical approval committees. When the requesters have

[45] Interview with participant nr 1 (2017, Titchfield). In that sense, analysts operate as 'regulatory stewards' who can help researchers 'navigate difficult regulatory spaces and improve the overall quality of research', see E Dove, *Regulatory Stewardship of Health Research: Navigating Participant Protection and Research Promotion* (Edward Elgar 2020) 183.

[46] Interview with participant nr 15 (2018, virtual).

[47] ibid.

prepared the documentation for submission, the analysts would again help to refine the application before it is formally considered by the public body.[48]

A colleague of theirs, who has worked as a data analyst for the ADRN (intermediary body), broke down the ways in which a request could be 'narrowed down' to satisfy managers:

> What we would do, we would have more expertise from the experience of helping them narrow it down to something that didn't involve the whole of the world. Temporal scoping, which years – geographical scoping, eg England & Wales, or England & Scotland.[49]

If, for example, researchers had a 'very vague idea' about the project,[50] such scoping would take longer, and would involve long e-mail exchanges and phone conversations. Another data analyst admitted that they would receive some really open-ended questions, eg 'I would like to do some research with some health data, can you do that for me?'[51] In these cases, the analysts would probe the researchers to clarify their interest in the data:

> With those people who have a very vague enquiry, is basically we send them back an awful lot of questions.[52]
>
> It is an 11-page word document, because there is quite a lot of information to catch on that. And basically, we would use that as the tool to try and make people clear about what they want.[53]

This does not mean that analysts require this information from the requesters without assisting them in the process of thinking about the difficult questions around data access. It will often be the case that requesters will use the feedback from data analysts while preparing their application forms. Another interviewee, who works in an information governance capacity for the Electronic Data Research and Innovation Service in Scotland, noted that they see their role as two-fold: help researchers and innovators make their requests more concrete, but also 'educate the decision-makers about the fact that sometimes you don't know what you need until you actually get into the analysis element of it'.[54] An information governance official, working for the Honest Broker Service (HBS) in Northern Ireland, described their own process of 'triaging' requests that HBS receives by external researchers. They explained that they oversee a team of analysts who first clarify with the researchers crucial parameters like 'variables' and the 'sample sizes', enabling them to engage in a 'preliminary exploration on the datasets, in terms of

[48] ibid.
[49] Interview with participant nr 5 (2017, Essex).
[50] ibid.
[51] Interview with participant nr 6 (2018, phone).
[52] ibid.
[53] ibid.
[54] Interview with participant nr 36 (2020, virtual).

quality, quantity of the data and the feasibility'.[55] They stressed the significance of this initial scoping exercise for the data sharing process to proceed:

> So, we (in the team with the analysts) have our discussion, an in-depth discussion, about what their intentions are, what the aims of the project are, perhaps tease out a bit more the variables they are interested in, sometimes they have only given a broad name and indication of what it is they are looking at. We need to tease out the actual variable name as it is coded and held on the database.[56]

After this initial stage, the HBS analysts, very much like their counterparts in other bodies, assist the researcher in 'drafting the application',[57] being themselves very familiar with the way in which the HBS governance board interpret the custodian requirements. The mediating role of data analysists in particularly highlighted in this case, since data analysts are also part of the data custodian organisation and provide a very helpful understanding of the organisational requirements to the researchers. A policymaker, working for the DWP, further explained the importance of this mediating role played by the analysts not only in respect of helping requesting parties, but also in terms of helping their own colleagues within a custodian organisation. This enhances the mediating influence of the analysts since both sides of the negotiation rely on their insights to make sense of the process. As the policy-making interviewee from DWP claimed, they ask data analysts to refine the requests 'into reasonable shape' before passing them on to their policy colleagues, expressing dissatisfaction at their previous lack of refinement:

> Some of the requests which come through are sometimes they are very vague, sometimes they ask for a huge amount of detail, it's not obvious why they need that amount of detail for all the research which they propose.[58]

Analysts do not exhaust their mediating role in helping requesters with properly articulating their requests. Crucially, analysts tend to see themselves as very close especially to researchers and often speak on behalf of researchers to their colleagues within custodian bodies. A data analyst, who has worked for the ADRN (intermediary body), attributed this to their background as data managers and users:

> You get more of the appreciation of the ability to get things done from the analysts, the data using people, (whereas) the people dealing with information governance … are more in the kind of defensive, cautious way … The analysts might give you interesting insight that I'd like to see, how to we go and make it work the right way.[59]

The background of analysts is contrasted here with the background of information governance officials who are more interested in limiting data uses for legal

[55] Interview with participant nr 11 (2018, Belfast).
[56] ibid.
[57] ibid.
[58] Interview with participant nr 7 (2017, Sheffield).
[59] Interview with participant nr 6 (2018, phone).

compliance and risk management reasons. An interviewee, who works in an information governance capacity for the Northern Irish Statistics and Research Agency (NISRA) explained that data analysts form an informal network across the Northern Irish public sector. Even if they are not formally the ultimate decision-makers, they often provide crucial 'buy-in' for a data sharing process to be established,[60] by convincing their policy-making colleagues about the merits of investing resources in that area. A data analyst, working for the Department for the Economy in Northern Ireland, provided some background on this very aspect of their role:

> A request would come to the analytical services, to ourselves, and … I myself am very open to doing an ADRC project. So, I think scepticism may be overcome … I would recommend it to policy folks if we felt there is sufficient benefit to it, sufficient merit … The Department would heavily rely on advice from us in terms of whether to share data.[61]

An information governance official, who works for the Electronic Data Research and Innovation Service (eDRIS) in Scotland described how their team of data analysts represent the interests of researchers in negotiating access to Scottish Government data. eDRIS analysts mediate between researchers and analysts working for the public bodies, ensuring that the latter have sufficient explanations about the requested data and the information governance concerns that they may have, 'avoiding questions going back to the applicants'.[62] Many researchers who have negotiated access to data in Scotland highlight the critical mediating role of eDRIS analysts. An administrative data researcher, with experience in negotiating access in the Scottish public sector, hailed eDRIS analysts for their sound understanding of governance issues like statistical disclosure control, expressing relief for being represented by them in access negotiations.[63] Another researcher, with experience in linking health with non-health data in Scotland, concurred that eDRIS analysts 'sort things out for you' and clarify things with the applicants in case they see problems in the application.[64] In a similar vein, a researcher, with experience in linking census data with health data in Scotland, expressed their admiration for eDRIS analysts:

> I'm absolutely beholden to my eDRIS co-ordinator who is incredible, I don't know how he does it. It's ridiculously messy.[65]

What makes analysts so motivated to act as liaisons between managers and researchers to help things move forward? While they are not necessarily researchers themselves, their knowledge about the datasets and their statistical expertise

[60] Interview with participant nr 9 (2018, Belfast).
[61] Interview with participant nr 16 (2018, phone).
[62] Interview with participant nr 36 (2020, virtual).
[63] Interview with participant nr 37 (2020, virtual).
[64] Interview with participant nr 39 (2020, virtual).
[65] Interview with participant nr 34 (2020, virtual).

makes them more sympathetic to research uses of administrative data. Due to this sympathy, in essence, analysts often aspire to broaden research data sharing frameworks, convincing custodians to make more of their data available for research use. An interviewee, who has worked for the ADRC – Northern Ireland in a policy-making capacity, described that their analysts perceive 'challenging the data providers along the lines of, well, why can we not have that?' as part of their remit.[66] An analyst colleague of theirs, indeed, took great pride in pressurising the data custodians of the NISRA to make more data available for research:

> I have spent a long time giving the NISRA guys hard time for why anything hadn't happened. … I would sort of argue back and say "look, you provided it here, you provided it there" and we would have an argument. Eventually, we would have a deal, somewhere in the middle usually.[67]

Another way in which analysts contribute to building bridges between requesting parties and custodians is by training requesters to use data safely and appropriately, helping them understand the existing best practices in data management. A data analyst, who has worked for the Administrative Data Research Network, reflected on their contributions to developing a bespoke 'safe researcher' training for applicants who were interested in accessing data through the ADRN:

> And we developed the training, the bit where the researchers come and have a day or half day session, teaching – learning sessions, when they are taught on ways to handle data, ways that they can make sure the data they give to the staff at the secure environment does not contain personal information.[68]

As the interviewee noted, this training was inspired by the ONS' 'approved researcher' training. A data analyst, who has previously worked for the ONS, clarified that this training framework, created by analysts, combined methodological knowledge around statistical analysis of administrative data and guidelines on how to conform with legal requirements and information governance standards.[69] Another analyst, working for the ADRC (intermediary body) in Northern Ireland, added that they might provide training sessions for requesting parties interested in improving their skills. They also offered 'a number of accreditation courses on data security and statistical disclosure control'.[70]

Through their expertise in the data and in statistical analysis, analysts perform crucial mediating roles in the data sharing space. Nonetheless, one might think that their crucial role is still limited by the fact that higher-ranked officials, such as information governance managers or policymakers, hold the ultimate decision-making authority. Analysts do not seem to hold any decision-making competences. Is this, indeed, the case?

[66] Interview with participant nr 10 (2018, Belfast).
[67] Interview with participant nr 15 (2018, virtual).
[68] Interview with participant nr 5 (2017, Essex).
[69] Interview with participant nr 28 (2020, London).
[70] Interview with participant nr 14 (2018, Belfast).

C. Analysts as Decision-Makers: Blurring the Lines between 'Recommending' and 'Deciding'

Analysts are the lowest-ranked officials in the organisational hierarchy of the decision-making space. Yet, their expertise and knowledge about the data, as well as their mediating role in building bridges between data custodians and requesting parties effectively blurs the boundaries between the notions of 'recommending' and 'deciding' when it comes to analysts' assessments.

Policymakers in public bodies reserve for themselves the final say on whether a data access request will be granted. It is a common perception among participants in the data sharing space that 'you need to have someone at the very top saying "make this happen"'.[71] A data analyst, who has worked for the DfE, explained that the power to establish and authorise a data sharing procedure belongs to the policymakers, ultimately pointing to the highest level of authority within the civil service, ie ministers:

> The policy team specify the policies that they are developing and how this will work – they would then come to my team and say we want to collect this data … In terms of making the data available, the ministers would have their say in that … They are the ones who have the power to make decisions.[72]

A policymaker, who has worked for HMRC, conceded that ministerial decisions can be 'a bit more complicated, a bit more whimsical perhaps'.[73] An information governance official, working for the DWP, caveated this by pointing out that there are 'certain protocols referring to decisions made by ministers'.[74] In practice, as an interviewee who sits at the Confidentiality Advisory Group explained, many of these decisions will be 'delegated to a senior civil servant' by the ministers, unless there is some 'political sensitivity to the decision'.[75] The DWP information governance official confirmed that it is their intention too to have as much data sharing decisions as possible delegated from the ministers to other officials:

> Ministers are still getting a feel for the benefits and the costs and risks. As this develops, what we would hope/expect to see is that Ministers go: 'I am fine with all the issues, you guys know what you are doing.' Potentially at some point they might go: 'don't bother me with these anymore'.[76]

In any case, as a data analyst working for the Department for the Economy in Northern Ireland stressed, there is a clear distinction between analysts and the

[71] Interview with participant nr 37 (2020, virtual).
[72] Interview with participant nr 30 (2020, virtual); it is important to clarify that this is only applicable to ministerial departments, since other public bodies do not have ministers.
[73] Interview with participant nr 32 (2020, Oxford).
[74] Interview with participant nr 8 (2017, Sheffield).
[75] Interview with participant nr 27 (2019, phone).
[76] Interview with participant nr 8 (2017, Sheffield).

'policy side of things' who are 'independent' from the analysts.[77] In other words, there is a clear division of roles between analysts and policymakers, with the latter having the final word on data access decisions. Another data analyst, who has worked for the DfE, confirmed that policymakers had the ultimate authority with regard to data sharing. They confessed that the policy people even had the authority to block an internal research project if it was 'politically difficult' for the government of the day:

> If you did stuff that was difficult for the government, it was unlikely to get published … the political situation at the time was also more sensitive. That naturally makes any minister more cautious. On occasion, getting stuff out was less about "is this good research?" and more about "what's the politics going on now?". Nothing is unaffected by the political side.[78]

A policymaker, who works for the ADRC – Scotland, similarly reflected on the difficulties created by the fact that policymakers are the ultimate decision-makers in data sharing for research and innovation. They lamented the lack of patience and more strategic vision on behalf of policy makers:

> They usually want an answer to something that week, or that month. My feeling is they are interested in quick answers to solve their particular issue that week or month, than actually engaging with a body of evidence that will help in the medium to long term evidence-based policy making across the board.[79]

A closer look at the micro-level dynamics of the space, however, somewhat nuances the picture of the almighty policymaker. While formally not holding decision-making powers, analysts do a lot of the work in refining and organising data sharing processes, effectively framing the way in which higher-ranked officials exercise their competences. The understanding of such officials is dependent, to a large extent, on the groundwork laid out by the analysts. This results in analysts becoming much more than simple advisers. To a data analyst, who has previously worked for the ONS, this is due to the fact that policymakers are detached from the data sharing process, whereas data analysts are really on top of it:

> Data access forms are usually designed by policy people who are a long way removed from the process … what you want is something that people can read and it makes sense to them and they can agree to.[80]

An administrative data researcher, who has negotiated access with Scottish data custodians, corroborated that policymakers are often unhelpful due to them missing the detail of data sharing like the 'specifics of the dataset'.[81] They recalled a paradigmatic incident where they had to negotiate with policymakers who were

[77] Interview with participant nr 16 (2018, phone).
[78] Interview with participant nr 33 (2020, virtual).
[79] Interview with participant nr 31 (2020, virtual).
[80] Interview with participant nr 42 (2020, virtual).
[81] Interview with participant nr 35 (2020, virtual).

unclear about the specifics and actually misled them about their possibilities to proceed with data sharing:

> We were told that you have to start at the (redacted) point of the system and you can't have before that. And then we start talking to the guy who would look after the big database and he said 'well that's not true, you can actually do that if you manually do this and give me some set parameters, I'll be able to stitch that dataset for you'. That kind of gap between the different people.[82]

The same interviewee added that senior, policy-making officials are also struggling to stay on top of data sharing specifics because they simply have 'other kind of priorities' and 'more things to do than facilitate an academic project'.[83] This is shared by a data analyst who has previously worked for the DfE. Policy makers are those with the competence to decide, yet they often 'don't have the time to invest in the level of detail'.[84] As another analyst, who works for the DfE in Northern Ireland, explained, this often results in policymakers 'heavily relying' on data analysts when making up their mind on whether to share data.[85] Another interviewee, who has previously worked for the ONS in an analyst capacity, explained that they were once able to convince some of their policy-making colleagues to delegate significant data sharing competences, like the statistical disclosure control,[86] invoking their expertise in the data:

> We said to the (redacted) team, why don't we do this disclosure control? We could make these decisions quickly – we'll send you what we've done, our decisions, and you can check it. You can keep an eye on this, but, basically, we will do the work … no one objected to that and no one thought that was a bad plan.[87]

Interestingly enough, another reason for delegating data sharing competences to analysts relates to political sensitivity, especially for policy-making departments. When a data access decision may become politicised, eg rejecting access to a project whose research questions can be interpreted as critical to the government of the day, it is more palatable for policymakers to keep themselves out of the decision. The rejecting decision can, then, be portrayed as a technical decision by technical stuff, ie the analysts. As an information governance official who works for the ONS explained, policy makers 'don't like having to be the person who gets to say no publicly'.[88] Essentially, a policy refusal of a request turns a supposedly technical procedure of data sharing into a political matter of endorsing or rejecting particular types of research agendas. A data analyst, who has worked for the ADRN, confirmed

[82] ibid.
[83] ibid.
[84] Interview with participant nr 30 (2020, virtual).
[85] Interview with participant nr 16 (2018, phone).
[86] Statistical disclosure control is a 'a technique used in data-driven research to ensure no person or organization is identifiable from the results of an analysis of survey or administrative data, or in the release of microdata', see C Skinner, 'Statistical Disclosure Control for Survey Data' (2009). Available at: http://personal.lse.ac.uk/skinnecj/SDC%20for%20survey%20data%20S3RI.pdf.
[87] Interview with participant nr 42 (2020, virtual).
[88] Interview with participant nr 1 (2017, Titchfield).

that, reflecting on some feedback they were given by their data analyst counterparts who work for the DWP. In their words, policy people 'never really want to find themselves in the position where they were asking their higher up, ie the minister, to refuse to do something'.[89] It would be preferable for them to have analysts responsible, or at least nominally responsible, for some aspects of the data sharing process.

Furthermore, analysts are much more centrally involved in the practicalities of data sharing compared to information governance officials who specialise in legal compliance and risk management of a data access request. Very much like policymakers, information governance officials hold significant decision-making competences, but their role is practically translated into a compliance check that takes place *after* most of the access negotiation has taken place, unless a request is 'clearly illegal'.[90] An administrative data researcher, with experience in negotiating access with Scottish data custodians, claimed that they have hardly reached the stage of liaising with information governance officials:

> Yeah, I guess, I was thinking about this question and I think it's never really come up, if you see what I mean. We never really got to the legal point in that process, it's always been trying to get people to agree – is this feasible and do you want to do this? Rather than, is this legal?[91]

A data analyst, who has worked for the ADRN, corroborated this picture of a separate and subsequent information governance participation in the data access negotiations. They recalled that information governance officials of the custodians were the only ones responsible for determining the lawfulness of the disclosure, with the requesting and intermediary parties often accepting the custodian determination.[92] A policymaker, working for the DWP, added that the information governance side is entirely distinct from the policy weighing of the merits and the risks related to an access request. Once policy makers have 'considered all of these requests and decide which ones have merit to pass on',[93] the request will be considered by the information governance officials who will opine on 'whether it is legal to do or not'.[94] A data analyst, who has worked for the DfE, explained that information governance officials do not have a more central role in designing a data sharing framework because their job is to 'reduce risk about making data available', not maximising the 'value of granting access to data'.[95]

As it has been shown, a humble group of data analysts plays a multi-faceted and central role in the research data sharing space. Interactions between analysts representing different actors, ie data managers and intermediary bodies or researchers, as well as interactions between analysts and policymakers or information governance officials within public bodies, matter. Through these interactions, analysts

[89] Interview with participant nr 6 (2018, phone).
[90] Interview with participant nr 5 (2017, Essex).
[91] Interview with participant nr 35 (2020, virtual).
[92] Interview with participant nr 5 (2017, Essex).
[93] Interview with participant nr 7 (2017, Sheffield).
[94] ibid.
[95] Interview with participant nr 30 (2020, virtual).

can leverage their expertise in the data and in statistical analysis to build bridges between different parties and offer authoritative recommendations. In so doing, they shape data sharing processes and, through that, the content of data sharing frameworks, often with a view to facilitating research data sharing. Higher-ranked officials, like policymakers and information governance officials, often find themselves implicitly or explicitly reliant on the understanding of data sharing processes that is offered to them by analysts. To complement this finding about low- rather than high-level officials setting the boundaries of the data sharing space, I now turn to the very nature of the interactions between the actors of the space as small-scale and informal, based on personal relationships.

II. Informal Communications and Small-Scale Interactions

Lower-ranked officials, ie analysts, play a central role in the research data sharing space because the regulatory issues of this space are often resolved through long-drawn-out conversations, often informal and involving a small number of individuals, rather than by the diktat of a high-ranking official. This is often facilitated by pre-existing relationships between actors in the data sharing space. After referring to the role of such relationships, I show that the crucial interactions which influence the implementation of data sharing frameworks and, thus, effectively shape the space happen at the 'micro' level, often take place outside formal governance structures and policy headlines.

A. 'Knowing the Right Person': Trust and relationships in the Data Sharing Space

The language used in data sharing frameworks is often technical and complex. Data managers need to ensure that the provision of access conforms to demanding data protection principles, intermediaries need to deliver sophisticated training programmes for requesters while requesters themselves need to observe the strict rules of secure environments. Interviewees of this study, however, felt that that the implementation of data sharing frameworks is neither neutral nor objective. Pre-existing relationships and the development of trust between participants in the space influence the way in which requirements are interpreted and issues are negotiated. As starkly put by an administrative data researcher with experience in the Scottish landscape:

> It's definitely the case that if you know the right person, you'll get things done faster.[96]

[96] Interview with participant nr 29 (2020, phone).

They added that the Scottish ADRC (intermediary body) was much more effective than its English counterpart in negotiating the establishment of research data sharing frameworks:

> When it came to demonstrating success in terms of data access, we were probably already ahead of the game in that sense. We already had access to a lot of the social care data and the education data that was, really, kind of the prize.[97]

Relationships between data custodians and requesting parties are often integral to triggering significant breakthroughs that allow a data sharing procedure to materialise. The devolved countries, being smaller and allowing the development of closer relationships, are very good examples in that regard. A policymaker, who works for the SAIL databank in Wales, provided some background on the establishment of it's much-hailed framework, which largely relies on an algorithm that splits and de-identifies the used datasets.[98] They recalled that the 'connections' of some of the academics with people working for the NHS Wales Informatics Service (NWIS) were crucial in NWIS taking the SAIL investment seriously and prioritising the development of the matching algorithm:

> I think (redacted) had some connections with them because they used to work on some projects in relation to clinical coding, you could easily check it with them. The people originally involved in the bid, they had some connections anyway.[99]

A data analyst, who works for the Knowledge and Analytical Services of the Welsh Government, claimed that the very possibility of data linkage, ie linking administrative datasets that belong to different public bodies,[100] arose out of established communicative channels between civil servants and academics. Since Wales is a 'small country', civil servants who manage datasets 'get to know the academics within their field quite well'.[101] This makes it easier for Welsh academics to influence the scope of data sharing agreements and, more generally, the interpretation of data sharing frameworks: they 'know who to talk to' and 'have already got relationships established'.[102]

Coming to Scotland, an administrative data researcher with experience in the Scottish landscape, explained that researchers had been largely relying on their relationships with individuals working for data custodians to influence the design of data sharing procedures. They invoked the example of one of their more experienced researcher colleagues who 'has been around' and 'has lots of experience and contacts'.[103] To manage relationships, this colleague was very keen on following up

[97] ibid.
[98] SAIL Databank (n 11).
[99] Interview with participant nr 21 (2019, Swansea).
[100] Harron et al (n 24).
[101] Interview with participant nr 25 (2019, Cardiff).
[102] ibid.
[103] Interview with participant nr 35 (2020, virtual).

on 'institutional rumours about who is up and who is down' within public bodies to understand who they 'need to talk to' for data access purposes.[104] Another researcher with a similar background recalled the establishment of a research data sharing process for the first time by a relatively small local council in Scotland. They explained that this particular local council had pre-existing relationships with their research centre, due to some previous collaboration which involved statistical analysis. To highlight the significance of these relationships, the interviewee drew a contrast with another local council, which they had approached without a prior relationship for data access:

> We also approached another council, a large council. We approached them, had a meeting with them and they were very cold. They said, you know, it's a great idea, but we don't have people to do it and we didn't even chase that up.[105]

A start-up founder in the Scottish landscape recalled one of the, arguably few, examples where a smooth and timely data sharing procedure was facilitated by the DWP. They attributed this to the previous relationship of one of their co-founders with DWP officials:

> I think it was an easier task for (redacted), because (redacted) was part of the research team that conducted the PSE survey for the DWP.[106]

In Northern Ireland, very much like Wales, the success of the local ADRC in agreeing the establishment of research data sharing procedures with public bodies is explained by virtue of the previous relationships between academics and civil servants. A data analyst, who works for the ADRC in Northern Ireland, recalled that their first administrative data research project came to fruition because their previous employer, a veterinary lab, had strong links with the government department that held some relevant data.[107] An interviewee, who works for the same ADRC in a policy-making capacity, explained how academics were often approached by civil servants who either knew them or had heard about them and wanted to discuss the establishment of a data sharing process:

> We had people with data come to us, … and say because they would know that there are academic experts in their area … we have data, would you like to use it?[108]

Although it is more difficult to establish trusting relationships in a bigger country like England, there are reasons to believe that pre-existing relationships have influenced the implementation of data sharing frameworks in the English landscape. A policymaker, who works for the Economic and Social Research Council with a background as an administrative data researcher, recalled that someone

[104] ibid.
[105] Interview with participant nr 37 (2020, virtual).
[106] Interview with participant nr 38 (2020, virtual).
[107] Interview with participant nr 15 (2018, virtual).
[108] Interview with participant nr 10 (2018, Belfast).

from their research team had 'good personal relationships' with the department of Communities and Local Government that would often 'help unlock things'.[109] A data analyst, who has worked for the DfE and now works for an independent research organisation, explained that their personal relationships were integral to them understanding how data sharing requirements would be interpreted:

> We have good contacts with DfE. Most people worked for me at one point or another and this comes as quite handy! Do I know how to do this with HMRC? No. With the DWP? No.[110]

In some cases, intermediary bodies may be better placed than researchers to handle relationships with data custodians with a view to broadening research data sharing frameworks, consistent with their organisational mission to promote research in the public interest. A data analyst, who works for the SAIL databank in Wales, noted that the databank leverages its good relationship with the National Statistician for Wales to convince other Welsh public bodies to subscribe to its data sharing framework.[111] Negotiations become easier when this key relationship was invoked:

> We can overcome a lot of their risk aversion by telling them who else is confident that we are a safe pair of hands with the data … they were reassured by the fact that the Welsh government already had a long relationship with us.[112]

If relationships are integral to progressing things in this space, the absence of relationships can really hamper the development of a data sharing procedure. A policymaker, who has worked for the ADRN, attributed the data sharing difficulties faced by the ADRN in England to the lack of 'contacts' and 'good working relationships' with data managers.[113] As their data analyst colleague working in Wales concurred, the more complicated organisational structures are, the more difficult relationship-building becomes:

> Certainly, you can't scale that model up to Whitehall very easily. DWP is eight times bigger itself than the Welsh government. There are many more factors in play, many more relationships.[114]

Relationships between data sharing actors are, then, critical to the development of research data sharing procedures. As it will now be shown, such relationships are, for the most part, not formed within formal organisational structures. Informal interactions are the most prominent facilitators of influential communications within the research data sharing space.

[109] Interview with participant nr 19 (2018, Swindon).
[110] Interview with participant nr 30 (2020, virtual).
[111] Interview with participant nr 22 (2019, Swansea).
[112] ibid.
[113] Interview with participant nr 21 (2019, Swansea).
[114] Interview with participant nr 22 (2019, Swansea).

B. Informal Interactions: Shaping Data Sharing Frameworks Far from the Spotlight

If connections and personal relationships are pivotal in developing research data sharing frameworks, then where does this process of development happen? As it will be suggested here, the *locus* of the negotiating process is not to be found in formal channels of communication and governance structures, but in informal interactions.

Momentous policy and legal decisions, like the establishment of the ADRN in 2012,[115] or the entry into force of the Digital Economy Act in 2017, are the first port of call for most writers reviewing the data sharing landscape in the UK.[116] Such decisions are, naturally, taken at the highest level of policy- or law-making and constitute the reflection of large organisational action over a long time. They reflect the collective intention of such large actors as the Department for Business, Enterprise and Skills or the UK Parliament to establish, amend or demarcate a framework governing data sharing for research and innovation. Stepping for a moment, however, outside of the formal structures that have been set up for this very purpose, one can notice that the dynamic development of data sharing framework often hinges on the commonplace and the informal.

A policymaker, who has worked for HMRC claimed that significant aspects of their department's uniform data sharing policy were decided in informal interactions with their colleagues:

> Going out and talking to people and high-jacking data shares that were in progress or new requests for other areas and applying our governance … That brought consistency.[117]

In designing the so-called 'front door' service at HMRC, which allows broader data sharing for research purposes compared to HMRC's Datalab,[118] the same interviewee admitted that they were influenced by some 'early exploration of potential proposals with the ADRN' through informal meetings with academics.[119] Another policymaker, working for the Health and Social Care department in Wales, welcomed the honesty and flexibility that is guaranteed by informal interactions, as opposed to formal and public meetings where everything is on the record. They felt that such interactions are the most productive in negotiating the development of a data sharing process with all interested stakeholders:

> In Wales we are small enough to put all these people in a room, often we have quite a good relationship in terms of engagement – it really is straightforward.[120]

[115] Administrative Data Taskforce (n 9).

[116] Laurie and Stevens (n 1); Jackson (n 1).

[117] Interview with participant nr 32 (2020, Oxford).

[118] D Bega, 'The HMRC Datalab: Sharing Administrative and Survey Data on Taxation with the Research Community' in A Dusa and others (eds), *Facing the Future: European Research Infrastructures for the Humanities and Social Sciences* (Scivero 2014).

[119] Interview with participant nr 32 (2020, Oxford).

[120] Interview with participant nr 24 (2019, phone).

They added that, through these interactions, thorny issues can be resolved that would otherwise necessitate years of formal negotiations, had official channels been used. For example, if a particular weakness in a research data sharing framework is to be ameliorated via legislative change, it would require 'a process of at least three years'.[121] By informally liaising with the appropriate stakeholders, a 'consensus around consistent single interpretations' can be reached and 'cut through the complexity' that is inherent in a sophisticated, robustly governed activity like research data sharing.[122]

A data analyst, working for the Knowledge and Analytical Services of the Welsh Government, recounted how significant their informal interactions with their higher-ups in government were for the initial establishment of data linkage processes for research purposes. They eloquently described the moment they started negotiating with their line manager within the civil service:

> When I first went to our chief statistician at the time and said, we should do this, (redacted) was like: 'well, I've got no money'. I said to (redacted), can I go and get some money? Do you mind if I do that? And (redacted) basically said, literally, fill your boots. This is how I started talking to the ESRC.[123]

Reflecting on that experience, the same interviewee admitted that they still rely on informal interactions to move things forward. For example, some months ago, they had noticed that information governance officials within local authorities were reluctant to proceed with data sharing due to worries about the limits imposed by the GDPR. To allay these worries, they brought these officers in touch with the Welsh Government data protection officers, setting up regular, weekly meeting to help 'building a common understanding of the GDPR and how they can share data for stats and research'.[124]

A start-up founder, with experience in the Scottish landscape, elaborated on the many aspects of the data sharing process that are predominantly shaped by informal interactions. To begin with, when constructing a proposal that will satisfy custodian requirements as to the 'public benefit', informal provision of advice from more experienced colleagues is often crucial:

> A lot of that is quite informal, not because there isn't provision, but, inevitably, informal support is a crucial component of any organisation.[125]

Following that stage, the extent to which the proposal will be deemed satisfactory by the decision-making panels within custodian bodies will, again, be significantly influenced by informal interactions. They recalled a particular example where they managed to negotiate a data sharing agreement thanks to

[121] ibid.
[122] ibid.
[123] Interview with participant nr 25 (2019, Cardiff).
[124] ibid.
[125] Interview with participant nr 34 (2020, virtual).

their personal relationship with data analysts working for the custodian body holding the data:

> I mentioned the informal there and I think that actually was crucial in moving forward the work. Lots of things just happened to align … Through individuals within National Records of Scotland, we were really able to start moving forward, thinking how we would enable the data to be made available for linkage and later for analysis.[126]

Based on this experience, they dismissed the view that 'more paperwork is the way forward'.[127] An information governance official, working for the DwP seemingly shared the opinion of the previous interviewee. They stressed that lots of clarifications and refinements are required when negotiating a data sharing process. Informal communication between the negotiating parties 'by telephone' allows all that to happen 'much more rapidly than it might happen if it was all written'.[128] In a similar vein, a data analyst, who has previously worked for the ONS, recalled that the establishment of a data access procedure happened after an informal, almost covert arrangement with one of their colleagues from IT:

> Luckily, I knew someone from ONS who was in IT and was very keen and was happy to work with me on this. We were lucky there, had no resistance at all. We basically pretended this was a pilot to get this up and running.[129]

To say that informal interactions very often shape the contents of data sharing frameworks is not to say that such interactions are always spontaneous or whimsical. Informality refers to the communications taking place outside the formal decision-making structures, not necessarily to the lack of organisation in such interactions. It may very well be the case that data sharing participants will set up informal teams in the interests of providing some structure and coherence to these interactions.

A prime example of such an informal team is the so-called 'Administrative Data Forum' (ADF) in Northern Ireland. This is a *sui generis* body, in that it is comprised of representatives from data managers, but it does not itself fall under any of the actors' categories of this space. An information governance official, who works for NISRA provided some background on the establishment and function of the ADF. As they explain, the forum is comprised of 'senior statisticians working for different government departments'[130] and was established by NISRA with a view to stimulate discussion about research data sharing in the Northern Irish public sector.[131] Crucially, data custodians were represented in the forum by their own data analysts. NISRA data analysts used this forum to 'build rapport' with

[126] ibid.
[127] ibid.
[128] Interview with participant nr 8 (2017, Sheffield).
[129] Interview with participant nr 42 (2020, virtual).
[130] Interview with participant nr 9 (2018, Belfast).
[131] ibid; NISRA were interested in doing so due to their mandate as the Northern Irish Statistics and Research Agency to promote statistical research.

their counterparts, thus securing critical 'buy-in' for the development of research-related access procedures.[132]

Some interviewees reflected on the significance of the ADF in the establishment of research data sharing procedures in the Northern Irish public sector. A policymaker, working for the HBS, recalled that they had previously participated in the ADF. They welcomed the 'information sharing' capacity of the forum with regard to making better use of government data and producing policy-relevant research.[133] A data analyst, working for the HBS, agreed that the forum had been 'very valuable' in making Northern Irish data managers more comfortable with the idea of data sharing:

> Once people come to grips with how it works in practice, a lot of the barriers will fall away I think. Having a forum where people can share information and address concerns is really important to this.[134]

Observing the utility of the ADF in establishing research data sharing frameworks in Northern Ireland, the ADRC – Northern Ireland adopted the idea of establishing informal teams and groups to effectively manage aspects of the data sharing process. They have agreed with NISRA analysts that they have a 'monthly team meeting … to discuss the state of play' for the progress of data access requests. While these meetings are not part of their official duties, they are always 'helpful' and 'well-structured', enabling them to stay on top of the most pressing data sharing challenges.[135]

In Wales, a data analyst, who works for the SAIL databank and the ADRC eloquently described the operation of an informal group which aims to bring together administrative data researchers, policymakers and data analysts from Welsh data custodians:

> We have developed the model … where one of my researchers, a policy person from Welsh government and a government researcher, they work as a team. The policy person has the emerging findings to make policy decisions, the government researcher is building the information base for the benefit of government research and the researcher here is deriving impact from the changes that the policy person is making.[136]

As in Northern Ireland, then, the Welsh and Scottish experience seems to reflect the significance of informal channels of communications like 'forums' as a facilitator of making data managers more confident in research data sharing. As another interviewee, who works as a data analyst for the KAS of the Welsh Government, explained, the Welsh Statistical Liaison Committee, 'brings together lots of the right professionals and lots of the local authorities',[137] enabling closer cooperation

[132] ibid.
[133] Interview with participant nr 13 (2018, Belfast).
[134] Interview with participant nr 16 (2018, phone).
[135] Interview with participant nr 14 (2018, Belfast).
[136] Interview with participant nr 22 (2019, Swansea).
[137] Interview with participant nr 26 (2019, Cardiff).

and better chances of promoting the idea of data sharing. An administrative data researcher, with experience in negotiating access with Scottish data custodians, described the establishment of an informal group to facilitate better communication between data custodians and researchers. There were also data analysts and policy people 'with a particular interest in data sharing' from Police Scotland and Fire Rescue Scotland.[138] Although they conceded that, in this particular case, the conversations were not very fruitful and the attempt to establish a data linkage framework eventually 'lost its momentum',[139] they expressed satisfaction about the efficiency of the communication outside a long, formal process.[140]

Informal interactions often unblock research data sharing negotiations and help participants overcome the state of standstill. As the next sub-section will show, interactions in the research data sharing space are also, to a large extent, routine and small-scale, with changes taking shape through long and incremental processes.

C. Small-Scale Interactions: Iteratively and Incrementally Shaping Data Sharing Frameworks

Some interactions in the data sharing space may receive significant attention and participation from interested stakeholders, being perceived as 'influential' and reflecting broader changes in the field.[141] By and large, however, interactions in this space take place between a few individuals as part of a daily organisational routine and require numerous iterations before yielding a particular output for the regulation of data sharing decisions.

An interviewee, who has previously worked for the ONS as a data analyst, recalled a particular data linkage negotiation with officials working for HMRC. They stressed the significance of multiple iterations for 'allowing people to talk and express … and address their concerns'.[142] In this particular case, they had to meet data analysts and policymakers from the VAT and PAYE departments within HMRC. Although initially happy, the custodians consulted with their colleagues and eventually came back with concerns about establishing a data sharing process. The interviewee had to go to great lengths and engage in multiple conversations to reboot the negotiations:

> So, I said, ok, can I talk to your bosses? And I went through the tree, I had two audio conferences, two physical trips to London, basically until I got to the directors responsible for these departments within HMRC.[143]

As the interviewee recalled, it was not really the substance of the conversations and their arguments that helped reassure data custodians and, eventually, convince

[138] Interview with participant nr 35 (2020, virtual).
[139] ibid.
[140] ibid.
[141] Thomas and Walport (n 2); Law Commission (n 2); Laurie and Stevens (n 1).
[142] Interview with participant nr 42 (2020, virtual).
[143] ibid.

them to proceed with the data sharing process. It was the very *method* of engaging in conversations, iteratively refining the proposals, and practically reassuring HMRC that all their worries are being carefully considered. In their own words:

> The conversations were exactly identical … Although there was no new information, I could have sent a document, but the document wouldn't have the same impact! … Doing all this in a personal way, particularly for senior people, is really really important. Because you really want to know about all of this stuff. I'll have you sign this off – are you happy to do this?[144]

The same interviewee recalled a series of iterations with the legal team at the ONS, when they were seeking to formalise the access of external researchers, who until then signed the so-called '1-pound contracts',[145] to ONS data. After some difficulties in the early conversations, they took some time to think and then 'went back' to the legal team at the ONS to frame their desired aim differently. This is when they realised that solutions to complex governance challenges may only come through multiple iterations:

> I went back to the lawyers and said, ok, can we treat academics as government researchers for the purposes of accessing this? And then they came up and said, yes, you do this, that and the other. That was the first time that I realised that getting the question right was really important and understanding how people are responding to the question.[146]

This is a really striking example of the importance of multiple iterations in the development of particular data sharing frameworks. Even if the substance of the request was the same, ie allow academics to be research users of the ONS data, a solution was only reached after numerous iterations that incrementally yielded a better mutual understanding. A policymaker, who works for the ADRC – Scotland, described a similarly iterative process of negotiating access to Police Scotland's data. They recall that one of the affiliated ADRC academics 'set up meetings with many people from Police Scotland for a long time',[147] aiming to make the data managers more comfortable with the ADRC's sponsored research. Over four years, they remember 'at least 35 meetings',[148] in which academic researchers would seek to demonstrate the impact that would be generated from establishing a research data access framework while the data custodians expressed their concerns. Eventually, patience and persistence through these iterations paid off:

> This finally bore fruit in that now what Police Scotland have done is they realised that they need to have someone who actually has got the authority to release data across the board and … as we speak, they are setting up a couple of cautious projects to test the water.[149]

[144] ibid.
[145] ibid.
[146] ibid.
[147] Interview with participant nr 31 (2020, virtual).
[148] ibid.
[149] ibid.

Iterations are not only critical in overcoming barriers during data access negotiations. In some cases, they might be necessary to even *start* a data access negotiation. One reason might be that there is lack of external knowledge about the available datasets. As an administrative data researcher, with experience in the Scottish landscape, explained, it may very well be the case that multiple iterations are needed for a researcher to even understand what kind of data is available and could potentially be used by them. With many data custodians in Scotland not having 'any discoverability for their datasets',[150] multiple inquiries to data analysts, who hold the datasets, becomes necessary to kickstart a data access request, especially when considering the level of detail that researchers have to include in their requests. Without this type of communication, or when such communication does not bear fruit, researchers are 'left in the dark'.[151]

Small-scale iterations can also help to establish whether datasets are available in terms of public bodies *desiring* to make them available for research use. An information governance official, who works for the electronic Data Research and Innovation Service in Scotland, noted that they are in 'regular contact' with data managers, so that they can then inform external parties when 'something is available'.[152] Another administrative data researcher with experience in Scotland added that there is often a need to go through multiple layers of communication with numerous individuals to get a grasp of what would public bodies actually make available:

> You need to send an email to one person, so that they can send an email to the second person and say they've been chased by us to show that there's some external pressure … I guess you have these organisational dynamics of people who are interested in different things within the Scottish government.[153]

Another reason why iterations are necessary relates to the fact that there is lack of knowledge about the potential benefits that data sharing can generate for a public body and, there are insufficient incentives to establish a data sharing framework. A policymaker who has previously worked for HMRC and currently works for the Cabinet Office noted that they see repeated conversations with data managers as the best way to help them realise how data sharing can address policy gaps:

> Perhaps you are in a department, and you have a fraud problem, but you might not necessarily know how to tackle it. We are trying to provide the little bit of extra information and handhold people through the governance process.[154]

The same interviewee recalled a particular example where repeated iterations with Ministry of Justice (MoJ) officials enabled establishing a data sharing process which was at the risk of being aborted. In that case, the process would be originally

[150] Interview with participant nr 29 (2020, phone).
[151] ibid.
[152] Interview with participant nr 36 (2020, virtual).
[153] Interview with participant nr 35 (2020, virtual).
[154] Interview with participant nr 32 (2020, Oxford).

established for the analytical benefit of a particular area within the MoJ who at some point 'ran out of money to actually land it'.[155] The interviewee recalled that they engaged in a series of conversations to 'salvage' this project and not allow it to be perceived as a 'complete waste of money'.[156] In their words:

> What I did was I went to the entire department, the MoJ, and asked them for the requirements of all their divisions. I knew that the prisoner probation service also had similar requirements – bringing them all together ... we could finish the solution that another part of the MoJ had funded.[157]

In this example, multiple iterations between small groups of individuals resulted in overcoming an impasse in a previously initiated data sharing procedure. It may also be the case that iterations provide the opportunity of striking a compromise between the negotiating parties as to the conditions under which data will be shared. A DWP policymaker suggested that applicants patient and persistent enough to chase DWP analysts are more likely to eventually agree on a data sharing agreement. In those cases, requesters 'would never get a flat no coming out of the blue'; there would normally be some back-and-forth discussion on whether alternative variables can work for the requesters, so that DWP analysts will be able 'to take it further'.[158]

A colleague of this interviewee, working in an information governance capacity for the DWP, agreed that discussing a data sharing agreement 'isn't just a yes or no, it is iterative, with revisions'.[159] They stressed that the 'human factor', through personal conversations, can often 'come in to get a way around' barriers to data sharing. Iterations between public bodies and requesting parties are important to 'catchup' or 'retrofit' to avoid rejection of a request.[160]

Even when iterations are internal within a public body, they can be of utmost importance for the eventual decision about a research data sharing procedure. A data analyst, who works for the DfE in Northern Ireland, claimed that 'scepticism' about data sharing for research and innovation can 'certainly be overcome' through iterations between analysts and policymakers.[161] They explained that a data access request, they would often be 'informally discussed' with their policy colleagues, asking them to 'raise any concerns' and trying to address these concerns to move the negotiation forward.[162] Another ONS data analyst confirmed that the 'most important dialogue' is that between the Office's analysts and policymakers who have the final word before an access request can be approved.[163] They stressed that it is of the utmost importance that both sides are patient during this dialogue,

[155] ibid.
[156] ibid.
[157] ibid.
[158] Interview with participant nr 7 (2017, Sheffield).
[159] Interview with participant nr 8 (2017, Sheffield).
[160] ibid.
[161] Interview with participant nr 16 (2018, phone).
[162] ibid.
[163] Interview with participant nr 2 (2017, Titchfield).

engaging in a series of iterations in a spirit of 'co-operating and trying to work through a mutually reasonable decision at the end of the process'.[164]

Apart from the more relational aspect of building rapport and allaying the worries of data managers, repeated iterations are often necessary due to the complexities of research data sharing from a technical and information governance perspective. An information governance official, working for the NHS Wales Informatics Service (NWIS), explained that handling risks of reidentification from the use of administrative data necessitates regular disclosure controls and oversight of researcher practices. In some cases, researchers may receive initial approval for a particular use of the data, but 'follow-up' later to amend 'certain statistical considerations from the initial request'.[165]

> So, they would come back, but the purpose and the original methodology has changed. We need to consider this slightly differently now ... you need to go back and reset some of this stuff ... With Wales being a smaller place, we are able to have a closer conversation with people in that line.[166]

Small-scale and repeated iterations, often as part of routine daily interactions between low-level officials working for public bodies, requesting and intermediary bodies, incrementally lead to the construction of data sharing frameworks. Even if such frameworks then receive the formal legal form or the imprimatur of a high-level data sharing strategy designed by a large ministerial department, they are often shaped through these informal and iterative communicative channels.

III. Conclusion: The Importance of Commonplace, Low-Level Interactions

Data access frameworks are shaped through interactions that are more complicated than meets the eye. In principle, high-ranked officials, like policymakers, who work for data custodians are the ultimate decision-makers and dictate the direction in which data sharing is headed, either resulting in broader and more permissive, or narrower and more restrictive frameworks.

A closer look, however, at the experiences of participants in the data sharing process has illuminated the interactive and relational character of decision-making. Decisions are neither solely taken at the high-level, nor are they unilateral in nature. Low-ranked officials, the data analysts, play a significant role in framing the realities of decision-making and mediating the dialogue between decision-makers and requesters. Analysts are the experts, the mediators, and the streamliners, often

[164] ibid.
[165] Interview with participant nr 23 (2019, Cardiff).
[166] ibid.

devising ingenuous solutions to enable higher-level officials to proceed with the creation and implementation of data sharing procedures.

Analysts can play such a pivotal role in unlocking the barriers to data sharing despite their lack of formal decision-making powers because the interactions in the research data sharing space are generally not always pursued with a view to a high-level, landmark legal or policy decision. Long-term relationships and mutual trust between data sharing participants offer critical assurances for a data sharing process to go ahead. Even if formally reflected in the legal framework or an officially published policy agenda, the requirements and the powers that constitute data sharing frameworks are constructed and negotiated in the commonplace, daily actions of the space's, often low-level, participants. Such interactions very often happen outside of formal decision-making channels and may require numerous iterations before incrementally resulting in the rules that govern data access. In the following, concluding chapters, I draw the tenets of the argument together and reflect on the future for the regulation of data sharing decisions for research and innovation in the UK.

PART 4

Looking Ahead

9

Legal Reform to Widen Access to Data for Research and Innovation

In the digital age, access to government data has become a critical resource for researchers and innovators seeking to address pressing societal challenges and drive evidence-based policymaking. However, as I have demonstrated in this book, there still exists a significant power imbalance between data controllers and requesting parties when it comes to accessing data for research and innovation purposes in the UK public sector. I now turn to a crucial question: Can legal reform alleviate these barriers and widen access to data for research and innovation? To answer this question, I draw inspiration from freedom of information legislation. The UK's Freedom of Information Act (FOIA) 2000 has long been a vital tool in enabling researchers to obtain previously undisclosed information about the inner workings of government. However, as public service delivery has evolved, becoming more data-driven and dynamic, the limitations of the FOIA have become increasingly apparent. By examining the successes and shortcomings of the FOIA, I propose establishing a legal presumption in favour of providing access to data for independent researchers and innovators for public interest purposes. This proposal recognises public-sector data as a 'public good' that should be utilised to benefit society as a whole. However, this chapter goes beyond mere legal prescriptions. In recognising that changing the letter of the law is not enough, I stress that we must also transform the culture and mindset of the public sector towards research data access. This cultural shift will require ongoing engagement, education, and incentives to ensure that the spirit of the reforms is embraced and implemented by data controllers and public officials. The implications of these proposed reforms are far reaching. By widening access to government data, we can unlock new possibilities for research and innovation that could lead to ground-breaking discoveries, more effective public policies, and improved social outcomes. Moreover, these reforms have the potential to enhance democratic accountability by enabling more robust scrutiny of government actions and decisions.

I begin by examining the legacy of the FOIA, highlighting its role in democratising access to information and facilitating independent research across various disciplines. I then turn to the limitations of the FOIA in the context of the digital state, where massive government datasets are continuously updated and shared across multiple public bodies. I argue that the current data sharing legislation and practices create significant barriers for independent researchers, particularly those without secure employment in academic or other organisations. To address these challenges, I propose a range of reforms, including amending the FOIA to expand its coverage to private providers of public services, requiring public bodies to maintain comprehensive statistics on data access requests, and reforming the Digital Economy Act (DEA) 2017 to establish a legal presumption in favour of providing access to data for independent researchers and innovators for public interest purposes. I also emphasise the importance of sectoral reforms and collaboration among data controllers to establish common baseline principles for granting access to public sector data.

I. Drawing Inspiration from the Freedom of Information Act (FOIA) 2000

A. The FOIA's Legacy

Chapter 4 has already elaborated on freedom of information legislation in the UK. In the present chapter, I draw on parts of this analysis before making a proposal for reforming the law. The inspiration for reforming public-sector data sharing law emerges from another area of administrative law that has enabled independent researchers to access public sector information in the past, that is freedom of information (FOI) legislation. Indeed, FOI legislation has facilitated independent research for the past two and a half decades in many countries, including the UK since the establishment of the Freedom of Information Act (FOIA) 2000.[1]

Many scholars have utilised Freedom of Information (FOI) laws to obtain formerly undisclosed details regarding the creation and execution of governmental policies that impact both individual citizens and various groups within society.[2] The FOIA, which was introduced in 1997 and enacted in 2000, aimed to position the United Kingdom as a global frontrunner in government transparency and information accessibility.[3] The Act, which came into effect in 2005, covered more than 110,000 public sector entities in the UK.[4] It grants the right to 'any person', including legal entities, to receive a written response regarding the presence of specific information within a public authority's records.[5] The requester's location need not be in the UK. If the public authority possesses the requested records, the requester has the right to obtain them. In cases where the information is exempt

[1] A Savage and R Hyde, 'Using Freedom of Information Requests to Facilitate Research' (2014) 17(3) *International Journal of Social Research Methodology* 303–17.

[2] K Walby and A Luscombe, 'Ethics Review and Freedom of Information Requests in Qualitative Research' (2018) 14(4) *Research Ethics* 1–15.

[3] D Vincent, *The Culture of Secrecy 1832–1997* (Oxford University Press, 1998).

[4] B Worthy, 'More Open but Not More Trusted? The Effect of the Freedom of Information Act 2000 on the United Kingdom Central Government' (2010) 23 *Governance* 561–82.

[5] C Bessant (ed), *Information Sharing Handbook* (The Law Society, 2009) 18.

from disclosure or the public authority does not possess it, the requester is entitled to a notice of denial.[6]

Exemptions are central to the functioning of the FOIA. There are two main types of exemptions: 'harm-based' and 'class-based'. 'Harm-based' exemptions, such as those related to defence and international relations (FOIA 2000, ss 26 and 27), require authorities to determine whether disclosing the information would lead to harm or prejudice to interests like national security, international relations, or national defence. In such cases, a balancing exercise must be conducted to assess whether the harm caused by releasing the information would outweigh the public interest in disclosure.[7] 'Class-based' exemptions, like section 32 of the Act concerning court records, apply when public authorities have determined that the requested information belongs to the class of information specified in the exemption, irrespective of any harm caused by disclosure. Importantly, under section 40(2) of the Act, an absolute exemption applies if disclosing the information would breach the principles of the UK GDPR, such as when there is no lawful basis for processing and disclosing personal data.[8]

Freedom of information legislation has been praised for its potential to 'democratise' independent research that effectively holds public power accountable. According to Savage and Hyde, FOI legislation can be used by anyone interested in scrutinising government policies through research, not just established institutional actors like universities or other research organisations and their affiliated researchers. It is no surprise that scholars in disciplines traditionally focused on power and accountability, such as law,[9] sociology,[10] criminology,[11] criminal justice,[12] and political science,[13] have been at the forefront of using this legislation for research purposes. Researchers in various countries have utilised freedom of information legislation. In Canada, freedom of information requests have been employed as a primary data source in diverse research contexts, including policing, national security, corporate security, and post-secondary education.[14] In the

[6] Savage and Hyde (n 1) 310.

[7] ibid.

[8] Information Commissioner's Office, 'The Guide to Freedom of Information' (updated July 2022). Available at: https://ico.org.uk/media/for-organisations/guide-to-freedom-of-information-4-9.pdf.

[9] K Walby and A Luscombe, 'Using Freedom of Information Requests in Socio-Legal Studies, Criminal Justice Studies, and Criminology' in M Deflem and D Silva (eds), *Methods of Criminology and Criminal Justice Research* (Emerald 2019) 33–46.

[10] P Greenberg, 'Strengthening Sociological Research Through Public Records Requests' (2016) 3(2) *Social Currents* 110–17.

[11] I Warren, 'Freedom of Information and Australian Criminology' in K Walby and A Luscombe (eds), *Freedom of Information and Social Science Research Design* (Routledge 2019) 75–85.

[12] L Cooke and P Sturges, 'Police and Media Relations in an Era of Freedom of Information' (2009) 19(4) *Policing & Society* 406–24.

[13] F Jiwani and T Krawchenko, 'Public Policy, Access to Government, and Qualitative Research Practices: Conducting Research Within a Culture of Information Control' (2014) 40(1) *Canadian Public Policy* 57–66.

[14] K Walby and A Luscombe, 'Criteria for Quality in Qualitative Research and Use of Freedom of Information Requests in the Social Sciences' (2017) 17(5) *Qualitative Research* 537–53;

United States, researchers used freedom of information requests to uncover information about the Federal Bureau of Investigation's (FBI) surveillance practices targeting academics believed to be radicals.[15] In the UK, scholars in the field of policing, particularly those with socio-legal and broader social-scientific perspectives, have made significant use of the FOIA. Savage used the FOIA to access the whistleblowing policies of 39 UK police constabularies in 2015.[16] Kingston and colleagues used the FOIA to investigate how cost calculations impede requests for information by the police in England and Wales in 2018.[17] Other researchers have employed FOIA requests to evaluate the resources allocated to combating economic crimes or the number of police station closures and reductions in opening hours.[18]

Despite the diverse use and democratising potential of freedom of information laws in research, relying on them is not yet a well-established scientific practice. Researchers have only recently begun to develop methodological aspects of using FOI requests[19] and there are many open questions regarding how to ensure research quality and implement best practices in submitting FOI requests and analysing the obtained data. Moreover, FOI requests do not automatically overcome government resistance to transparency and accountability. Many researchers have reported abuses of power by public officials, such as characterising FOI requests as vexatious or citing resource constraints to avoid responding to requests.[20] Significant barriers may also exist in accessing the desired data. Researchers have reported delays exceeding estimates, redactions, overextension of exemptions, and poor data quality.[21] Despite the challenges, freedom of information legislation provides access to a wealth of information that researchers would otherwise be unable to obtain, particularly in security-sensitive research contexts requiring access to confidential government documents such as internal communiqués, reports, policy agenda drafts, emails, and other classified information.[22] For certain

J Piché, 'Accessing the State of Imprisonment in Canada: Information Barriers and Negotiation Strategies. Brokering Access: Politics, Power, and Freedom of Information in Canada' (2012) 234–60.

[15] S Diamond, *Compromised Campus: The Collaboration of Universities with the Intelligence Community* (Oxford University Press, 1992); J Keen and J Appleby, 'Freedom of information. Quietly Does It' (1999) 109(5678) *The Health Service Journal* 24–26.

[16] A Savage, 'Whistle Blowing in the Police Service: Developments and Challenges' (2016) 22(1) *European Journal of Current Legal Issues*.

[17] S Kingston and others, '"Cost" Calculations as a Barrier to Gaining Information under the Freedom of Information Act 2000 from the Police in England and Wales' (2019) 29(7) *Policing and Society* 834.

[18] R Smith and P Somerville, 'The Long Goodbye: A Note on the Closure of Rural Police Stations and the Decline of Rural Policing in Britain' (2013) 7(4) *Policing: A Journal of Policy and Practice* 348–58; M Button and others, '"The Not So Thin Blue Line After All?" Investigative Resources Dedicated to Fighting Fraud/Economic Crime in the United Kingdom' (2015) 9(2) *Policing: A Journal of Policy and Practice* 129–42.

[19] Walby and Luscombe (n 9) 33.

[20] ibid.

[21] D Clément, '"Freedom" of Information in Canada: Implications for Historical Research' (2015) 75 *Labour: JouD* democracy: The Critical Relationship between Academics and the Access to Information Act' (2011) 26(3) *Canadian Journal of Law and Society/La Revue Canadienne Droit et Société* 613–22; Piché (n 14).

[22] Walby and Luscombe (n 9) 33.

research questions, especially in fields like political science, international relations, or the sociology of organisations, officially produced state documents can be invaluable sources of information.[23] Another significant advantage of FOI is its ability to generate large amounts of data, particularly when researchers submit multiple relevant requests to numerous public authorities simultaneously.[24] Considering the time pressures inherent in publicly funded academic research projects, effectively utilising FOI may allow researchers to optimally allocate their efforts and time to developing other aspects of the research design while awaiting responses from public authorities to access the data.

B. The FOIA's Limitations

While the FOIA has undeniably played a crucial role in enabling independent research that critically examines government policies, the emergence of the "digital state" in the UK and other countries has significantly limited this empowering capacity. The FOIA is designed to provide access to information in a more static manner, allowing researchers to identify and request access to specific pieces of information or databases, which often reflect public service delivery from previous years. However, the modernised State collects and produces information in a much more dynamic fashion. Massive government datasets are updated daily and require organisation and curation to ensure that the contributions of thousands of civil servants and the data points of millions of citizens are coherently and meaningfully registered during routine government operations.[25] For instance, to scrutinise the fairness of immigration decisions made by UK border control authorities, one would need ongoing access to massive datasets that are continuously updated through daily border control activities and bureaucratic decisions, such as those related to the settled status of EU citizens in the UK. Many of the relevant datasets will belong to different public bodies besides the main decision-maker (in this case, the Home Office), such as HM Revenue and Customs (HMRC) and the Department for Work and Pensions (DWP).[26]

As public bodies increasingly share data to make service delivery more cost-efficient and tailored to actual needs,[27] ongoing access to up-to-date government information becomes essential for researchers to gain a complete understanding of the progress made in public policymaking and delivery. The automation of certain civil service processes further complicates matters by blurring the

[23] Savage and Hyde (n 1) 310.

[24] ibid.

[25] S Lowe, 'The Value of Safe Settings in Evidence-Based Policy Making' (2018). Available at: http://eprints.ncrm.ac.uk/4255/.

[26] J Tomlinson, 'Quick and Uneasy Justice: An Administrative Justice Analysis of the EU Settlement Scheme' (2019) The Public Law Project. Available at: https://publiclawproject.org.uk/content/uploads/2019/07/Joe-Tomlinson-Quick-and-Uneasy-Justice-Full-Report-2019.pdf.

[27] Law Commission, *Data Sharing Between Public Bodies: A Scoping Report* (2014), Law Com No 351. Available at: www.lawcom.gov.uk/app/uploads/2015/03/lc351_data-sharing.pdf.

boundaries between human decision-makers and algorithms, making it challenging to map information flows. Public bodies may use automated systems to triage user requests or augment (or even make) decisions that affect citizens' rights and obligations, such as those related to social welfare benefits.[28] With powerful private actors often involved in deploying these systems,[29] researchers may struggle to hold the exercise of public power accountable without ongoing and regularly updated knowledge of existing data sharing practices. Ongoing knowledge requires established and predictable data access arrangements. Large government datasets, which were not originally collected for research purposes, must be edited before researchers can use them. This process demands significant efforts from the data controller. Officials with statistical expertise and knowledge of the subject area must identify the most appropriate datasets and variables within these datasets for research use. The datasets then need to be curated and 'cleaned'[30] to ensure that missing or poor-quality data do not hinder research. Even if the datasets are usable, the data controller must make specific arrangements for researchers to access personal data. Issues such as the need for an accreditation system to ensure responsible data use, both in terms of the individuals accessing the data and the projects they wish to pursue, must be thoroughly considered, and incorporated into legally binding data sharing agreements between the data controllers and researchers. Finally, even after researchers have extracted the necessary information, controls, and oversight, known as Statistical Disclosure Control,[31] must be performed to ensure that no identifiable data of living individuals are included in the research outputs.

The description above provides a general overview of the various stages involved in government data sharing for independent research purposes, and depending on the specific data controller, even more sub-phases and processes could be identified. However, this overview already highlights the nature of the data sharing relationship between public bodies and researchers: it is a complex and prolonged process, characterised by intricate technical requirements as well as legal and ethical safeguards. To navigate the various requirements and establish a long-term relationship based on trust, both parties must maintain smooth and efficient communication. As will be demonstrated, building this trust is just as crucial as fulfilling the formal data access requirements to make progress. The lack of an appropriate legal instrument, such as the limitations of the Freedom

[28] R Booth, 'Benefits system automation could plunge claimants deeper into poverty' *The Guardian* 14 October 2019. Available at: www.theguardian.com/technology/2019/oct/14/fears-rise-in-benefits-system-automation-could-plunge-claimants-deeper-into-poverty.

[29] UN Special Rapporteur on Extreme Poverty and Human Rights, 'Digital technology, social protection and human rights: Report' (2019). Available at: www.ohchr.org/EN/Issues/Poverty/Pages/DigitalTechnology.aspx; HM Government, 'Guidelines for AI procurement' (8 June 2020). Available at: www.gov.uk/government/publications/guidelines-for-ai-procurement/guidelines-for-ai-procurement.

[30] S Randall and others, 'The Effect of Data Cleaning on Record Linkage Quality' (2013) 13(1) *British Medical Council Medical Informatics and Decision Making* 1–10.

[31] L Willenborg and T de Waal, *Elements of Statistical Disclosure Control* (Springer 2012).

of Information Act (FOIA), is not the only source of difficulties for independent researchers seeking to produce critical research that effectively holds public power accountable. The incentive structure of the contemporary academic world also introduces constraints on how relationships between independent researchers and public bodies are managed. For example, researchers are often required to demonstrate the impact of their work on policy-making activities.[32] In practice, adopting a highly critical approach is likely to result in the closing of several doors, which can have detrimental effects on one's research and career ambitions.

II. A Legal Presumption for Data Availability for Research and Innovation

The Freedom of Information Act (FOIA) has played a crucial role in democratising information and increasing transparency in the UK Government. However, the rise of the digital State has limited the FOIA's effectiveness in supporting modern-day, data-driven research that scrutinises government work. As a non-profit research group points out, the FOIA 'is static while the ways in which public services are delivered are changing'.[33] This book, showing the power imbalance between data controllers and requesting parties, demonstrates that, without a regulatory instrument that serves the same accountability function as the FOIA, the current data sharing legislation and practices create a complex maze that is often difficult for independent researchers to navigate, especially those who do not have secure employment in academic or other organisations and are under strict time constraints to complete their projects. In the absence of relevant legal regulations, efficiency-driven new public management rationales are likely to overshadow democratic ideals of government accountability, leaving independent researchers with a stark choice: compromise with the data controller's demands or face inertia and lack of access to the data.

Legal reform can help improve the situation. Both legislative and regulatory reforms can be considered, either at the central government level or on a sectoral level. Legislative reform could start with amending the FOIA itself. Several proposals directly relevant to data sharing for independent research should be considered.[34] Since many public services in the UK are contracted out,[35] it would be significant for the UK Government to follow that of the Scottish Government

[32] S Smith and others, ''Impact' in the proposals for the UK's Research Excellence Framework: Shifting the Boundaries of Academic Autonomy' (2011) 40(10) *Research Policy* 1369–79.

[33] See mySociety, 'Reforming Freedom of Information' (2022) for a comprehensive list of proposed reform of the FOIA framework in its own terms, and with a clearer focus on investigative journalism. Available at: https://research.mysociety.org/html/reforming-foi/#conclusion.

[34] ibid.

[35] B Meggitt, 'Partnering with Agents: How the Covid-19 Pandemic Changed Relations between the UK Government and Public Service Contractors' (2022) 93(2) *The Political Quarterly* 244–52.

and expand FOI obligations to private providers of public services under section 5 of the Scottish FOIA.[36] Additionally, in line with the existing government commitment to promote transparency about the use of government data,[37] the FOIA should be amended to require public bodies to maintain comprehensive statistics on the volume and processing of data access requests, covering both FOIA requests and requests based on the Digital Economy Act (DEA) 2017.[38] This would enhance the accountability of public bodies, revealing which bodies are more open to enabling independent research using their datasets compared to those that are more reluctant. These reforms would empower independent researchers and innovators to assert their rights to access information more effectively and gather a complete picture by relying on both FOI legislation and the DEA for ongoing access.

Moreover, government regulators should initiate reforms to enable researchers and innovators to rely more convincingly on both the FOIA and a reformed version of the Digital Economy Act (DEA) 2017. This reform could be part of the new National Data Strategy proclaimed by the UK Government to unlock 'not only economic benefits but wider societal benefits' through greater personal data use.[39] This would enhance the third mission of the Strategy, which is 'transforming government's use of data to drive efficiency and improve public services',[40] by ensuring that independent researchers can evaluate government policies, scrutinise shortcomings and contribute to improvements in public services. While the government has primarily focused on STEM scientists, such as those in life sciences,[41] researchers who can produce other types of 'life-enhancing research', such as sociologists and economists, should also be considered beneficiaries of the reform. Current proposals to 'improve the delivery of government services through better use and sharing of personal data'[42] aim to reform the data sharing powers in the DEA 2017, primarily by expanding powers currently available to government departments for businesses.[43]

However, more fundamental legal changes would be required to enhance the right to access public-sector data for independent researchers and innovators for public interest purposes. It is proposed that a legal presumption in favour of providing access to data for independent researchers and innovators for public interest purposes should be established, similar to the presumption in the FOIA that government information shall be disclosed to interested parties unless an exemption applies or there is a legally protected interest (eg, national security)

[36] Freedom of Information (Scotland) Act 2002 (FOISA), s 5.

[37] Department for Digital, Culture, Media and Sport (DCMS), *National Data Strategy* (9 December 2020) para 7.1.

[38] mySociety (n 33).

[39] DCMS, 'Data: A New Direction – Government Response to Consultation'. Available at: www.gov.uk/government/consultations/data-a-new-direction/outcome/data-a-new-direction-government-response-to-consultation#executive-summary.

[40] ibid para 3.

[41] ibid.

[42] ibid.

[43] ibid para 104.

outweighing the public interest in the disclosure of information. In practical terms, this would require defining public-sector data as a 'public good' that is to be used in the interest of society, departing from the approach in section 64(1) of the DEA 2017. This section currently leaves it entirely to the discretion of the public body to decide whether information that is 'in connection with' its 'functions' will be disclosed to another person for research purposes.[44] The Act should clearly express the political will for government data to serve the public interest more effectively through independent research and also add the notion of 'innovation' as an explicit additional legitimate purpose as long as it serves public interest goals. In other words, it should be established that, in principle and under reasonable conditions, public interest data of the UK Government shall be made available on an ongoing basis, allowing researchers to cross-validate, interrogate, and challenge existing government work or innovate in a way that creates more economic opportunities for the broader society. This would change the current situation where access to data is a privilege, not a right for researchers and innovators, and would require public bodies to justify when it is reasonable not to provide access to the data. This way, researchers will not be subject to the whims of public-sector data controllers, and the research community will be able to contribute to improved collective economic and social knowledge and, often, improved policy making and delivery.

Lastly, sectoral reforms and collaboration via guidance for data controllers and soft law regulatory instruments should be explored to delineate common baseline principles for granting access to public sector data for research and innovators. This would follow the idea established in the UK's national AI strategy,[45] where sectoral regulators are asked to collaborate and establish cross-sectoral principles for regulating AI. Experienced and better-resourced public bodies, such as the DWP, could lead the way and initiate communication and policymaking to frame the researcher-data controller relationship in a way that mitigates the risk of arbitrary decision-making by data controllers. Such policymaking activity would also fall within the scope of Mission 4 of the National Data Strategy, which is 'ensuring the security and resilience of the infrastructure on which data relies', by encouraging the consideration of research uses of data at the level of infrastructure design, such as collecting and storing data in a research-friendly format.

In short, while the FOIA has been a vital tool for promoting government transparency and enabling independent research, its effectiveness has been limited by the rise of the digital State. The current data sharing legislation and practices create significant barriers for independent researchers seeking to scrutinise government work. To address these challenges, both legislative and regulatory reforms are needed. Amending the FOIA to expand its coverage to private providers of public services and requiring public bodies to maintain comprehensive statistics on data

[44] DEA 2017, s 64(1).

[45] DCMS, *Establishing a Pro-innovation Approach to Regulating AI* (20 July 2022).

access requests would be important steps forward. Additionally, the DEA 2017 should be reformed to establish a legal presumption in favour of providing access to data for independent researchers and innovators for public interest purposes, recognising public-sector data as a 'public good'. Sectoral reforms and collaboration among data controllers should also be pursued to establish common baseline principles for granting access to public sector data. By implementing these reforms, the UK Government can create a more conducive environment for independent researchers to contribute to improved policy making and delivery, ultimately serving the public interest more effectively.

III. The Need for Organisational Change

While legal reform is a necessary step towards improving research data access, it is important to recognise that it will not solve all problems immediately. Research and innovation data access is governed by technically complex and lengthy interactions among various organisations, and it is negotiated through the interactions between data sharing participants within and outside of formal decision-making channels. Even if reform aims to prescribe more facilitative conditions for researchers' data access, controllers may use their interpretative latitude to resist disclosure when it goes against their established views, such as their entitlements over administrative data or the appropriateness of research without clear policy relevance as an activity that uses public resources.

To address this, civil service leadership should actively work to shift the culture in the UK public sector, providing incentives for public officials to become more transparent about their management of administrative data. Small steps can lead to substantial change, such as requiring the publication of research data sharing decision-making criteria and steps, as well as making comprehensive catalogues of the datasets held by departments that can be used by researchers publicly available. The perception that public-sector data is a 'public good', to be managed and shared in the interest of the public, should be gradually infused across the civil service.

Changing the culture and mindset of the public sector towards research and innovation data access will take time and consistent effort. It is essential to recognise that reform alone is not a panacea, and that ongoing engagement, education, and incentives will be necessary to ensure that the spirit of the reforms is embraced and implemented by data controllers and public officials. By fostering a culture of transparency and openness, and by promoting the idea that administrative data is a valuable resource that should be shared for the public good, the UK Government can create a more conducive environment for independent researchers to access and utilise this data for the benefit of society as a whole.

Ultimately, the success of reforms aimed at improving research data access will depend on the willingness of all stakeholders, including data controllers, public officials, and researchers, to work together towards a common goal. By engaging in open dialogue, sharing best practices, and continuously evaluating and refining the processes and protocols surrounding research data access, the UK can make significant strides towards creating a more transparent, accountable, and evidence-based system of governance.

IV. Conclusion

The Freedom of Information Act (FOIA) has been a vital tool for promoting government transparency and enabling independent research in the UK. However, the rise of the digital state has exposed the limitations of the FOIA in facilitating access to modern-day, data-driven research that scrutinises government work or innovates in the public interest. To address these challenges and create a more conducive environment for independent research and innovation, both legislative and regulatory reforms are necessary. Amending the FOIA to expand its coverage to private providers of public services and requiring public bodies to maintain comprehensive statistics on data access requests would enhance transparency and accountability. Additionally, the DEA 2017 should be reformed to establish a legal presumption in favour of providing access to data for independent researchers and innovators, recognising public-sector data as a 'public good' that should be used in the interest of society.

Sectoral reforms and collaboration among data controllers should also be pursued to establish common baseline principles for granting access to public sector data. By fostering a culture of transparency and openness, and by promoting the idea that administrative data is a valuable resource that should be shared for the public good, the UK Government can enable independent researchers and innovators to access and utilise this data for the benefit of society as a whole. However, it is important to recognise that legal reform alone is not sufficient. Changing the culture and mindset of the public sector towards research data access will require ongoing engagement, education, and incentives to ensure that the spirit of the reforms is embraced and implemented by both data controllers and public officials.

Ultimately, the success of reforms aimed at improving research and innovation data access will depend on the willingness of all stakeholders to work together towards a common goal. By engaging in open dialogue, sharing best practices, and continuously evaluating and refining the processes and protocols surrounding research data access, the UK can make significant strides towards creating a more transparent, accountable, and evidence-based system of governance. This will not only benefit independent researchers but also contribute to improved policy making and delivery, ultimately serving the public interest more effectively. As the digital state continues to evolve, it is crucial that the legal and regulatory frameworks keep pace to ensure that the principles of transparency, accountability and public interest are upheld.

10

Research Data Access and Automating Public Services

As the conclusion to this book is being drafted, winds of change are blowing through the UK public sector. According to a recent report by the National Audit Office,[1] most (74%) public bodies in the UK have either deployed artificial intelligence (AI) or are planning to deploy AI in the short term. At the same time, a similar majority (70%) of public bodies concedes that AI adoption in their organisation is made more difficult due to lack of relevant skills in their workforce.[2] Reading these findings together, it becomes evident that a lot of AI adoption in the UK public sector will be a matter of experimentation rather than a matter of certainty. In these circumstances, critical, independent research requiring access to public-sector data for scrutinising the ongoing automation in the UK public sector will be on the one hand much needed, but, on the other, very much a matter of negotiation between data controllers and requesting researchers, as per the evidence presented previously in this book.

In this chapter, I examine the intersection of big public-sector data, automation, and research access in the United Kingdom. I argue that while the UK Government is rapidly adopting artificial intelligence (AI) and automated systems across various public services, there is a critical lack of transparency and independent research access to these systems. This opacity not only hinders innovation and scrutiny but also raises significant concerns about accountability, fairness, and the potential for unchecked algorithmic bias in public service delivery. The rapid adoption of artificial intelligence and automated systems in the UK public sector presents both significant opportunities and considerable challenges. While the government's push for AI integration across various departments and services is reshaping the landscape of public administration, this transformation is occurring against a backdrop of skill shortages, fragmented governance structures, and a concerning lack of transparency. Automated systems deployed across crime and criminal justice, housing, immigration, policing, and welfare demonstrate the wide-ranging impact of these technologies on citizens' lives.

[1] National Audit Office, 'Use of Artificial Intelligence in Government' (15 March 2024). Available at: www.nao.org.uk/wp-content/uploads/2024/03/use-of-artificial-intelligence-in-government.pdf 4.

[2] ibid.

From the National Fraud Initiative to the controversial Gangs Matrix, these tools are increasingly influencing decision-making processes that affect vulnerable populations. The potential for bias, error, and unintended consequences in these systems underscores the critical need for robust oversight, ethical considerations, and independent scrutiny.

A stark contrast emerges when comparing the UK public sector's approach to research access with that of major technology companies. While firms like OpenAI, Microsoft, and Google have established structured programs for third-party researcher access, the UK Government's automated systems remain largely opaque. The fact that the majority of information about these tools has only come to light through freedom of information requests is deeply concerning. This lack of transparency not only hinders independent research and innovation but also raises questions about accountability and the potential for unchecked algorithmic bias. The absence of dedicated researcher access policies for UK public sector AI systems is a missed opportunity. Such policies could contribute to improved safety, alignment with human values, and accelerated innovation. They could also help level the playing field between government agencies and external researchers, fostering a more diverse and robust ecosystem of AI development and oversight.

The chapter is structured into three main sections, each building upon the previous to construct a comprehensive picture of the current landscape and its implications. First, I explore the path to adoption of AI and automated systems in the UK public sector. I outline the government's initiatives and strategies for integrating these technologies into public services, from the 2018 AI Sector Deal to the more recent National AI Strategy and Public Sector Productivity Programme. I also highlight the challenges faced in this adoption process, including skill shortages and fragmented governance structures. In the second section, I provide a detailed overview of the applications of big public-sector data and automation across various policy areas. Through case studies from crime and criminal justice, housing, immigration, policing, and welfare, I illustrate the wide-ranging impact of these technologies on citizens' lives. This section underscores the potential risks and ethical considerations associated with these automated systems, particularly their effects on vulnerable populations. In the final section, I focus on the critical issue of research access to these automated systems. My analysis contrasts the approach of major technology companies, which have established structured programmes for third-party researcher access, with the UK public sector's lack of transparency and access policies. I argue for the importance of independent scrutiny and research access in ensuring the safety, fairness, and effectiveness of public sector AI systems. Throughout these sections, I emphasise the tension between the drive for innovation and efficiency in public services and the need for responsible deployment, transparency, and accountability, highlighting the potential consequences of opaque AI systems on democratic governance and citizens' rights.

I. Big Public-Sector Data and Automation: The Path to Adoption

The UK Government has consistently promoted the adoption of automation and data-driven AI systems in the public sector over recent years. This effort began with the 2018 AI Sector Deal and a 2019 review of AI's potential in government.[3] The 2021 National AI Strategy emphasised safe and ethical AI deployment in public services.[4] In 2023, the UK Science and Technology Framework highlighted AI as a critical technology,[5] with public sector innovation as a key focus. The framework aimed to leverage generative AI for public services. The 2023 Autumn Statement noted significant potential productivity gains from AI in routine government tasks.[6] Building on this, the 2024 Spring Budget allocated funds for AI initiatives within the Public Sector Productivity Programme, further solidifying the government's commitment to AI-driven public sector transformation.[7]

While AI integration in government operations offers substantial potential to enhance public services and boost efficiency, implementing these changes comes with considerable challenges. To achieve widespread benefits, it is not enough to simply introduce new technology; significant shifts in operational practices are also necessary. For successful AI implementation, the government must establish crucial groundwork, including ensuring access to skilled personnel, appropriate infrastructure, and high-quality data resources.[8] According to the National Audit Office, however, the government's efforts to promote AI adoption in the public sector have been lacking a cohesive strategy and proper governance structures.[9] The strategy's goal of making the public sector a model for safe and ethical AI deployment was hampered by fragmented responsibilities across various bodies, without robust oversight, clear accountability, implementation plans, or progress metrics. The July 2022 AI Action Plan,[10] while summarizing activities, failed to establish outcome measures or detailed implementation strategies. An initial AI Strategy Delivery Group, set up by the Office for Artificial

[3] UK Government, 'AI Sector Deal' (21 May 2019). Available at: www.gov.uk/government/publications/artificial-intelligence-sector-deal/ai-sector-deal.

[4] UK Government, 'National AI Strategy'. Available at: https://assets.publishing.service.gov.uk/media/614db4d1e90e077a2cbdf3c4/National_AI_Strategy_-_PDF_version.pdf.

[5] UK Government, 'The UK Science and Technology Framework' (Updated 9 February 2024). Available at: www.gov.uk/government/publications/uk-science-and-technology-framework/the-uk-science-and-technology-framework.

[6] HM Treasury, 'Autumn Statement 2023'. Available at: www.gov.uk/government/publications/autumn-statement-2023/autumn-statement-2023-html.

[7] HM Treasury, 'Spring Budget 2024'. Available at:www.gov.uk/government/topical-events/spring-budget-2024.

[8] National Audit Office, '(n 1) 16.

[9] ibid.

[10] UK Government, 'National AI Strategy – AI Action Plan' (18 July 2022). Available at: www.gov.uk/government/publications/national-ai-strategy-ai-action-plan.

Intelligence to oversee implementation, was dissolved in March 2022, further undermining coordinated efforts.[11]

The UK governance arrangements for AI adoption in government involve a complex network of departments and entities, each with specific roles and responsibilities. The Cabinet Office plays a central role through its Central Digital and Data Office, which leads the Government Digital and Data function. This office is responsible for setting the strategic direction and standards for digital, data, and technology initiatives, including AI, across the government.[12] In November 2023, the Cabinet Office established the Incubator for Artificial Intelligence (i.AI) to help departments harness the potential of AI for improving productivity and public services.[13] This incubator, staffed by approximately 70 people, is set to receive significant funding over five years to support its mission. The Government Digital Service, another entity within the Cabinet Office, supports AI adoption by building common digital products and platforms for use across government.[14] The Department for Science, Innovation & Technology houses several key entities involved in AI governance. The Artificial Intelligence Policy Directorate, formerly known as the Office for Artificial Intelligence, oversees the implementation of the National AI Strategy. This directorate focuses on long-term planning for the AI ecosystem, supporting the transition to an AI-enabled economy, and ensuring proper governance of AI technologies.[15] Within the same department, the Responsible Technology Adoption Unit enables trustworthy innovation using data and AI, developing tools and frameworks to build public trust in these technologies.[16] The National Technology Adviser, also part of this department, leads work on the UK Science and Technology Framework's vision for an innovative public sector.[17] Additionally, the Artificial Intelligence Safety Institute was established in 2023 with a mission to minimise risks from rapid AI advancements. This institute conducts safety evaluations on advanced AI systems and drives foundational AI safety research.[18]

This is an emerging picture, as government bodies are still developing their oversight mechanisms for AI. Among the 32 organisations that have implemented

[11] National Audit Office (n 1) 16.

[12] UK Government, 'Central Digital and Data Office'. Available at: www.gov.uk/government/organisations/central-digital-and-data-office.

[13] Incubator for Artificial Intelligence, 'About us'. Available at: www.gov.uk/government/organisations/incubator-for-artificial-intelligence/about.

[14] UK Government, 'Government Digital Service'. Available at: www.gov.uk/government/organisations/government-digital-service.

[15] UK Government, 'Office for Artificial Intelligence'. Available at: www.gov.uk/government/organisations/office-for-artificial-intelligence.

[16] UK Government, 'The CDEI is Now the Responsible Technology Adoption Unit'. Available at: www.gov.uk/government/news/the-cdei-is-now-the-responsible-technology-adoption-unit.

[17] UK Government, 'Dr Dave Smith Takes Helm as UK's National Technology Adviser'. Available at: www.gov.uk/government/news/dr-dave-smith-takes-helm-as-uks-national-technology-adviser.

[18] AI Safety Institute, 'Rigorous AI Research to Enable Advanced AI Governance'. Available at: www.aisi.gov.uk/.

AI according to a recent National Audit Office report,[19] 24 reported that their AI applications typically or always have a designated accountable owner. However, only 15 of these bodies stated that AI use cases are consistently or usually identified at an organisational level prior to deployment.[20] What kind of data-driven AI applications have, however, been rolled out in the UK public sector?

II. Big Public-Sector Data and Automation: Applications

The Public Law Project has made an immense contribution to the study of automation in the UK public sector by creating a database which currently tracks 55 automated tools utilising public-sector data to, allegedly, improve the quality and efficiency of public service.[21] These tools are employed in a wide variety of policy areas including crime & fraud, law enforcement, education, housing, immigration, legal aid, military, policing, and welfare. Without aiming to present all the tools, this section will focus on some prominent examples that have already been deployed within the most intensely automated policy areas of crime and criminal justice, housing, immigration, policing, and welfare.

Starting with crime and criminal justice, the National Fraud Initiative (NFI) is one of the most prominent and longest in use automation initiatives to detect and prevent fraud.[22] The NFI gathers over 8,000 datasets encompassing more than 20 different data types from 1,300 participating organisations. These datasets include information such as public sector payroll, housing benefit, social housing waiting lists, parking permits, council tax, local authority pension payments, the electoral register, right to buy, and public sector housing.[23] The Cabinet Office is responsible for determining which datasets should be matched based on its evaluation of the likelihood that the comparison will reveal pertinent information. For instance, the NFI compares pension payment records with those of deceased individuals to detect instances where someone might be fraudulently or mistakenly receiving a deceased person's pension.[24] Another example is the comparison of housing benefit payments with payroll records to identify cases where an individual may be inappropriately receiving housing benefit despite earning a sufficient income, either due to fraud or error.[25]

[19] National Audit Office (n 1) 20.

[20] ibid.

[21] Public Law Project, 'Tracking Automated Government (TAG) Register' (accessed 19 June 2024). Available at: https://trackautomatedgovernment.shinyapps.io/register/.

[22] Public Sector Fraud Authority, 'National Fraud Initiative' (2 April 2024). Available at: www.gov.uk/government/collections/national-fraud-initiative.

[23] Public Law Project (n 21).

[24] Cabinet Office, 'NFI: public sector case studies and testimonials' (21 March 2023). Available at: www.gov.uk/government/publications/national-fraud-initiative-case-studies/nfi-public-sector-case-studies.

[25] ibid.

Moving to housing, since April 2021, the Department for Work and Pensions (DWP), has, with the help of local authorities, rolled out the Housing Benefit Award Accuracy Indicator.[26] Using a variety of data sources, such as the claimant's personal data, number of dependents and total income,[27] the model forecasts the likelihood that a person receiving Housing Benefit will experience a change in their situation or circumstances. As per the relevant guidance of the DWP, local authorities are advised to prioritise and examine cases that have been flagged by the risk assessment system. They should rely on this risk score as the primary indicator, rather than using any alternative risk evaluation methods that the local authority might have employed previously.[28] The DWP mandates that local authorities perform a comprehensive review of the 400,000 cases deemed to be at the greatest risk, as determined by the risk assessment model.[29] Of particular concern is the fact that the system factors in age and sex, both protected characteristics under the Equality Act 2010, with the DWP dismissing in their equality impact assessment that this can lead to disproportionate outcomes.[30]

Immigration is one of the most intensely automated areas of policy and the Home Office has been particularly active in investing energy and resources in that regard. Following the Windrush scandal and the recommendations in the subsequent report which recommended that the Home Office should improve the quality and management of its data,[31] the Home Office invested in 2022 in an augmented data catalogue to assist government officials in gaining a deeper understanding of the information in their possession and to establish a centralised database that will serve as the main source of evidence to inform and guide their decision-making processes.[32] On the decision-support side, one of the main automated in tools currently in use (since 2002) is the Electronic Monitoring Review Tool (EMRT). The EMRT is a system that employs automated business rules and adheres to the guidelines outlined in the Immigration Bail guidance. Its purpose is to offer recommendations for decisions in cases where an electronic monitoring condition is under review.[33] Caseworkers are required to consider the recommendation provided by the decision support tool in conjunction with the guidelines outlined in the Home Office's official caseworker guidance when making their final

[26] Public Law Project (n 21).

[27] ibid.

[28] Department for Work and Pensions, 'A5/2020: Housing Benefit Award Accuracy Initiative' (10 February 2021). Available at: www.gov.uk/government/publications/housing-benefit-adjudication-circulars-2020/a52020-housing-benefit-award-accuracy-initiative.

[29] ibid.

[30] Big Brother Watch, 'Poverty Panopticon: The Hidden Algorithms Shaping Britain's Welfare State'. Available at: https://bigbrotherwatch.org.uk/wp-content/uploads/2021/07/Poverty-Panopticon.pdf 43.

[31] W Williams, 'Windrush Lessons Learned Review' (31 March 2020). Available at: www.gov.uk/government/publications/windrush-lessons-learned-review 18.

[32] Mark Say, 'Home Office plans augmented data catalogue' (22 February 2022). Available at: www.ukauthority.com/articles/home-office-plans-augmented-data-catalogue.

[33] Home Office, 'Immigration Bail' (Version 19.0). Available at: https://assets.publishing.service.gov.uk/media/65f4260efa1851001a0117bf/Immigration+bail.pdf 49.

determinations.[34] Another tool that the Home Office plans to use is the Asylum Initial Decision Model.[35] The analytical model examines the progression of cases through the asylum system. It employs probability distributions to forecast how the initial decision-making process is expected to function when presented with a specific influx of cases.[36] The model's predictions regarding the effect on the asylum system and its resources (eg, available interview slots) are utilised to assess the potential costs associated with the caseload. The model allows for adjustments to accommodate internal procedural changes, such as specifying which types of cases should be given priority at any particular time.[37] Beyond these tools, there is a wide variety of other automated tools in the immigration context, such as the Visa streaming tool, the Modern Slavery risk profiles, the Windrush compensation scheme model and the Border Risk and Targeting Capability.[38]

Policing is another intensely automated area in the UK public sector and one which shows how experimentation with algorithms is often quite harmful, especially for minorities. The Gangs Matrix,[39] used by the London Metropolitan Police between 2011 and 2024, was one of the longest running, if not the longest running, automated tool in the UK before it was scrapped in February 2024. The gangs matrix was a database maintained by the police that stored personal information about individuals who the Metropolitan Police Service believed to be gang members and considered likely to engage in violent behaviour.[40] The tool was suspended after many years of campaigns and legal action over the disproportionate representation of young Black males in the outcomes of the model.[41] Similarly problematic was the Harm Assessment Risk Tool (HART) employed by the Durham Constabulary between 2016 and 2020. The system was employed to forecast the probability of an individual engaging in either a violent or non-violent criminal act within the upcoming two-year period.[42] HART assigned the person a 'risk score' of low, medium, or high, and was designed to overestimate the risk. It based its prediction on 34 pieces of data, 29 of which related to the person's past criminal history. The other pieces of data included personal characteristics such as age, gender, and postcode.[43] In April 2018, it was revealed that an Experian dataset called 'Mosaic' was used to supplement the police data being fed into the HART

[34] Public Law Project (n 21).
[35] ibid.
[36] Home Office, 'Annex to Home Office's response to Public Law Project's FOI request'. Available at: www.whatdotheyknow.com/request/aqa_assessments_of_home_office_s/response/2229983/attach/4/FOI%2073704%20Annex%20A.pdf.
[37] Public Law Project (n 21).
[38] ibid.
[39] StopWatch, 'The gangs matrix*'. Available at: www.stop-watch.org/what-we-do/projects/the-gangs-matrix/.
[40] ibid.
[41] Metropolitan Police, 'Violence Harm Assessment'. Available at: www.met.police.uk/police-forces/metropolitan-police/areas/about-us/about-the-met/violence-harm-assessment.
[42] Public Law Project (n 21).
[43] ibid.

system. Mosaic profiled and classified people into groups, even linking specific names to stereotypes.[44] Following scholarly and civil society criticism,[45] the tool was scrapped in 2020. Other projects, such as Project Alpha or NeoFace Live Facial Recognition (LFR) are currently in use, but there is not enough information to assess their operation or impact.[46]

Finally, yet importantly, welfare is another area of intense automation with massive potential impacts for the affected individuals, who are often quite vulnerable and struggle with information literacy aspects. Like housing, the DWP have been the main force behind automating welfare, which has been called, in more critical terms, as 'automating poverty'.[47] The Fraud Risk Model, currently in use, is a machine learning model trained on data from historical benefits claims. The model assigns each claim a score. Claims above a certain threshold are referred to caseworkers for review and payment of the benefit is paused until a caseworker issues a decision on the referral.[48] A selection of claims are flagged at random and caseworkers are not told the reason for referral. The National Audit Office highlighted the existence of an 'inherent risk of bias' when employing machine learning tools like this one.[49] In response, the DWP acknowledged that its ability to assess and test for bias is restricted. This limitation stems from two factors: first, claimants often opt not to provide demographic information that is considered optional, and second, the DWP segregates personal data as a security measure. Another tool developed by the DWP is the General Matching Service (GMS) and Fraud Referral and Intervention Management System (FRAIMS), although there is not enough information on its deployment.[50] These systems are used as a component of DWP strategy to tackle benefit fraud and minimize errors in the system. Specifically, the GMS seems to be utilised to pinpoint claimants or their dependents who might possess undeclared capital or additional sources of income that have not been disclosed to the department.[51] More specifically, the DWP regularly extracts data from its systems and matches it against savings data stored in the 'Database & Matching Service'. The General Matching Service (GMS)

[44] ibid.

[45] M Oswald and others 'Algorithmic Risk Assessment Policing Models: Lessons from the Durham HART Model and 'Experimental' Proportionality' (2018) 27(2) *Information & Communications Technology Law* 223–50; A Harkens, 'Fairness in Algorithmic Decision-Making: Trade-offs, Policy Choices, and Procedural Protections' (2019) *Series 2 Vol. 1 Amicus Curiae* 84; FairTrials, 'FOI reveals over 12,000 People Profiled by Flawed Durham Police Predictive AI Tool' (15 August 2022). Available at: www.fairtrials.org/articles/news/foi-reveals-over-12000-people-profiled-by-flawed-durham-police-predictive-ai-tool/.

[46] Public Law Project (n 21).

[47] The Guardian, 'Automating Poverty'. Available at: www.theguardian.com/technology/series/automating-poverty.

[48] Department for Work and Pensions, 'Annual Report & Accounts 2022–23'. Available at: https://assets.publishing.service.gov.uk/government/uploads/system/uploads/attachment_data/file/1167946/annual-report-accounts-2022-23-web-ready.pdf.

[49] National Audit Office, 'Report on Accounts – Department for Work and Pensions' (July 2023). Available at: www.nao.org.uk/wp-content/uploads/2023/07/dwp-report-on-accounts-2022-23.pdf.

[50] Public Law Project (n 21).

[51] ibid.

automatically downloads any identified referrals onto the Fraud Referral and Intervention Management System (FRAIMS). Prior to interviewing the claimant about the alleged undeclared capital, additional intelligence gathering may be necessary. Case papers must be reviewed, considering several factors: the timing of the data match; whether the claimant was receiving benefits at that time; whether the claimant has obtained capital from any government-funded Trusts and Funds that may be exempt; and whether the claimant has previously declared the capital in question.[52] Other initiatives that are less known about in this area of policy are the Common Risk Engine, the housing fraud and error detection pilot and the people living together fraud and error detection pilot.[53]

While there is a rich literature about the potentially negative impacts of experimenting with algorithms in the UK public sector,[54] the focus in this chapter is on the data access for research and innovation arrangements. The next section explains the idea of researcher data access in the context of AI and automation before demonstrating the lack of transparency in the UK public sector.

III. Automation and Research (Data) Access: Rationale and Challenges

When it comes to AI and automated algorithmic models, there is a rich discourse about the significance and benefits of providing access routes for third-party research.[55] There are many arguments in favour of providing third-party researchers access to algorithmic models and the data on which they have been trained. To begin with, there is the idea that third-party researcher access can result in improved safety and alignment. External researchers can help identify potential risks, biases, or unintended behaviours in the models, contributing to making them safer and better aligned with human values.[56] This can also diversify AI development, as third-party researchers bring varied backgrounds and viewpoints, which can uncover blind spots and lead to more robust and ethical AI systems.[57]

[52] Department for Work & Pensions, 'Fraud Investigations Staff Guide – Part 1'. Available at: www.gov.uk/government/publications/fraud-investigations-staff-guide 135–6.

[53] Public Law Project (n 21).

[54] Among others see Oswald et others (n 45); Joe Tomlinson, *Justice in the Digital State* (Bristol 2019); K Yeung,'The New Public Analytics as an Emerging Paradigm in Public Sector Administration'(2022) 27(2) *Tilburg Law Review* 1–32.

[55] T Shevlane, 'Structured Access: An Emerging Paradigm for Safe AI Deployment' (2022) *arXiv preprint arXiv:2201.05159*; S Bucknall and F Trager, 'Structured Access for Third-party Research on Frontier Ai Models: Investigating Researchers' Model Access Requirements' (2023); M van Drunen and A Noroozian, 'How to Design Data Access for Researchers: A Legal and Software Development Perspective' (2022) 52 *Computer Law & Security Review* 105946.

[56] D Leslie, 'Understanding Artificial Intelligence Ethics and Safety' (2022) arXiv preprint arXiv:1906.05684.

[57] M Cheong and others, 'Computer Science Communities: Who is Speaking, and Who is Listening to the Women? Using an Ethics of Care to Promote Diverse Voices' in *Proceedings of the 2021 ACM Conference on Fairness, Accountability, and Transparency* 106–15.

Then, there is the idea that third-party research can bolster innovation and accelerate scientific progress, as broader access allows more minds to work on advancing AI capabilities and applications, potentially leading to faster breakthroughs.[58] Innovation is also encouraged by the fact that wider access helps level the playing field and reduces the gap between large tech companies and smaller research institutions or individual researchers.

Some of the most prominent technology companies have made commitments to establish and implement third-party researcher access policies. For example, OpenAI has established a Researcher Access Program to support studies related to the responsible deployment of AI, mitigation of associated risks, and understanding of AI's societal impact. The program offers subsidised access to OpenAI's products through API credits.[59] The application process is managed through a third-party provider, SurveyMonkey Apply, where researchers must create an account to apply. OpenAI particularly encourages applications from early-stage researchers in countries supported by their API, with a special interest in subsidising work from those with limited financial and institutional resources.[60] OpenAI has outlined several key areas of research interest. These include AI alignment, focusing on understanding and aligning model objectives with human preferences; fairness and representation in language models; methods for measuring AI's societal impact; interdisciplinary research drawing insights from fields like philosophy, cognitive science, and sociolinguistics; interpretability and transparency of AI models; potential misuse of AI systems and development of 'red teaming' approaches; and robustness of large generative models to various perturbations and inputs.[61]

In a similar vein, Microsoft's Bing Qualified Researcher program offers access to publicly accessible Bing data for researchers who meet specific criteria. This program is designed to support research that contributes to understanding systemic risks in the European Union, as outlined in the EU Digital Services Act.[62] To qualify, researchers or research organisations must be independent from commercial interests and fully disclose their research funding. They must also demonstrate the capability to meet data security and confidentiality requirements, including the protection of personal data. The application should outline the technical and organisational measures in place to ensure data protection.[63] The program requires that the proposed research access and timeframes are necessary and proportionate

[58] D Mundy, 'Strengthening Third-Party Data Collaborations in AI-Driven Enterprises' (1 February 2024). Available at: www.dasera.com/blog/strengthening-third-party-data-collaborations-in-ai-driven-enterprises.

[59] OpenAI, 'Researcher Access Program Application'. Available at: https://openai.com/form/researcher-access-program/.

[60] ibid.

[61] ibid.

[62] Microsoft, 'Bing Qualified Researcher Program'. Available at: https://support.microsoft.com/en-us/topic/bing-qualified-researcher-program-b1c5a4b6-3ad6-4c8c-963d-a395c7766c85.

[63] ibid.

to the research objectives. Crucially, the expected research outcomes must contribute to detecting, identifying, and understanding systemic risks in the EU. These risks include the dissemination of illegal content through Bing services, potential negative effects on fundamental rights (as outlined in the EU Charter), impacts on civic discourse and electoral processes, public security, and issues related to gender-based violence, public health, and the well-being of minors.[64]

Similarly, Google's Researcher Program is designed to provide qualified researchers with access to data from various Google services to advance public understanding of these platforms and their impact.[65] Currently, the program is available only to researchers based in the European Union, though there are indications it may be expanded in the future. The program welcomes researchers from diverse disciplines, emphasizing a broad approach to studying Google's services. Participation in the program is governed by a comprehensive Acceptable Use Policy.[66] This policy defines key terms and sets out the conditions under which researchers can access and use the provided data. Researchers are strictly limited to using the data for approved research purposes only. The policy explicitly prohibits using the data for product development, private interests, personal use, or any harmful or illegal activities. In addition, data security and privacy are paramount in the program. Researchers must implement appropriate security controls and have a clear privacy policy describing how they will handle the data.[67]

When comparing these researcher access policies to the picture in UK public sector automation, the difference is striking. According to the thorough survey by the Public Law Project on the matter, government automation in the UK lacks transparency.[68] Of the 55 tools registered in the tracker, the overwhelming majority (83.6%) were only uncovered or more fully understood through freedom of information requests.[69] As one might expect, there is no tool accompanied by a researcher access policy at the moment of writing, making data access for researchers (let alone innovators) quite unpredictable and wholly subject to the driving forces of research data sharing analysed previously in this book. While this has not been explicitly conceded by the UK government, one might assume that members of the AI Safety Institute will enjoy privileged access to data and AI systems used by the UK government, in an effort to guarantee their robustness and safety as per its institutional remit.[70] Whether this kind of gatekeeping access will yield the results that the UK Government is seeking will be for the readers of this book to assess in a few years' time.

[64] ibid.

[65] Google, 'Researcher Engagement'. Available at: https://transparency.google/researcher-engagement/#learn-researcher-program.

[66] Google, 'Google Researcher Program Acceptable Use Policy'. Available at: https://requestrecords.google.com/researcher/policy.

[67] ibid.

[68] Public Law Project (n 21).

[69] ibid.

[70] AI Safety Institute, 'Rigorous AI research to enable advanced AI governance'. Available at: www.aisi.gov.uk/.

IV. Conclusion

Looking forward, the UK Government must prioritise transparency and establish clear pathways for independent research access to its AI systems. This could involve developing comprehensive researcher access policies and creating a centralised registry of all AI and automated systems used in the public sector, complete with detailed documentation. Furthermore, establishing an independent body to oversee and facilitate research access requests would be crucial in ensuring fair and efficient access for researchers. As the UK continues to navigate the complex terrain of public sector AI adoption, the balance between innovation and responsible deployment will be crucial. Transparency, accountability, and robust research access will be key to ensuring that these powerful tools serve the public interest, protect individual rights, and maintain public trust in government institutions. This approach would not only enhance the quality and effectiveness of AI systems in public services but also contribute to building public trust in these technologies. As AI continues to play an increasingly significant role in governance and public administration, ensuring that its deployment is subject to rigorous, independent scrutiny will be essential for maintaining democratic accountability and protecting citizens' rights in the digital age.

BIBLIOGRAPHY

Books

Baldwin R, Cave M and Lodge M, *Understanding Regulation: Theory, Strategy and Practice* (OUP 1999).

Bessant C (ed), *Information sharing handbook* (The Law Society 2009).

Davenport T and others, *Information Politics* (Taylor & Francis 1997).

Diamond S, *Compromised Campus: The Collaboration of Universities with the Intelligence Community* (Oxford University Press, 1992).

Dove E, *Regulatory Stewardship of Health Research: Navigating Participant Protection and Research Promotion* (Edward Elgar 2020).

Edelman L, *Working Law: Courts, Corporations and Symbolic Civil Rights* (Chicago University Press 2016).

Ferlie E and others, *The New Public Management in Action* (Oxford University Press 1996).

Fezer K-H, *Repräsentatives Dateneigentum. Ein zivilgesellschaftliches Bürgerrecht.* (Konrad-Adenauer-Stiftung 2018).

Floridi L, *The Fourth Revolution How the Infosphere Is Reshaping Human Reality* (Oxford University Press 2014).

Jay R, *Data Protection Law and Practice* (Sweet & Maxwell 2012).

Keyser T and Dainty C, *The Information Governance Toolkit: Data Protection, Caldicott, Confidentiality* (CRC 2016).

Lynskey O, *Foundations of EU Data Protection Law* (Oxford University Press 2015).

Mason, *Qualitative Researching* (Sage 1996).

McLaughlin K and others (eds), *New Public Management: Current Trends and Future Prospects* (Routledge 2005).

Morgan B and Yeung K, *An Introduction to Law and Regulation* (CUP 2012).

Munné R, 'Big Data in the Public Sector' in Jose Cavanillas (ed), *New Horizons for a Data-Driven Economy: A Roadmap for Usage and Exploitation of Big Data in Europe* (Springer Berlin Heidelberg 2015).

Ostrom E, *Governing the Commons: The Evolution of Institutions for Collective Action [Nobel Prize Winner 2009]* (Cambridge University Press 2011).

Savas E S, *Privatization and Public-Private Partnerships* (Chatham House, New York 2000).

Scott R, *Institutions and Organizations* (Sage 1995).

Silverman D, *Interpreting Qualitative Data* (Sage 2015).

Taylor L and others (eds), *Group Privacy: New Challenges of Data Technologies* (Springer International Publishing 2017).

Tomlinson J, *Justice in the Digital State* (Bristol 2019).

Vibert F, *The New Regulatory Space: Reframing Democratic Governance* (Edward Elgar 2014).

Vincent D, *The Culture of Secrecy 1832–1997* (Oxford University Press, 1998).

Wade W and Forsyth C, *Administrative Law* (OUP 2014).

Waldron J, *The Right to Private Property* (Clarendon Press 1988).

Weiss R, *Learning from Strangers: The Art and Methods of Qualitative Interview Studies* (The Free Press 1994).

Willenborg L and de Waal T, *Elements of Statistical Disclosure Control* (Springer 2012).

Zuboff S, *The Age of Surveillance Capitalism* (London: Profile 2019).

Book Chapters

Aidinlis S, 'Government-to-Business (G2B) Research Data Sharing and the GDPR: Reconciling the "Public" with the "Private"?' in Kosta E and Leenes R, *Research Handbook on EU Data Protection Law* (Edward Elgar 2022).

Bega D, 'The HMRC Datalab: Sharing Administrative and Survey Data on Taxation with the Research Community' in Dusa A et al (eds), *Facing the Future: European Research Infrastructures for the Humanities and Social Sciences* (Scivero 2014).

Burdon M and others, 'Access Control in Federated Databases: How Legal Issues Shape Security' in Wimmer M and others (eds), *Electronic Government: 6th International Conference, EGOV 2007* (Springer 2007) 235.

Cheong M and others, 'Computer Science Communities: Who is Speaking, and Who Is Listening to the Women? Using an Ethics of Care to Promote Diverse Voices' in *Proceedings of the 2021 ACM Conference on Fairness, Accountability, and Transparency* 106.

Douven R and others, 'Microdata and Policy Evaluation at CPB' in Crato N and Paruolo P (eds), *Data-Driven Policy Impact Evaluation* (Springer 2018).

Figlio D and others, 'Education Research and Administrative Data', in Hanushek E and others (eds), *Handbook of the Economics of Education, vol 5* (Elsevier 2016).

Goerge R and Joo Lee B, 'Matching and Cleaning Administrative Data' in Ver Ploeg et al M (eds), *Studies of Welfare Populations: Data Collection and Research Issues* (NAP 2002) 197.

Hancher L and Moran M, 'Organizing Regulatory Space' in Baldwin R, Scott C and Hood C (eds), *A Reader on Regulation* (OUP 1998).

Harbinja E, 'Posthumous Medical Data Donation: The Case for a Legal Framework' in Krutzinna J and Floridi L (eds), *The Ethics of Medical Data Donation* (Springer Open 2019) 103.

Honoré T, 'Ownership' in Guest AG (Ed.), *Oxford Essays in Jurisprudence* (Oxford University Press 1961) 107.

Jackson P, 'From "Intruders' to 'Partners": The Evolution of the Relationship Between the Research Community and Sources of Official Administrative Data' in Crato N and Paruolo P, *Data-Driven Policy Impact Evaluation* (Springer 2019).

Krizan T and others, 'In-Situ Anonymization of Big Data', *2015 38th International Convention on Information and Communication Technology, Electronics and Microelectronics (MIPRO)* (IEEE 2015). Available at: http://ieeexplore.ieee.org/document/7160282/.

Lange B and Haines F, 'Regulatory Transformations: An Introduction' in B Lange and others (eds), *Regulatory Transformations: Rethinking Economy-Society Interactions* (Hart 2015).

Mueller D and Moeller J, 'Giving the International Scientific Community Access to German Labor Market Data: A Success Story' in Crato N and Paruolo P (eds), *Data-Driven Policy Impact Evaluation* (Springer 2018) 101.

Powell W and Colyvas J, 'Microfoundations of Institutional Theory' in Greenwood R and others (eds), *The Sage Handbook of Organizational Institutionalism* (Sage 2008).

Ritchie F, 'Access to Business Microdata in the UK: Dealing with the Irreducible Risk' in Eurostat, *Monographs of Official Statistics: Work session on statistical data confidentiality* (2005).

Thelen K and Steinmo S, 'Historical Institutionalism in Comparative Politics' in Thelen K and others (eds), *Structuring Politics: Historical Institutionalism in Comparative Analysis* (Cambridge University Press 1992).

Thouvenin F and others, 'Data Ownership: Taking Stock and Mapping the Issues' in Dehmer M and Emmert-Streib F (eds), *Frontiers in Data Science* (CRC Press 2017).

Walby K and Luscombe A, 'Using Freedom of Information Requests in Socio-Legal Studies, Criminal Justice Studies, and Criminology' in Deflem M and Silva D (eds), *Methods of Criminology and Criminal Justice Research* (Emerald 2019).

Warren I, 'Freedom of Information and Australian Criminology' in Walby K and Luscombe A (eds), *Freedom of Information and Social Science Research Design* (Routledge 2019).

Webber G, 'On the Loss of Rights' in Huscroft G and others (eds), *Proportionality and the Rule of Law Rights, Justification, Reasoning* (Cambridge University Press 2014).

Woolard M, 'Administrative Data: Problems and Benefits. A Perspective from the United Kingdom' in Dusa A et al (eds), *Facing the Future: European Research Infrastructures for the Humanities and Social Sciences* (Scivero 2014).

Journal Articles

Abd Hadi Z and McBride N, 'The Commercialisation of Public Sector Information within UK Government Departments' (2000) 13 *International Journal of Public Sector Management* 552.

Aberbach J and Rockman B, 'Conducting and Coding Elite Interviews' (2002) 35(4) *Political Science & Politics* 673.

Alamgir Hossain M and Chan C, 'Open Data Adoption in Australian Government Agencies: An Exploratory Study' (2015) *ACIS 2015 Proceedings* 60. Available at: https://aisel.aisnet.org/acis2015/60.

Aletras and others, 'Predicting Judicial Decisions of the European Court of Human Rights: A Natural Language Processing Perspective' (2016) *Peer J Computer Science* 2:e93. Available at: https://doi.org/10.7717/peerj-cs.93.

Almunia M and others, 'Expanding access to administrative data: the case of tax authorities in Finland and the UK' (2019) 26 *International Tax Public Finance* 661.

Arzberger P and others, 'Promoting Access to Public Research Data for Scientific, Economic, and Social Development' (2004) 3 *Data Science Journal* 135.

Ballantyne A and Stewart C, 'Big Data and Public-Private Partnerships in Healthcare and Research' (2019) 11 *Asian Bioethics Review* 315.

Bell J and others, 'Balancing Data Subjects' Rights and Public Interest Research' (2019) 5 *European Data Protection Law Review* 43.

Black J, 'Decentring Regulation: Understanding the Role of Regulation and Self-Regulation in a "Post-Regulatory" World' (2001) 54 *Current Legal Problems* 103.

Black J, 'Regulatory Conversations' (2002) 29 *Journal of Law and Society* 163.

Braun V and Clarke V, 'Using Thematic Analysis in Psychology' (2006) 3 *Qualitative Research in Psychology* 77–101.

Brett C and Deary I, 'Realising Health Data Linkage from a Researcher's Perspective: Following up the 6-Day Sample of the Scottish Mental Survey 1947' (2014) 5(3) *Longitudinal Life Course Studies* 283.

Button M and others, '"The Not So Thin Blue Line After All?' Investigative Resources Dedicated To Fighting Fraud/Economic Crime In The United Kingdom' (2015) 9(2) *Policing: A Journal of Policy and Practice* 129.

Carroll Rainie S and others, 'Data as a Strategic Resource: Self-Determination, Governance, and the Data Challenge for Indigenous Nations in the United States' (2017) 8(2) *International Indigenous Policy Journal* 1–29.

Carter P and others, 'The Social License for Research: Why Care.data Ran into Trouble' (2015) 41(5) *Journal of Medical Ethics* 404–409.

Cascade E and others, 'Combining Electronic Health Records and Patient-Reported Information in the UK: Preliminary Results from the WASPS (Wales SAIL + PRO Study) (2012) *Value in Health* A134–A35.

Clément D, '"Freedom" of Information in Canada: Implications for Historical Research' (2015) 75 *Labour: Journal of Canadian Labour Studies* 101.

Cooper C, 'Quantitative Models of Well-Being to Inform Policy: Problems and Opportunities' (2020) 12 *Sustainability* 3180.

Chowdhury G and others, 'Measuring the Impact of Research: Lessons from the UK's Research Excellence Framework 2014' (2016) 11(6) Public Library of Science ONE.

Chowdury N and Wessel R, 'Conceptualizing Multilevel Regulation in the EU: A Legal Translation of Multilevel Governance?' (2012) 18(3) *European Law Journal* 335.

Connelly R and others, 'The Role of Administrative Data in the Big Data Revolution in Social Science Research' (2016) 59 *Social Science Research* 1.

Conradie P and Choenni S, 'On the Barriers for Local Government Releasing Open Data' (2014) 31 *Government Information Quarterly* S10.

Contreras J and others, 'Patient Data Ownership' (2018) 319 *Journal of the American Medical Association* 935.

Cooke L and Sturges P, 'Police and Media Relations in an Era of Freedom of Information' (2009) 19(4) *Policing & Society* 406.

De Hert P and others, 'The Right to Data Portability in the GDPR: Towards User-Centric Interoperability of Digital Services' (2018) 34 *Computer Law & Security Review* 19.

De Montjoye Y and others, 'Unique in the Crowd: The Privacy Bounds of Human Mobility' (2013) 3 *Scientific Reports* 1376.

Donald Shao D and Saxena S, 'Barriers to Open Government Data (OGD) Initiative in Tanzania: Stakeholders' Perspectives' (2019) 50 *Growth and Change* 470.

Dyke SO and others, 'Registered Access: A "Triple-A" Approach' (2016) 24 *European Journal of Human Genetics* 1676–80.

Dyke SO and others, 'Registered Access: Authorizing Data Access' (2018) *European Journal of Human Genetics* (published online).

Einav L and Levin J, 'The Data Revolution and Economic Analysis' (2014) 14(1) *Innovation Policy and the Economy* 1.

Elias P, 'The UK Administrative Data Research Network: Its Genesis, Progress, and Future' (2018) 675(1) *The Annals of the American Academy of Political and Social Science* 184.

Erdos D, 'Systematically Handicapped? Social Research in the Data Protection Framework' (2011) 20 *Information & Communications Technology Law* 83.

Evans B, 'Much Ado about Data Ownership' (2011) 25 *Harvard Journal of Law & Technology* 69.

Farrelly R and Chew E, 'Designing a Primary Personal Information Market as an Industry Platform: a Service Innovation Approach' (2017) *AIS Electronic Library*.

Fezer K-H, 'Ein originäres Immaterialgüterrecht sui generis an verhaltensgenerierten Informationsdaten der Bürger' (2017) 3 *Zeitschrift für Datenschutz* 99.

Finck M and Pallas F, 'They Who Must Not Be Identified – Distinguishing Personal from Non-Personal Data under the GDPR' (2020) 10 *International Data Privacy Law* 11.

Ford D and others, 'The SAIL Databank: Building a National Architecture for E-health Research and Evaluation' (2009) 9 *BMC Health Services Research* 157.

Greenberg P, 'Strengthening Sociological Research through Public Records Requests' (2016) 3(2) *Social Currents* 110.

Hall P and Taylor R, 'Political Science and the Three New Institutionalisms' (1996) *Political Studies* 936.

Harkens A, 'Fairness in Algorithmic Decision-Making: Trade-offs, Policy Choices, and Procedural Protections' (2019) *Series 2 Vol. 1 Amicus Curiae* 84–96.

Harron K and others, 'Challenges in Administrative Data Linkage for Research' (2017) 4(2) *Big Data & Society* 1134.

Hicks J, 'The Future of Data Ownership: An Uncommon Research Agenda' (2023) 71 *The Sociological Review* 544.

Hintze M, 'Viewing the GDPR through a De-Identification Lens: A Tool for Compliance, Clarification, and Consistency' (2018) 8 *International Data Privacy Law* 86.

Hummel P and others, Own Data? Ethical Reflections on Data Ownership (2020) 34(3) *Philosophy and Technology* 545.

Iveson MH and Deary IJ, 'Navigating the Landscape of Non-Health Administrative Data in Scotland: A Researcher's Narrative' (2019) *Wellcome Open Research* 97.

Jiwani F and Krawchenko T, 'Public Policy, Access to Government, and Qualitative Research Practices: Conducting Research within a Culture of Information Control' (2014) 40(1) *Canadian Public Policy* 57.

Jones KH and others, 'The Good, the Bad, the Clunky: Addressing Challenges in Using Administrative Data for Research' (2019) 4(1) *International Journal of Data Population Science* 587.

Jonnergård K and Larsson-Olaison U, 'Developing Codes of Conduct: Regulatory Conversations as Means for Detecting Institutional Change' (2007) 29(4) *Law & Policy* 460.

Kaye J and Gibbons S, 'Mapping the Regulatory Space for Genetic Databases and Biobanks In England and Wales' (2008) 9(2) *Medical Law International* 111.

Kazmierski V, 'Accessing democracy: The critical relationship between academics and the access to information act' (2011) 26(3) *Canadian Journal of Law and Society/La Revue Canadienne Droit et Société* 613.

Keen J and Appleby J, 'Freedom of information. Quietly does it' (1999) 109(5678) *The Health Service Journal* 24.

Kelle U and others, 'How to Use Mixed-methods and Triangulation Designs: An Introduction to History Education Research' (2019) 16(1) *History Education Research Journal* 5–23.

King J, 'The Justiciability of Resource Allocation' (2007) 70(2) *The Modern Law Review* 197.

Kingston S and others, '"Cost" Calculations as a Barrier to Gaining Information under the Freedom of Information Act 2000 from the Police in England and Wales" (2019) 29(7) *Policing and Society* 834–837.

Kleiman F and others, 'Changing Civil Servants' Behaviour Concerning the Opening of Governmental Data: Evaluating the Effect of a Game by Comparing Civil Servants' Intentions before and after a Game Intervention' (2022) 88 *International Review of Administrative Sciences* 921.

Kramer A and others, 'Experimental Evidence of Massive-scale Emotional Contagion Through Social Networks' (2014) 111 *The Proceedings of the Natural Academy of Sciences* 8788.

Kuner C, 'Protecting EU Data Outside EU Borders under the GDPR' (2023) 60 *Common Market Law Review* 77.

Lane J, 'Building an Infrastructure to Support the Use of Government Administrative Data for Program Performance and Social Science Research' (2017) 1 *The ANNALS of the American Academy of Political and Social Science* 240.

Lange B and Cook C, 'Mapping a Developing Governance Space: Managing Drought in the UK' (2015) 68 *Current Legal Problems* 229.

Laurie G and Stevens L, 'Developing a Public Interest Mandate for the Governance and Use of Administrative Data in the United Kingdom' (2016) 43 *Journal of Law & Society* 360.

Li S and Chen Y, 'Explaining the Resistance of Data Providers to Open Government Data' (2021) 73 *Aslib Journal of Information Management* 560.

Lyon F and others, 'Opening Access to Administrative Data for Evaluating Public Services: The Case of the Justice Data Lab' (2015) 21(2) *Evaluation* 232.

MacKenzie R and Martinez Lucio M, 'The Colonisation of Employment Regulation and Industrial Relations? Dynamics and Developments over Five Decades of Change' (2014) 55(2) *Labour History* 189.

Mahieu R and others, 'Collectively Exercising the Right of Access: Individual Effort, Societal Effect' (2018) 7 *Internet Policy Review* https://policyreview.info/node/927.

Martin C, 'Barriers to the Open Government Data Agenda: Taking a Multi-Level Perspective: Barriers to the Open Government Data Agenda' (2014) 6 *Policy & Internet* 217.

Meggitt B, 'Partnering with Agents: How the Covid-19 Pandemic changed Relations between the UK Government and Public Service Contractors' (2022) 93(2) *The Political Quarterly* 244.

Meszaros J and Ho C, 'AI Research and Data Protection: Can the Same Rules Apply for Commercial and Academic Research under the GDPR?' (2021) 41 *Computer Law & Security Review* 105532.

Moberly T, 'Should We Be Worried about the NHS Selling Patient Data?' [2020] British Medical Journal m113.

Montgomery J, 'Data Sharing and the Idea of Ownership' (2017) 23 *The New Bioethics* 81.

Morris H and others al, 'Challenges of Administrative Data Linkages: Experiences of Administrative Data Research Centre for England (ADRC-E) Researchers' (2018) 3(2) *International Journal of Population Data Science* 97.

Mourby M and others, 'Are 'Pseudonymised' Data Always Personal Data? Implications of the GDPR for Administrative Data Research in the UK' (2018) 34(2) *Computer Law & Security Review* 222.

Mourby M and others, 'Governance of Academic Research Data under the GDPR – Lessons from the UK' (2019) 9(3) *International Data Privacy Law* 192.

O'Reilly D and others, 'Administrative Data Research Northern Ireland (ADR NI)' (2020) 4(2) *International Journal of Data Population Science* 1148.

Oswald M, 'Share and Share Alike? An Examination of Trust, Anonymisation and Data Sharing with Particular Reference to an Exploratory Research Project Investigating Attitudes to Sharing Personal Data with the Public Sector' (2014) 11(3) *SCRIPTed* 245.

Oswald M and other 'Algorithmic Risk Assessment Policing Models: Lessons from the Durham HART Model and 'Experimental' Proportionality' (2018) 27(2) *Information & Communications Technology Law* 223.

Ottolia A and Sappa C, 'A Topography of Data Commons: From Regulation to Private Dynamism' (2022) 71 *GRUR International – Journal of European and International IP Law* 335.

Parvathaneni V and others, 'Drug Repurposing: A Promising Tool to Accelerate the Drug Discovery Process' (2019) 24 *Drug Discovery Today* 2076.

Pearce H, 'Personality, Property and Other Provocations' (2018) 4 *European Data Protection Law Review* 190.

Perry A, 'The Crown's Administrative Powers' (2015) *Law Quarterly Review* 652.

Powell W and Dimaggio P, 'The Iron Cage Revisited: Institutional Isomorphism and Collective Rationality in Organizational Fields' (1983) 48(2) *American Sociological Review* 147.

Prainsack B, 'Logged Out: Ownership, Exclusion and Public Value in the Digital Data and Information Commons' (2019) 6 *Big Data & Society* 1.

Price S, 'Academic and Commercial Research: Bridging the Gap' (2015) 12(2) *Participations* 168.

Purtova N, 'Property in Personal Data. A European Perspective on the Instrumentalist Theory of Propertisation' (2010) 2 *European Journal of Legal Studies* 193.

Ramos EM and others, 'A Mechanism for Controlled Access to GWAS Data: Experience of the GAIN Data Access Committee' (2013) 92 *American Journal of Human Genetics* 479.

Randall S and others, 'The effect of Data Cleaning on Record Linkage Quality' (2013) 13(1) *British Medical Council Medical Informatics and Decision Making* 1.

Rankin D and others, 'Reliability of Supervised Machine Learning Using Synthetic Data in Health Care: Model to Preserve Privacy for Data Sharing' (2020) 8(7) *JMIR Medical Informatics* 1.

Ritchie, 'Business Data Linking – Recent UK Experience' (2004) 33(1–2) *Austrian Journal of Statistics* 89.

Ritchie F, 'Secure Access to Confidential Microdata: Four Years of the Virtual Microdata Laboratory' (2008) 2 *Economic & Labour Market Review* 29.

Ritchie F, 'UK Release Practices for Official Microdata' (2010) 26(3) *Statistical Journal of the IAOS* 103.

Ruijer E and others, 'The Politics of Open Government Data: Understanding Organizational Responses to Pressure for More Transparency' (2020) 50 *The American Review of Public Administration* 260.

Sabeel Rahman K, 'The New Utilities: Private Power, Social Infrastructure, and the Revival of the Public Utility Concept' (2017) 39 *Cardozo Law Review* 1621.

Savage A and Hyde R, 'Using Freedom of Information Requests to Facilitate Research'(2014) 17(3) *International Journal of Social Research Methodology* 303.

Savage A, 'Whistle Blowing in the Police Service: Developments and Challenges' (2016) 22(1) *European Journal of Current Legal Issues*.

Schwartz P and Solove D, 'The PII Problem: Privacy and a New Concept of Personally Identifiable Information' (2011) 86 *NYU Law Review* 1814.

Scott C, 'Analysing Regulatory Space: Fragmented Resources and Institutional Design' (2001) Public Law 283.

Sexton A and others, 'A Balance of Trust in the Use of Government Administrative Data' (2017) 17(4) *Archival Science* 305.

Shkabatur J, 'The Global Commons of Data' (2019) 22 *Stanford Technology Law Review* 354.

Smith R and Somerville P, 'The Long Goodbye: A Note on the Closure of Rural Police-stations and the Decline of Rural Policing in Britain' (2013) 7(4) *Policing: A Journal of Policy and Practice* 348.

Smith S and others, ''Impact' in the Proposals for the UK's Research Excellence Framework: Shifting the Boundaries of Academic Autonomy' (2011) 40(10) *Research Policy* 1369.

Suddaby R, 'How Communication Institutionalizes: A Response to Lammers' (2011) 25(1) *Management Communication Quarterly* 183.

Susha I and others, 'Achieving Voluntary Data Sharing in Cross-sector Partnerships: Three Partnership Models' (2023) 33(1) *Information and Organization* 100448.

Tavmen G, 'Data/Infrastructure in the Smart City: Understanding the Infrastructural Power of Citymapper App through Technicity of Data' (2020) 7 *Big Data & Society* 1.

Taylor L, 'The Ethics of Big Data as a Public Good: Which Public? Whose Good?' (2016) 374 *Philosophical Transactions of the Royal Society A: Mathematical, Physical and Engineering Sciences* 374: 20160126.

Taylor MJ and others, 'Developing a Data Sharing Framework: A Case Study' (2014) 8 *Transforming Government: People, Process and Policy* 151.

Taylor MJ, 'Legal Bases for Disclosing Confidential Patient Information for Public Health: Distinguishing between Health Protection and Health Improvement' (2015) 23(3) *Medical Law Review* 348.

Tsakyrakis S, 'Proportionality: An Assault on Human Rights?' (2009) 7(3) *International Journal of Constitutional Law* 468.

Tzanou M, 'Data Protection as a Fundamental Right next to Privacy? "Reconstructing" a Not so New Right' (2013) 3 *International Data Privacy Law* 88.

van Drunen M and Noroozian A, 'How to Design Data Access for Researchers: A Legal and Software Development Perspective' (2022) 52 *Computer Law & Security Review* 105946.

Vezyridis P and Timmons S, 'Understanding the care.data Conundrum: New Information Flows for Economic Growth' (2017) 4(1) *Big Data & Society* 1.

Victor J, 'The EU General Data Protection Regulation: Toward a Property Regime for Protecting Data Privacy' (2013) 123(2) *Yale Law Journal* 513.

Wagner B, 'Accountability by Design in Technology Research' (2020) 37 *Computer Law & Security Review* 10.

Waithira N and others, 'Data Management and Sharing Policy: The First Step Towards Promoting Data Sharing' (2019) 17(1) *BMC Medicine* 80.

Walby K and Luscombe A, 'Criteria for Quality in Qualitative Research and Use of Freedom of Information Requests in the Social Sciences' (2017) 17(5) *Qualitative Research* 537.

White R and van Koten H, 'Co-designing for Sustainability: Strategizing Community Carbon Emission Reduction Through Socio-ecological Innovation' (2016) 19(1) *The Design Journal* 25.

Williamson O, 'Comparative Economic Organization: The Analysis of Discrete Structural Alternatives' (1991) 36 *Administrative Science Quarterly* 269.

Wong J and others, 'Data Protection for the Common Good: Developing a Framework for a Data Protection-Focused Data Commons' (2022) 4 *Data & Policy* e3.

Worthy B, 'More Open but Not More Trusted? The Effect of the Freedom of Information Act 2000 on the United Kingdom Central Government' (2010) 23 *Governance* 561.

Yeung K, 'The New Public Analytics as an Emerging Paradigm in Public Sector Administration'(2022) 27(2) *Tilburg Law Review* 1.

Young J, 'Outlining Regulatory Space: Agenda Issues and the FASB' (1994) 19(1) *Accounting, Organizations and Society* 83.

Zygmuntowski J and others, 'Embedding European Values in Data Governance: A Case for Public Data Commons' (2021) 10(3) *Internet Policy Review* 1.

Miscellanea

Article 29 Working Party, 'Opinion 06/2014 on the 'Notion of legitimate interests of the data controller under Article 7 of Directive 95/46/EC'.

Ball J and Marland M, 'Male Earnings Mobility in the Lifetime Labour Market Database' (1996) (Analytical Services Division, Department of Social Security Working Paper Series).

Bass T, 'It's time to think about our data as a common good. British Council' (2020). Available at: www.britishcouncil.org/anyone-anywhere/explore/communities-connections/rethinking-data.

European Data Protection Supervisor, 'A preliminary opinion on data protection and scientific research'. Available at: https://edps.europa.eu/sites/edp/files/publication/20-01-06_opinion_research_en.pdf.

Hales J and others, 'Evaluation of Employment Zones: Report on a Cohort Study of Long-Term Unemployed people in the Zones and a Matched Set of Comparison Areas' (2003) (National Centre for Social Research).

Hand, 'The Role of the ADRN Governing Board' (2013). Available at: https://esrc.ukri.org/files/research/administrative-data-taskforce-adt/the-role-of-the-adrn-governing-board-david-hand/.

Jackson P, 'The Route to Better Knowledge for a Better Society' (2017). Available at: https://prezi.com/6pe-8m2u9ad0/the-route-to-better-knowledge-for-a-better-society/?utm_campaign=share&utm_medium=copy. These cover: children, world of work, ageing, productive society, and health and society.

Jones P and Elias P, 'Administrative Data as a Research Resource: A Selected Audit' (Report to the ESRC) (2006) 17.

Kushwaha N, 'Up in the Air: Ensuring Government Data Sovereignty in the Cloud', 2020 *12th International Conference on Cyber Conflict (CyCon)* (IEEE 2020). Available at: https://ieeexplore.ieee.org/document/9131718/.

Manzoni J, 'Big Data in Government: The Challenges and Opportunities' (21 February 2017). Available at: www.gov.uk/government/speeches/big-data-in-government-the-challenges-and-opportunities.

Mazzucato M, 'Let's Make Private Data into a Public Good' (2018) 121(4) *MIT Technology Review* 74–75.

Petel A, 'Chapter 5 of the Data Act – What Is the European Concept of "B2G Data Sharing" in the Data Act Proposal?' (*KU Leuven CITIP Blog*, 21 June 2022).

Purtova N, 'Important Questions to Answer before Talking of Data Commons' (2021). Available at: https://itforchange.net/sites/default/files/2021-06/Nadezhda-Purtova-Socializing-Data-Value-Provocation.pdf.

Richards, 'Introducing the Administrative Data Research Centre Wales (ADRC-W)' (Blogs Wales Institute of Social & Economic Research, Data & Methods).

Ritchie F and Welpton R, 'Addressing the Human Factor in Data Access: Incentive Compatibility, Legitimacy and Cost-effectiveness in Public Data Resources' (UWE Economics Working Paper Series) (2014).

Skinner C, 'Statistical Disclosure Control for Survey Data' (2009). Available at: http://personal.lse.ac.uk/skinnecj/SDC%20for%20survey%20data%20S3RI.pdf.

Smith G and others, 'The Value of Linked Administrative Records for Longitudinal Analysis' (ESRC National Longitudinal Strategy Committee) (2004).

Stephenson P, 'The Future of Public Services Means Giving Citizens Control Over Their Own Data'. Available at: www.openaccessgovernment.org/giving-citizens-control-own-data/71660/.

Tennison J, 'We Need a More Collective Approach to Data Governance. How Might It Look?' (14 March 2022).

Tennison J, 'Beyond Ownership: We Need Better Control and Rights over Data' (*ODI Knowledge and Opinion*). Available at: https://theodi.org/article/data-rights-we-need-to-build-a-coherent-framework/.

Tomlinson J, 'Quick and Uneasy Justice: An Administrative Justice Analysis of the EU Settlement Scheme' (2019) The Public Law Project.

UK Statistics Authority, 'Research Code of Practice and Accreditation Criteria' (12 February 2020). Available at: www.gov.uk/government/publications/digital-economy-act-2017-part-5-codes-of-practice/research-code-of-practice-and-accreditation-criteria.

Welpton R and Wright M, 'HMRC Datalab: Engaging with the External Research Community' (2011) (ESRC) 1.

Pre-prints

Aral A and others, 'Building a data ecosystem for using telecom data to inform the COVID-19 response efforts' (Data for Policy 2020). Available at: https://zenodo.org/record/3992420#.X7auxi0Rry9.

Bommasani R and others, 'On the Opportunities and Risks of Foundation Models'. Available at: https://arxiv.org/abs/2108.07258.

Buckee C and Engø-Monsen K, 'Mobile phone data for public health: towards data-sharing solutions that protect individual privacy and national security' (2016) arXiv:1606.00864.

Bucknall S and Trager F, 'Structured Access for Third-Party Research on Frontier AI Models: Investigating Researchers' Model Access Requirements' (2023).

Emilsson C and others, 'The Interdependency of Data Governance and Open Government Data: Lessons From COVID-19' (Data for Policy 2020). Available at: https://zenodo.org/record/3978270#.X7avHS0Rry9.

Heeks R, 'Government Data: Understanding the Barriers to Citizen Access and Use' [2000] SSRN Electronic Journal. Available at: www.ssrn.com/abstract=3540061.

Jacobson M, 'Who "Owns" Public Data?' Available at: https://mrsc.org/stay-informed/mrsc-insight/october/who-owns-public-data.

Kilkelly U, 'The Right to Respect for Private and Family Life' (Council of Europe 2003).

Leslie D, 'Understanding Artificial Intelligence Ethics and Safety' (2022) arXiv preprint. Available at: arXiv:1906.05684.

Lowe S, 'The value of safe settings in evidence-based policy making' (2018). Available at: http://eprints.ncrm.ac.uk/4255/.

Marcowitz-Bitton M, 'Commercializing Public Sector Information' [2015] SSRN Electronic Journal. Available at: www.ssrn.com/abstract=2653555.

Micheli M, 'Accessing Privately Held Data: Public/Private Sector Relations in Twelve European Cities' (Data for Policy 2020). Available at: https://zenodo.org/record/3967044#.X7as6i0Rry9 2.

Mills S, 'Who Owns the Future? Data Trusts, Data Commons, and the Future of Data Ownership' [2019] SSRN Electronic Journal. Available at: www.ssrn.com/abstract=3437936.

Pattaro S and others, 'Labour Market and Wider Impacts of Benefit Sanctions: A Scoping Review' (2019) 17th Annual ESPAnet Conference, Stockholm, Sweden, 5–7 Sept 2019.

Piché J, 'Accessing the State of Imprisonment in Canada: Information Barriers and Negotiation Strategies. Brokering Access: Politics, Power, and Freedom of Information in Canada' (2012) 234–260.

Ritchie F, 'Can a Change in Attitudes Improve Effective Access to Administrative Data for Research?'. Available at: www2.uwe.ac.uk/faculties/BBS/BUS/Research/General/Economics%20papers%202016/1607.pdf.

Ritchie F, 'UK Official Microdata Release Practices'. Available at: www.academia.edu/1336375/UK_Official_Microdata_Release_Practices.

Robinson G and others, 'Public Attitudes to Data Sharing in Northern Ireland: Findings from the 2015 Northern Ireland Life and Times Survey' (2018) (ADRC-Northern Ireland).

Scassa T, 'Data Ownership' [2018] SSRN Electronic Journal. Available at: www.ssrn.com/abstract=3251542.

Shevlane T, 'Structured Access: An Emerging Paradigm for Safe AI Deployment' (2022) arXiv preprint arXiv:2201.05159.

Ubaldi BC and others, 'Towards a New Data-driven Service Design and Delivery Model?' (Data for Policy 2020). Available at: https://zenodo.org/record/3978179#.X7auPC0Rry9.

Villalobos P and others, 'Will We Run out of Data? An Analysis of the Limits of Scaling Datasets in Machine Learning'. Available at: https://arxiv.org/abs/2211.04325.

Waind E, 'Trust, Security & Public Interest: Striking the Balance. A Review of Previous Literature on Public Attitudes Towards the Sharing, Linking and Use of Administrative Data for Research' (Data for Policy 2020). Available at: https://zenodo.org/record/3971006#.X76I2C0RrRZ 1.

Weber I and others, 'Real-Time Mobility Analysis Through Google Maps' (Data for Policy 2020). Available at: https://zenodo.org/record/3965386#.X7fmai0RrRZ.

White M, 'Macro Evaluation of the New Deal for Young People' (2000) (PSI briefing note).

Zamenopoulos T and Alexiou K, 'Co-design As Collaborative Research' (2018) (Connected Communities Foundation Series, Bristol). Available at: http://oro.open.ac.uk/58301/1/Co-Design_CCFoundationSeries_PUBLISHED.pdf.

Policy Reports

Administrative Data Taskforce, 'The UK Administrative Data Research Network: Improving Access for Research and Policy' (December 2012).

Aidinlis S and others, 'Building a Justice Data Infrastructure'. Available at: www.law.ox.ac.uk/news/2020-10-08-building-justice-data-infrastructure.

Allsopp C, 'Review of Statistics for Economic Policymaking: Final Report to the Chancellor of the Exchequer, the Governor of the Bank of England and the National Statistician' (2003).

Barbero and others, 'Big Data Analytics for Policy Making' (EU Commission DG DIGIT). Available at: https://joinup.ec.europa.eu/sites/default/files/document/2016-07/dg_digit_study_big_data_analytics_for_policy_making.pdf 2.

Birmingham Safeguarding Children Board, 'Serious Case Review in respect of the death of Keanu Williams' (2013). Available at: www.cscb-new.co.uk/downloads/Serious%20Case%20Reviews%20%20exec.%20summaries/SCR_Archive/Birmingham%20SCR%20-%20KW%20(2013).pdf.

Byrom N, 'Digital Justice: HMCTS data strategy and delivering access to justice Report and recommendations' (October 2019). Available at: https://research.thelegaleducationfoundation.org/blog/digital-justice-hmcts-data-strategy-and-delivering-access-to-justice.

Cabinet Office, 'Departments, agencies and public bodies'. Available at: www.gov.uk/government/organisations.

Cabinet Office, 'Open Data: unleashing the potential' (28 June 2012).

Cabinet Office, 'Departments, Agencies and Public Bodies'. Available at: www.gov.uk/government/organisations.

Centre for Excellence for Information Sharing, 'Overcoming cultural barriers to information sharing within regulatory services' (2016). Available at: https://assets.publishing.service.gov.uk/government/uploads/system/uploads/attachment_data/file/535439.

Collington R, 'Digital Public Assets' (Commonwealth) (October 2019).

Department for Digital, Culture, Media & Sport, 'UK National Action Plan for Open Government 2019–2021' (2019).

Department of Health, 'Research Governance Framework for Health and Social Care' (2nd edn, 2005).

Desai T, Ritchie F and Welpton R, 'Five Safes: Designing Data Access for Research' (UWE Economics Working Paper Series) (2016).

Endicott T, 'Parliament and the Prerogative: From the Case of Proclamations to Miller' (2016) Judicial Power Project. Available at: http://judicialpowerproject.org.uk/wp-content/uploads/2016/12/Endicott-2016-Parliament-and-the-Prerogative.pdf.

European Commission, 'The New European Innovation Agenda' (2022). Available at: https://research-and-innovation.ec.europa.eu/strategy/support-policy-making/shaping-eu-research-and-innovation-policy/new-european-innovation-agenda_en.

European Data Protection Board, 'Opinion 3/2019 concerning the Questions and Answers on the interplay between the Clinical Trials Regulation (CTR) and the General Data Protection regulation (GDPR) (art. 70.1.b))' (23 January 2019). Available at: edpb.europa.eu/sites/edpb/files/files/file1/edpb_opinionctrq_a_final_en.pdf 8.

Flynn M, 'South Gloucestershire Safeguarding Adults Board, Winterbourne View Hospital, A Serious Case Review' (2012). Available at: https://hosted.southglos.gov.uk/wv/report.pdf.

High-Level Expert Group, 'Towards a European strategy on business-to- government data sharing for the public interest. Final report prepared by the High-Level Expert Group on Business-to-Government Data Sharing' (European Union). Available at: www.euractiv.com/wp-content/uploads/sites/2/2020/02/B2GDataSharingExpertGroupReport-1.pdf.

HMCTS, 'Access to courts and tribunals for academic researchers'. Available at: www.gov.uk/guidance/access-to-courts-and-tribunals-for-academic-researchers.

House of Commons, 'The Bichard Inquiry Report' (2004). Available at: https://dera.ioe.ac.uk/6394/1/report.pdf.

House of Commons Science and Technology Committee, 'The Big Data Dilemma: Fourth Report of Session 2015–16'.

House of Lords Constitution Committee, 'Constitution – First Report' (2000-01). Available at: https://publications.parliament.uk/pa/ld200102/ldselect/ldconst/11/1101.htm ch2.

Information Commissioner's Office, 'Data Sharing Code of Practice'. Available at: https://ico.org.uk/media/fororganisations/documents/1068/data_sharing_code_of_practice.pdf.

Information Commissioner's Office, 'The Guide to Freedom of Information' (updated July 2022). Available at: https://ico.org.uk/media/for-organisations/guide-to-freedom-of-information-4-9.pdf.

Intellectual Property Office and Government Digital Service, 'Sui generis database rights' (2020).

IPSOS Mori, 'Commercial Access to Health Data' (2016). Available at: https://perma.cc/9TK2-JWEB.

Laurie G and Sethi N, 'Information Governance of Use of Health-Related Data in Medical Research In Scotland: Current Practices And Future Scenarios' (SHIP Core Programme 2 Working Paper No 1) 9.

Law Commission, `Data Sharing Between Public Bodies: A Scoping Report' (2014). Available at: www.lawcom.gov.uk/app/uploads/2015/03/lc351_data-sharing.pdf.

Morozov E and Bria F, 'Rethinking the Smart City' (Rosa Luxembourg Stiftung). Available at: https://onlineopen.org/media/article/583/open_essay_2018_morozov_rethinking.pdf.

National Audit Office, 'Challenges in using data across government' (21 June 2019). Available at: https://nao.org.uk/wp-content/uploads/2019/06/Challenges-in-using-data-across-government.pdf 11.

National Institute for Social Care and Health Research Wales, 'Maximising the Use of Routine Data for Research in Wales' (2013). Available at: www.healthandcareresearch.gov.wales/uploads/Policy%20%26%20Strategy/Use%20of%20routine%20data/Maximising%20the%20Use%20of%20Routine%20Data%20for%20Research%20in%20Wales.pdf.

OECD, 'A Data-Driven Public Sector: Enabling the Strategic Use of Data for Productive, Inclusive and Trustworthy Governance', vol 33 (2019) OECD Working Papers on Public Governance 33. Available at: www.oecd-ilibrary.org/governance/a-data-driven-public-sector_09ab162c-en.

REFORM, 'Sharing the Benefits: How to Use Data Effectively in The Public Sector'. Available at: https://reform.uk/research/sharing-benefits-how-use-data-effectively-public-sector.

Research Project Management, 'Administrative Data Research Network (ADRN) Mid-Term Review Report' (8 November 2016). Available at: https://esrc.ukri.org/files/research/research-and-impact-evaluation/adrn-mid-term-review-report-8-november-2016/ 8.

Scottish Government, 'Linking Social Care, Housing & Health Data' (2010). Available at: www.gov.scot/binaries/content/documents/govscot/publications/statistics/2019/01/health-community-care-data-linkage/documents/linking-social-care-housing-and-health-data-social-care-clients-and-patients-views/linking-social-care-housing-and-health-data-social-care-clients-and-patients-views/govscot%3Adocument/Linking%2BSocial%2BCare%252C%2BHousing%2Band%2BHealth%2BData%2BSocial%2BCare%2BClients%2527%2Band%2BPatients%2527%2BViews.pdf.

Shakespeare S, 'Shakespeare Review: An Independent Review of Public Sector Information' (May 2013).

Singapore Government, 'Bringing Data into the Heart of Digital Government' (Singapore Civil Service College). Available at: https://knowledge.csc.gov.sg/ethos-issue-21/bring-data-in-the-heart-of-digital-government/.

Tarkowski A and Vogelezang F, 'Public Data Commons: A Public Interest Framework for Business-to-Government Data Sharing in the Data Act.' (Open Future Policy Brief). Available at: https://openfuture.eu/wp-content/uploads/2022/05/Public-data-commons-A-public-interest-framework-for-B2G-data-sharing-in-the-Data-Act.1.pdf.

Thomas R and Walport M, `Data Sharing Review Report' (2008). Available at: https://webarchive.nationalarchives.gov.uk/+/http:/www.justice.gov.uk/docs/data-sharing-review.pdf.

Ubaldi BC, 'Open Government Data: Towards Empirical Analysis of Open Government Data Initiatives', vol 22 (2013) *OECD Working Papers on Public Governance* 22. Available at: www.oecd-ilibrary.org/governance/open-government-data_5k46bj4f03s7-en.

Ubaldi BC and others, 'A Data-Driven Public Sector: Enabling the Strategic Use of Data for Productive, Inclusive and Trustworthy Governance' (2019). Available at: www.sipotra.it/wp-content/uploads/2019/05/A-data-driven-public-sector-Enabling-the-strategic-use-of-data-for-productive-inclusive-and-trustworthy-governance.pdf 34.

UK Competition and Markets Authority, 'AI Foundation Models: Initial Review'. Available at: https://assets.publishing.service.gov.uk/media/650449e86771b90014fdab4c/Full_Non-Confidential_Report_PDFA.pdf.

UK Statistics Authority, 'Research Code of Practice and Accreditation Criteria' (1 March 2018).

UN Special Rapporteur on Extreme Poverty and Human Rights, 'Digital technology, social protection and human rights: Report' (2019). Available at: www.ohchr.org/EN/Issues/Poverty/Pages/DigitalTechnology.aspx.

US Government, 'Federal data strategy. Available at:' https://strategy.data.gov.

Welsh Government, 'Data Linking Demonstration Project: Examining Fuel Poverty Using Home Energy Efficiency Data (HEED) and Routinely Collected Health Data' (2013). Available at: www.gov.wales/sites/default/files/statistics-and-research/2019-01/data-linking-demonstration-project-examining-fuel-poverty-using-home-energy-efficiency-data-and-routinely-collected-health-data.pdf.

Welsh Government, 'The Fuel Poverty Data Linking Project'. Available at: https://gov.wales/fuel-poverty-data-linking-project-impact-health-welsh-government-warm-homes.

World Health Organization, 'Health Data as a Global Public Good – A Call for Health Data Governance' (29 July 2021).

Websites

ADRN, 'History'. Available at: https://uksa.statisticsauthority.gov.uk/about-the-authority/committees/adrn/.

AI Safety Institute, 'Rigorous AI Research to Enable Advanced AI Governance'. Available at: www.aisi.gov.uk/.

Besse P and Laurent B, 'From Statistician to Data Scientist'. Available at: https://arxiv.org/abs/1509.07804.

Big Brother Watch, 'Poverty Panopticon: The Hidden Algorithms Shaping Britain's Welfare State'. Available at: https://bigbrotherwatch.org.uk/wp-content/uploads/2021/07/Poverty-Panopticon.pdf.

Booth R, 'Benefits System Automation Could Plunge Claimants Deeper into Poverty' *The Guardian* 14 October 2019. Available at: www.theguardian.com/technology/2019/oct/14/fears-rise-in-benefits-system-automation-could-plunge-claimants-deeper-into-poverty.

Cabinet Office, 'NFI: public sector case studies and testimonials' (21 March 2023). Available at: www.gov.uk/government/publications/national-fraud-initiative-case-studies/nfi-public-sector-case-studies.

Centre for Market and Public Organisation, 'NPD User Group'. Available at: www.bristol.ac.uk/cmpo/npd-user-group/.
Centre of Excellence for Information Sharing, 'Information Governance'. Available at: https://informationsharing.org.uk/infogovernance/.
CNIL, 'Coronavirus (COVID-19): Reminders from the CNIL on the Collection of Personal Data by Employers'. Available at: www.cnil.fr/fr/coronavirus-covid-19-les-rappels-de-la-cnil-sur-la-collecte-de-donnees-personnelles-par-les.
Data Science Campus. Available at: www.ons.gov.uk/aboutus/whatwedo/datasciencecampus.
Department for Education, 'DfE External Data Shares' (18 July 2019). Available at: https://gov.uk/government/publications/dfe-external-data-shares.
DCMS, 'Data: A New Direction – Government Response to Consultation'. Available at: www.gov.uk/government/consultations/data-a-new-direction/outcome/data-a-new-direction-government-response-to-consultation#executive-summary.
Department for Work and Pensions, 'Research at DWP'. Available at: www.gov.uk/government/organisations/department-for-work-pensions/about/research.
Department for Work and Pensions, 'Work and Pensions Longitudinal Study'. Available at: www.gov.uk/government/statistics/work-and-pensions-longitudinal-study.
Department for Work and Pensions, 'DWP Open Data: Case Studies' (2013). Available at: https://assets.publishing.service.gov.uk/government/uploads/system/uploads/attachment_data/file/221159/dwp-open-data-case-studies.pdf.
Department for Work and Pensions, 'Annual Report & Accounts 2022–23'. Available at: https://assets.publishing.service.gov.uk/government/uploads/system/uploads/attachment_data/file/1167946/annual-report-accounts-2022-23-web-ready.pdf.
Department for Work & Pensions, 'Fraud Investigations Staff Guide – Part 1'. Available at: www.gov.uk/government/publications/fraud-investigations-staff-guide 135-6.
Department for Work and Pensions, 'A5/2020: Housing Benefit Award Accuracy Initiative' (10 February 2021). Available at: www.gov.uk/government/publications/housing-benefit-adjudication-circulars-2020/a52020-housing-benefit-award-accuracy-initiative.
Education Policy Institute, 'About Us'. Available at: https://epi.org.uk/our-mission-and-purpose/.
ESRC Big Data Network. Available at: https://esrc.ukri.org/research/our-research/big-data-network/.
FairTrials, 'FOI reveals over 12,000 people profiled by flawed Durham police predictive AI tool' (15 August 2022). Available at: www.fairtrials.org/articles/news/foi-reveals-over-12000-people-profiled-by-flawed-durham-police-predictive-ai-tool/.
Garante, 'Coronavirus: No do-it-yourself (DIY) data collection, says the Italian DPA'. Available at: www.garanteprivacy.it/web/guest/home/docweb/-/docweb-display/docweb/9282117#1.
Giannopoulos N, 'The Greek Government-CISCO Data Sharing Agreement: The Lost Atlantis' (3 October 2020). Available at: www.news247.gr/koinonia/symvasi-cisco-dimosioy-apdpch-tin-zitise-kerameos-den-tin-edose-pote.9005665.html.
Greek Government, 'data.gov.gr'. Available at: www.data.gov.gr.
Google, 'Researcher Engagement'. Available at: https://transparency.google/researcher-engagement/#learn-researcher-program.
Google, 'Google Researcher Program Acceptable Use Policy'. Available at: https://requestrecords.google.com/researcher/policy.
Health and Social Care Northern Ireland, 'Honest Broker Service'. Available at: www.hscbusiness.hscni.net/services/2454.htm.
HMCTS Chief Executive, 'Modernising the Courts and Tribunals Service: Future of Justice Conference' (14 May 2018). Available at: www.ucl. ac.uk/laws/sites/laws/files/ucl_ foj_01_03_acland-hood.pdf.
HM Government, 'HMRC Publication Scheme'. Available at: www.gov.uk/government/organisations/hm-revenue-customs/about/publication-scheme.
HM Government, 'How to Access Department for Education (DfE) Data Extracts' (2018). Available at: www.gov.uk/guidance/how-to-access-department-for-education-dfe-data-extracts.
HMRC, 'Research at HMRC'. Available at: https://gov.uk/government/organisations/hm-revenue-customs/about/research.

HM Treasury, 'Autumn Statement 2023'. Available at: www.gov.uk/government/publications/autumn-statement-2023/autumn-statement-2023-html.
HM Treasury, 'Spring Budget 2024'. Available at: www.gov.uk/government/topical-events/spring-budget-2024.
Home Office, 'Immigration Bail' (Version 19.0). Available at: https://assets.publishing.service.gov.uk/media/65f4260efa1851001a0117bf/Immigration+bail.pdf 49.
Home Office, 'Annex to Home Office's response to Public Law Project's FOI request'. Available at: www.whatdotheyknow.com/request/aqa_assessments_of_home_office_s/response/2229983/attach/4/FOI%2073704%20Annex%20A.pdf.
Incubator for Artificial Intelligence, 'About us'. Available at: www.gov.uk/government/organisations/incubator-for-artificial-intelligence/about.
Information Commissioner's Office, 'What Information Do We Need to Publish?'. Available at: https://ico.org.uk/for-organisations/foi-eir-and-access-to-information/guide-to-freedom-of-information/publication-scheme/.
Information Commissioner's Office, 'Data Sharing Checklists'. Available at: https://ico.org.uk/media/for-organisations/documents/1067/data_sharing_checklists.pdf.
Information Commissioner's Office, 'Anonymisation: Managing Data Protection Risk Code of Practice'. Available at: https://ico.org.uk/media/for-organisations/documents/1061/anonymisation-code.pdf.
Information Commissioner's Office, 'Principle (e): Storage limitation'. Available at: https://ico.org.uk/for-organisations/guide-to-data-protection/guide-to-the-general-data-protection-regulation-gdpr/principles/storage-limitation/.
JUST: Access, 'JUST: Transcription'. Available at: www.just-access.org/just-transcription.
Klein N, 'How Big Tech Plans to Profit from the Pandemic', The Guardian (13 May 2020). Available at: www.theguardian.com/news/2020/may/13/naomi-klein-how-big-tech-plans-to-profit-from-coronavirus-pandemic.
KPMG, 'Building Trust in Government's Use of Data'. Available at: https://kpmg.com/xx/en/home/insights/2018/06/building-trust-in-governments-use-of-data.html.
Lindner C, 'Where do Data Scientists Come From?'. Available at: https://medium.com/indeed-engineering/where-do-data-scientists-come-from-fc526023ace.
Lewis P and others, 'Cambridge Analytica Academic's Work Upset University Colleagues' The Guardian (2018). Available at: www.theguardian.com/education/2018/mar/24/cambridge-analytica-academics-work-upset-university-colleagues.
Metropolitan Police, 'Violence Harm Assessment'. Available at: www.met.police.uk/police-forces/metropolitan-police/areas/about-us/about-the-met/violence-harm-assessment.
Microsoft, 'Bing Qualified Researcher Program'. Available at: https://support.microsoft.com/en-us/topic/bing-qualified-researcher-program-b1c5a4b6-3ad6-4c8c-963d-a395c7766c85.
Ministry of Justice, 'Evaluating our reforms: Response to PAC Recommendation 4, January 2019'. Available at: www.gov.uk/government/news/moj-response-to-public-accounts-committee-transforming-courts-and-tribunals.
Mundy D, 'Strengthening Third-Party Data Collaborations in AI-Driven Enterprises' (1 February 2024). Available at: www.dasera.com/blog/strengthening-third-party-data-collaborations-in-ai-driven-enterprises.
Murray M, 'Users angered at Facebook Emotion-Manipulation Study'. Available at: www.today.com/tech/users-angered-facebook-emotion-manipulation-study-1D79863049.
mySociety, 'Reforming Freedom of Information' (2022). Available at: https://research.mysociety.org/html/reforming-foi/#conclusion.
National Archives, 'Information Management Assessment: Department for Work and Pensions' (2015). Available at: www.nationalarchives.gov.uk/documents/information-management/dwp-ima-report-2015.pdf.
National Audit Office, 'Use of Artificial Intelligence in Government' (15 March 2024). Available at: www.nao.org.uk/wp-content/uploads/2024/03/use-of-artificial-intelligence-in-government.pdf.
National Audit Office, 'Report on Accounts – Department for Work and Pensions' (July 2023). Available at: www.nao.org.uk/wp-content/uploads/2023/07/dwp-report-on-accounts-2022-23.pdf.

OpenAI, 'Researcher Access Program Application' https://openai.com/form/researcher-access-program/.

Open Democracy, 'Under Pressure, UK Government Releases NHS COVID Data Deals with Big Tech'. Available at: www.opendemocracy.net/en/ournhs/under-pressure-uk-government-releases-nhs-covid-data-deals-big-tech/.

Public Law Project, 'Tracking Automated Government (TAG) Register' (accessed 19 June 2024). Available at: https://trackautomatedgovernment.shinyapps.io/register/.

Public Sector Fraud Authority, 'National Fraud Initiative' (2 April 2024). Available at: www.gov.uk/government/collections/national-fraud-initiative.

SAIL Databank, 'The Anonymisation Process'. Available at: http://saildatabank.com/saildata/data-privacy-security/#anonymisation-process.

Say M, 'Home Office plans augmented data catalogue' (22 February 2022). Available at: www.ukauthority.com/articles/home-office-plans-augmented-data-catalogue.

Scottish Government, 'Data linkage for research in Scotland'. Available at: www.gov.scot/publications/data-linkage-for-research-in-scotland/pages/scottish-government-funded-linkage-projects/.

Scottish Longitudinal Study Development & Support Unit, 'Introduction to the Scottish Longitudinal Study'. Available at: https://sls.lscs.ac.uk/about/.

StopWatch, 'The Gangs Matrix*'. Available at: www.stop-watch.org/what-we-do/projects/the-gangs-matrix/.

The Guardian, 'Automating poverty'. Available at: www.theguardian.com/technology/series/automating-poverty.

Tromans R, 'France Bans Judge Analytics, 5 Years in Prison For Rule Breakers' (2019). Available at: www.artificiallawyer.com/2019/06/04/france-bans-judge-analytics-5-years-in-prison-for-rule-breakers/.

UK Data Service, 'Registration'. Available at: https://ukdataservice.ac.uk/get-data/how-to-access/registration/commercialusers.aspx.

UK Government, 'AI Sector Deal' (21 May 2019). Available at: www.gov.uk/government/publications/artificial-intelligence-sector-deal/ai-sector-deal.

UK Government, 'National AI Strategy'. Available at: https://assets.publishing.service.gov.uk/media/614db4d1e90e077a2cbdf3c4/National_AI_Strategy_-_PDF_version.pdf.

UK Government, 'The UK Science and Technology Framework' (Updated 9 February 2024). Available at: www.gov.uk/government/publications/uk-science-and-technology-framework/the-uk-science-and-technology-framework.

UK Government, 'National AI Strategy – AI Action Plan' (18 July 2022). Available at: www.gov.uk/government/publications/national-ai-strategy-ai-action-plan.

UK Government, 'Central Digital and Data Office'. Available at: www.gov.uk/government/organisations/central-digital-and-data-office.

UK Office for National Statistics, 'ONS Research and Data Access Policy'. Available at: www.ons.gov.uk/aboutus/transparencyandgovernance/datastrategy/datapolicies/onsresearchanddataaccesspolicy.

UK Government, 'Government Digital Service'. Available at: www.gov.uk/government/organisations/government-digital-service.

UK Government, 'Office for Artificial Intelligence'. Available at: www.gov.uk/government/organisations/office-for-artificial-intelligence.

UK Government, 'The CDEI is now the Responsible Technology Adoption Unit. Available at:' www.gov.uk/government/news/the-cdei-is-now-the-responsible-technology-adoption-unit.

UK Government, 'Dr Dave Smith takes helm as UK's National Technology Adviser'. Available at: www.gov.uk/government/news/dr-dave-smith-takes-helm-as-uks-national-technology-adviser.

UK Statistics Authority, 'First Meeting of the Administrative Data Research Network Board' (2014). Available at: https://uksa.statisticsauthority.gov.uk/wp-content/uploads/2015/12/images-minutesandpapersfromadrnboardon14april201_tcm97-43879.pdf.

UK Statistics Authority, 'Meet the ADRN Board'. Available at: https://uksa.statisticsauthority.gov.uk/about-the-authority/committees/adrn/meet-the-adrn-board/.

UK Statistics Authority, 'Thirteenth Meeting of the ADRN Board: Agenda and Papers' (2017). Available at: www.statisticsauthority.gov.uk/wp-content/uploads/2017/06/ADRN-05-06-2017.pdf.

Understanding Patient Data, 'Putting people at the centre of decisions about patient data'. Available at: https://understandingpatientdata.org.uk/.

Wigglesworth R, 'Hedge Funds See a Gold Rush in Data Mining' *Financial Times* (28 August 2017). Available at: www.ft.com/content/d86ad460-8802-11e7-bf50-e1c239b4578.

Williams W, 'Windrush Lessons Learned Review' (31 March 2020). Available at: www.gov.uk/government/publications/windrush-lessons-learned-review.

INDEX

access, 3–4, 32–33, 45–46
data sharing, 6–12
formalising access to data, *see* formalising access to data
inequality of access, *see* unequal access to data
limitations
data protection law, 59–61
human rights law, 61–63
processes and frameworks, 34–35
regulatory space, 35–36
actors, 36–37
data access negotiations, 36
institutions, 37–38
interactions and interdependencies, 38–39
regulation, 33–34
research and innovation distinguished, 46–47
right to access (GDPR Article 15), 29
status of those seeking access, 47–48
widening access, 100–1
see also widening access to data
see also commercial access to public sector data; public sector data access
accountability of data sharing procedures, 101–6
failures, 117–19
actors as drivers of access within regulatory space, 36–37
Administrative Data Research Network (ADRN), 7, 109–12
Administrative Data Taskforce (ADT), 109
anonymisation, 17–18, 59–60, 69, 71, 81, 105, 107–9
artificial intelligence (AI), 190–91, 193–94
autonomy, 29, 77
automation of public services, 190
transparency issues, 190–91
AI integration in government operations, 192–94
applications, 194–98
significance and benefits, 198–200
challenges, 198–200
brigading research projects, 135–39
British Economic and Social Research Council, 7
British Market Research Bureau International, 95

Canada:
FOI requests, 49, 181–82
co-designing research projects, 139–43
collective control over data, 23–24
commercial access to public sector data, 66–67
organisational challenges, 66–69
public interest, 69–72
commercialisation of data, 26–28
common law, 57–58
common-pool resources (CPR) framework, 24
conceptualisation of data as a public asset, 21–22
contracting-out research, 92–93
control of data, 16, 30–31
collective control over data, 23–24
data as a public good, 21–25
collective control over data, 23–24
conceptualisation of data as a public asset, 21–22
health data as a global public good, 22
public interest, 22
individual citizens, 28–30
legal framework in the UK, 19–21
meaning of control, 18
ownership of data, 19, 29–30
personal and non-personal data distinguished, 17–18
public sector data controlled by public sector bodies, 25–28
controlled access to data for research and innovation, 90
cost of providing access data, 91
data breach incidents and disclosure of identifiable data, 90–91
organisational inertia, 92
suspicion of external researchers, 91

Copyright and Rights in Databases Regulations 1997, 25–26
coronavirus:
data sharing, 7–8, 67
health data as a global public good, 22
cost-effectiveness, 183–84

data analysts, 11, 145–46
analysts as decision-makers, 158–62
analysts as experts, 146–53
analysts as mediators, 153–57
data collection, 4–5, 19, 40–41
data commons, 24–25
data minimisation, 35, 60–61, 81–82, 147, 149–52, 153
data portability:
right to data portability (GDPR Article 20), 29
Data Protection Act 2018, 29, 60–61, 62, 83
research and innovation distinguished, 46–47
data protection law:
anonymisation, 59–60
data minimisation, 61
lawful basis for processing, 60
purpose limitation, 60
data sharing, 6–12, 87–88
efficiency, 88
accountability, 88–89
public interest, 69–72
data sovereignty, 28
public sector data controlled by public sector bodies, 28
data subjects' rights, 29, 62, 73–74, 81
Department for Business, Energy, and Industrial Strategy (BEIS), 7, 36–37
Department for Education (DfE), 88
communication and interaction, 164–65
data as property, 130–31, 132–33
data sharing, 92–97, 99, 108, 114–16, 123–24, 127–28, 158–61, 173
Department for Work and Pensions (DWP):
ADRN Board, 110
co-design research projects, 140–41
data as property, 130, 132, 133–34
data sharing, 57–58, 88, 90–91, 116, 135–36, 149–50, 173
information governance, 160–61
New Deal for the Long Term Unemployed, 95
partnerships with academia, 98–99
Work and Pensions Longitudinal Study, 93–95
Digital Economy Act (DEA) 2017, 9, 19, 53–54
digitalisation strategy, 6–8
disclosure, *see* **duties to disclose public sector information**
discretionary legal powers to share information, 48, 53
common law powers, 57–58
implied powers, 55–56
prerogative powers, 58
statutory gateways, 53–55
Driver and Vehicle Licensing Agency (DVLA):
commercialisation of data, 26
duties to disclose public sector information, 48
private disclosure mandates, 52–53
public disclosure mandates, 51–53

Economic and Social Research Council (ESRC), 107, 134
ADRN, 109–10, 112–13
ADT, 109
Electronic Data Research and Innovation Service (eDRIS) (Scotland), 156
Environmental Information Regulations (EIRs) 2004, 51–52
erasure:
right to erasure (right to be forgotten) (GDPR Article 17), 29
EU:
public sector big data analysis projects, 70–72
see also General Data Protection Regulation
European Convention on Human Rights (ECHR):
qualified rights, 62
right to private life (Art. 8), 61–62
proportionality, 62–63
European Data Protection Supervisor (EDPS), 72

financial data, 51–52
Finland:
public control of privately held data, 23
formalising access to data, 101
accountability, 101–6
Administrative Data Research Network, 7, 109–12
digitisation, 105–6
efficiency, 101–6

independent research on government data, 106–9
limits of formalisation, 112–16
public benefit narrative, 104–5
transparency and open government, 103–6

France:
data protection authorities, 73
public control of privately held data, 23

Freedom of Information (FOI) Act 2000, 48
harm-based and class-based exemptions distinguished, 48–49
individual rights of access, 48–52

General Data Protection Regulation (GDPR), 17
commercial access to public sector data, 72–75
data subjects' rights, 29
legitimate interests, 73
personal or proprietary rights, 29
public and private interests distinguished, 72–75
public interest, 72
research and innovation distinguished, 46–47

Germany:
public sector big data analysis projects, 71–72

Greece:
data sharing arrangements with private entities, 79
public sector big data analysis projects, 71

Health and Social Care Act 2012, 9

health data, 9, 90, 149–50
ADRN, 111
longitudinal studies, 95
public good, as, 22
Scotland, 119, 148, 156
Wales, 128–29, 151

His Majesty's Revenue and Customs (HMRC), 90–91, 94, 100–1, 105–8, 114, 130, 132, 136–37, 166, 170–71, 183

HM Courts and Tribunals (HMCTS), 7, 105–6

HM Customs:
commercialisation of data, 26

HM Treasury, 95

Honest Broker Service (HBS), 108–9, 124, 129, 149–50, 154–55, 169

human rights law:
data protection
proportionality, 62–63
right to private life, 61–63

in-house research, 92–93

independent research, 97–100

individual rights of access, 48
Freedom of Information Act 2000, 48–51

informal access to data for research and innovation, 89–90
data sharing frameworks, 166–74
low-level interactions, 144–45
data sharing frameworks, 166–74
relationships, 162–65

Information Commissioner's Office, 9–10, 36
FOI publication schemes, 51–52

information governance officials, 12

institutions as drivers of access within regulatory space, 37–38

intellectual property rights:
public sector data controlled by public sector bodies, 25–26

interactions and interdependencies as drivers of access within regulatory space, 38–39

interoperability, 67, 150

judicial review, 19–21, 61, 126

Law Commission:
data sharing between public and private bodies, 9–10

law enforcement, 28, 70, 74, 194

lawful basis for processing, 60

legitimate interests, 14
GDPR, 66, 73–74

limitations to access rights:
data protection law
anonymisation, 59–60
data minimisation, 61
lawful basis for processing, 60
purpose limitation, 60
human rights law, 61–63
right to private life, 61–63

low-level interactions and informal communications, 144–45
data sharing frameworks, 166–74
relationships, 162–65

Micro-Data Release Panel (MRP), 106–8, 125, 126
microdata:
Micro-Data Release Panel, 106–8, 125, 126
National Pupil Database, 99
Netherlands, 71
Virtual Microdata Laboratory, 91–92, 106–7, 125, 126

National Health Service Act 2006, 9, 53
national security, 28, 48–50, 78, 181–82, 186–87
Netherlands:
microdata, 71
public sector big data analysis projects, 70–72
new public management, 88–89, 93, 101, 185
NHS data:
commercialisation of data, 26
see also health data
non-justiciability doctrine, 20–21
non-personal data:
personal data distinguished, 17–18
Northern Ireland, 52
Administrative Data Forum, 168–69
ADRC, 116, 130–31, 137, 141–42, 149–50, 152, 153–54, 157, 164, 169
Honest Broker Service, 104–5, 108–9, 113–14, 124, 129, 149–50, 154–55, 169
longitudinal studies, 95
Northern Irish Statistics and Research Agency, 131, 156–57, 168–69

Office for National Statistics (ONS), 90–92, 94–95, 97–98, 102, 103–5, 106–9, 113–15, 123–24, 125–28, 136, 140, 147, 170–71
open government data (OGD) initiatives:
public sector data controlled by public sector bodies, 26–27
Organisation for Economic Co-operation and Development (OECD), 67
comprehensive model for data governance, 82–83
public integrity principle, 80
public sector data analysis and public value, 70
oversight bodies, 37
ownership of data, 19, 29–30, 122
public good, data as
accountability mechanisms, 125–29
facilitating research, 122–24
scrutinising government, 124

patient information for medical research purposes, 8–9
see also health data
personal data:
non-personal data distinguished, 17–18
policymakers, 12
prerogative powers, 53, 57, 58
private interest, 8, 14, 200
GDPR
commercial access to public sector data, 72–75
justification for public/private interests divide, 75–83
see also public/private interests divide
private sector researchers and innovators:
involvement in digitisation, 7–8
property, data as, 130–31
accountability issues, 131–34
policy relevance of government data research, 135
brigading research projects, 135–39
co-designing research projects, 139–43
proportionality, 30, 35, 62–63, 80–81, 153
public/private interests divide and its challenges, 82–83
balance of interests, 75–76
classification of types of research
hybrid research, 78–79
proprietary research, 78
public interest research, 78
data security measures, 81–82
data subjects' rights, respect for, 80–81
proof of common good/collective welfare, 79–80
public engagement, 82
public integrity principle, 80
public suspicion of data sharing initiatives, 76–77
surveillance capitalism, 76
public good, data as, 21–25
public interest:
data as a public good, 22
justification for public/private interests divide, 75–83
research projects, 54–55
commercial access to public sector data, 72–75
GDPR, 72–75
see also public/private interests divide

public records, 54, 130
public sector big data analysis projects, 70–72
public sector data access, 3–4
commercialisation of data, 26
control of, 16
collective control over data, 23–24
individual citizens, 28–30
legal framework in the UK, 19–21
meaning of control, 18
ownership of data, 19, 29–30
personal and non-personal data distinguished, 17–18
public sector bodies, 25–28
data sharing, 6–12
definition, 4–6
limitations
data protection law, 59–61
human rights law, 61–63
research and innovation distinguished, 46–47
status of those seeking access, 47–48
see also access; commercial access to public sector data
purpose limitation, 46, 60, 72–74

Qatar:
public sector big data analysis projects, 70–72

regulatory space approach:
actors as drivers of access, 36–37
institutions as drivers of access, 37–38
interactions and interdependencies as drivers of access, 38–39
responsibilisation of data protection, 23

Scotland, 52, 62, 91, 99–100, 128–29
ADRC Scotland, 138–39, 147, 159, 163–64, 171
ADRN Scotland, 154
co-design research projects, 142–43
data as property, 132–34
discoverability, 171–72
eDRIS, 156
Fire Rescue Scotland, 170
fragmentation and limits of formalisation, 114–15, 119
health data, 119, 148, 151–52, 156
Police Scotland, 142, 170, 171
Scottish Government, 119
access decisions, 129
ADRC Scotland, 138–39, 147, 159, 163–64, 171
centralisation of data, 128
co-design research projects, 142–43
duties to disclose information, 52
facilitation of data access, 114
Secure Data Service (SDS), 107
Singapore:
public sector big data analysis projects, 71
Statistics and Registration Services Act 2007, 19, 20, 53
surveillance capitalism, 18, 76

Tariff and Statistical Office:
commercialisation of data, 26
tax data, 108, 112–13, 130, 194
transparency, 14–15, 30, 35
open government, 25–27, 103–6
see also accountability of data sharing procedures; duties to disclose public sector information; Environmental Information Regulations; Freedom of Information Act
TRIPS agreement, 25
trusted third parties, 37, 39, 59, 128

unequal access to data:
accountability failures, 117–19
limitations
data protection law, 59–61
human rights law, 61–63
limits of formalisation, 112–16
United States:
FOI requests, 49, 181–82
government data and evidence-based policymaking, 71
Government-to-Business research data sharing, 81–82

Virtual Microdata Laboratory (VML), 91–92, 106–7, 125, 126

Wales:
ADRC Wales, 124, 137–38, 163–65, 166–67, 169
data linkage studies, 94–95, 103
data sharing, 114–15
FOI requests, 49–50, 182
longitudinal studies, 94–95
NHS Wales Informatics Service, 128–29, 174
SAIL Databank, 95, 128–29, 163–65, 169

Welsh Government, 115–16, 165
data linkage studies, 94–95, 103
Knowledge and Analytical Services, 129, 138, 151–52, 163, 167, 169–70
policy making, 70–71
SAIL Databank, 95, 128–29, 163–65, 169
widening access to data, 100–1
legal reform proposals, 179–80, 189
FOIA's legacy, 180–83
FOIA's limitations, 183–85
organisational reforms, need for, 188–89
presumption of data availability, 185–88

www.ingramcontent.com/pod-product-compliance
Ingram Content Group UK Ltd.
Pitfield, Milton Keynes, MK11 3LW, UK
UKHW020810290926
15470UKWH00003B/1071